A NOBLE PURSUIT

English Silver from
the Rita Gans Collection
at the Virginia Museum of Fine Arts

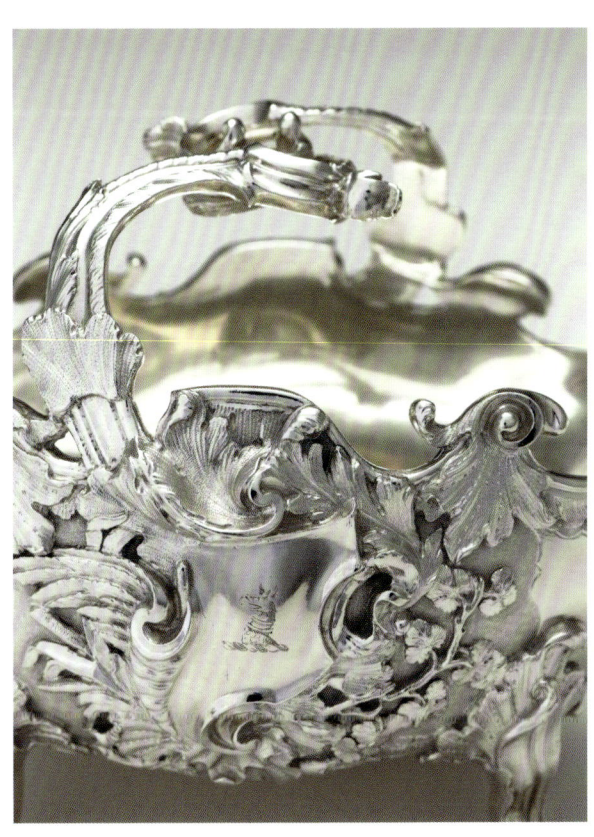

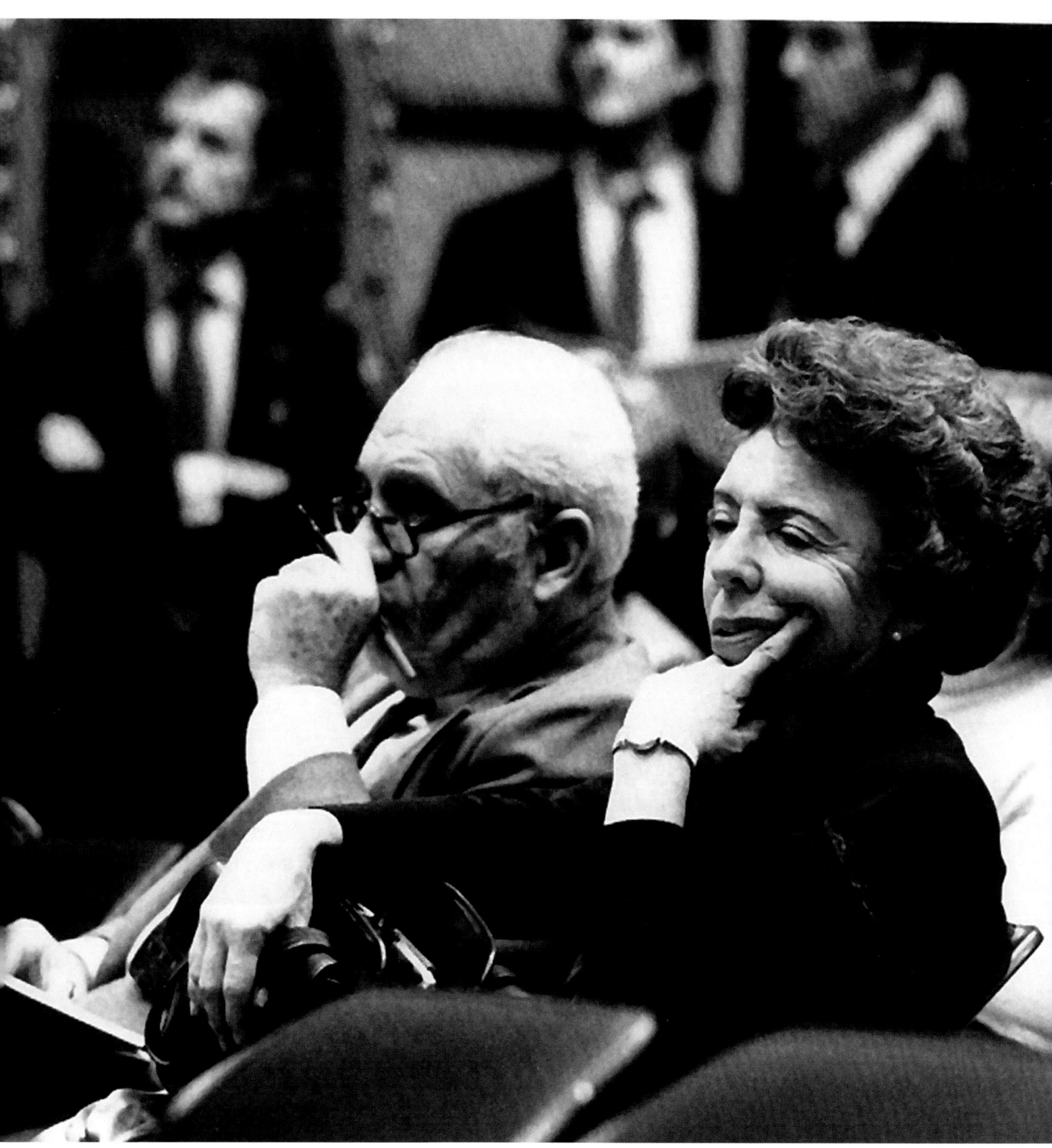

Jerry and Rita Gans in pursuit of silver at the auction sale of the Morgan Collection at Christie's in New York, October 26, 1982. In the background on the left is David Bathurst, president of Christie's in North America.

A NOBLE PURSUIT

ENGLISH SILVER FROM
THE RITA GANS COLLECTION
at the Virginia Museum of Fine Arts

by Christopher Hartop
with a preface by Ellenor Alcorn

VIRGINIA MUSEUM OF FINE ARTS
Richmond, Virginia
in association with
JOHN ADAMSON
Cambridge, England

Published to mark the gift of Rita R. Gans and the opening
of a new Silver Gallery at the Virginia Museum of Fine Arts,
September 24, 2010

Edited and produced by John Adamson

Co-published by
Virginia Museum of Fine Arts
200 N. Boulevard
Richmond, Virginia, 23220-4007
and
John Adamson
90 Hertford Street
Cambridge CB4 3AQ, England

Distributed by University of Virginia Press, Charlottesville
and London

First published 2010
ISBN 978-0-917046-90-2

Copyediting and index by Monica S. Rumsey, Richmond,
Virginia
Designed by Design4Science Ltd., London, England
Printed on Burgo Larius 170 gsm matt by Conti Tipocolor,
Florence, Italy

Half-title:
Cat. no. 27 (detail)

Contents page:
Cat. nos. 4, 31, 20 and 49

Library of Congress Cataloging-in-Publications Data
Virginia Museum of Fine Arts.
A noble pursuit : English silver from the Rita Gans collection at
the Virginia Museum of Fine Arts / by Christopher Hartop ; with
an introduction by Ellenor Alcorn. — 1st ed.
p. cm.
Published to mark the opening of the new Silver Gallery at the
Virginia Museum of Fine Arts, September 24, 2010.
Bound with the companion title: " A noble feast : English silver
from the Rita Gans collection at the Virginia Museum of Fine Arts.
Includes bibliographical references and index.
ISBN 978-0-917046-90-2 — ISBN 978-0-917046-91-9 (shrink-
wrapped with companion title "A noble feast : English silver from
the Rita Gans collection at the Virginia Museum of Fine Arts"
ISBN 9780917046834)
1. Silverwork—England—Catalogs. 2. Gans, Jerome—Art
collections—Catalogs. 3. Gans, Rita—Art collections—Catalogs.
4. Silverwork—Private collections—Virginia—Richmond—
Catalogs. 5. Virginia Museum of Fine Arts—Catalogs. I.
Hartop, Christopher. II. Virginia Museum of Fine Arts. Noble
feast. 2007. III. Title. IV. Title: English silver from the Rita Gans
collection at the Virginia Museum of Fine Arts.
NK7143.A1V58 2010
739.2'30942047755451--dc22
2010034214

CONTENTS

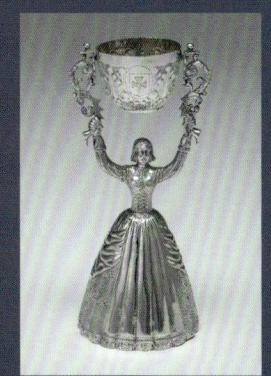

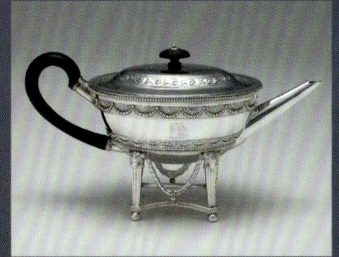

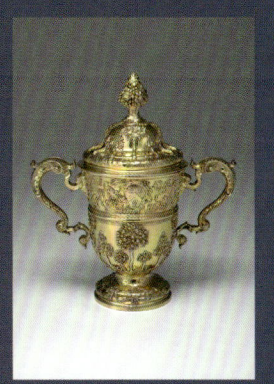

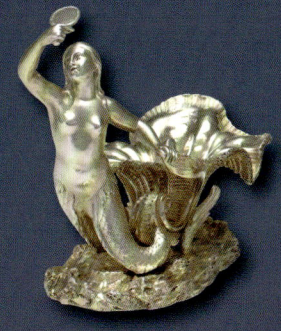

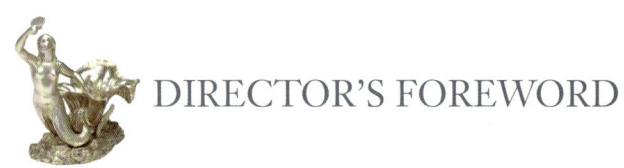

DIRECTOR'S FOREWORD

This book celebrates Rita Gans's gift to the Virginia Museum of Fine Arts of fifty magnificent pieces of English silver. This extraordinarily generous offering will join the collection formed by Rita and her late husband, Jerry, which was first installed in 1988 and given to the museum in 1997. Their collection has been one of the glories of the museum, beloved both by scholars and our visitors. In 2007, the Gans Collection opened an installation entitled "A Noble Feast," the first new gallery of the museum's architectural transformation. This year, as we cut the ribbon on architect Rick Mather's stunning new wing, the museum also announces with pride and gratitude Rita's exceptional gift of a second collection of silver.

Though Rita had announced that her collecting days were over after her husband's death, she soon found herself drawn back to the pursuit of great works. Her lively and engaging personal style is vividly reflected in her silver. The refinement of the neoclassical tureen (cat. 30), the gravitas of the Chesterfield wine coolers (cat. 41), and the exuberance of the rock-crystal standing cup (cat. 44) all reflect facets of her character. Most striking, perhaps, is the energetic zeal with which the pieces were gathered together: she assembled this exceptional group of fifty pieces in the years between 1997 and 2009—little more than a decade. Christopher Hartop explores that very theme—the impulse to collect—in this engaging book. He writes about how art collections reveal the character of the individuals behind them and examines in depth the history of silver collecting. I am grateful to him for sharing his expertise so generously.

The museum's staff brought their usual high standards of professionalism to their contributions to this catalogue. Mitchell Merling, Paul Mellon Curator and Head of European Art, deftly managed not only the publication, but a complex gallery installation as well. Stephen Bonadies's diplomacy ensured the smooth co-ordination of all involved. Corey Piper ably served as project assistant. Under the direction of Kathy Z. Gillis, Mary Scott Andrews and Cheryl Sumner prepared the silver for photography. Katherine Wetzel was responsible for the superb photographs, with assistance from Susie Rock, Travis Fullerton, and Howell Perkins. Jennie Runnels was the registrar responsible for the incoming gift, and Roy Thompson meticulously recorded the marks and measurements of each piece. Monica Rumsey did an exemplary job in her role as copyeditor, working with Rosalie West. I am grateful to Ellenor Alcorn, formerly Consulting Curator for the Gans Collection, for her stewardship of the collection over several years. John Adamson, who has published the book, has been a superb collaborator, and we are proud to add to the bookshelves a second volume with our shared imprints.

Our greatest debt of gratitude, of course, goes to Rita Gans herself. This publication is a tribute to her exceptional eye, to her generosity, and to her noble pursuit of the finest English silver.

Alex Nyerges
Director, Virginia Museum of Fine Arts
Richmond

ACKNOWLEDGMENTS

Colleagues in the world of silver have once again been most generous with their time and help. In particular, I wish to thank Vanessa Brett, former editor of *Silver Studies: The Journal of the Silver Society*, for her many kindnesses, Philippa Glanville for lively discussions about drinking bowls, Gale Glynn for her help with some heraldic conundrums, Anna Keay who enlightened me about Charles II's coronation, Robert Barker for sharing some bibliographical discoveries, and Timothy Kent and David Constable for useful insights into woodwose spoons. My thanks go to Christopher Grimwade and John Lumley for kindly allowing me to reproduce photographs of their respective fathers, and to Richard Southall the photograph of his grandmother, Mrs How. I am grateful to Jan Trestik, director of the Galerie Středočeského kraje, Kutna Horá, for allowing us to reproduce the newly discovered image of the Bohemian silver mine. Lucy Morton, current editor of *Silver Studies: The Journal of the Silver Society*, was most helpful in sharing her expertise with me, and thanks are also due to Tim Bolton and Cynthia Harris of Sotheby's, Alastair Dickenson, and Ian and Neil Franklin in London, and to James McConnaughy of S.J. Shrubsole Corp. in New York.

All books and catalogues stand on the shoulders of those that came before, and for this second volume of the Gans Collection I have relied heavily on the published work of John Culme, Timothy Schroder and the late Eric J.G. Smith.

Once again it has been a pleasure to work with Ellenor Alcorn, since spring 2010 Associate Curator of European Sculpture and Decorative Arts at the Metropolitan Museum of Art in New York but until then consulting curator of the Gans Collection at the Virginia Museum of Fine Arts. Her knowledge and experience have been the mainstay of the project. In Richmond, much help and encouragement have been received from a team headed by Mitchell Merling, Paul Mellon Curator and Head of European Art. Katherine Wetzel of the museum's photographic studio worked calmly under pressure, as did Monica Rumsey, who acted as copyeditor in Virginia and, working with Emily J. Salmon, compiled the index which covers this volume and its companion, *A Noble Feast*.

I have been lucky to have the same production team as with *A Noble Feast*, namely Chris Jones of Design4Science, Conti Tipocolor in Florence for printing and binding, and John Adamson for editing and production management. My wife, Juliet, has, as always, been my vital support. To all of them my heartfelt thanks, but the biggest thank you must go to Rita Gans, not only for her generosity in giving this second collection to the Virginia Museum of Fine Arts and making this second volume possible, but also for the support and encouragement she has given the world of silver scholarship during the past thirteen years. Her enthusiasm has been contagious.

Christopher Hartop

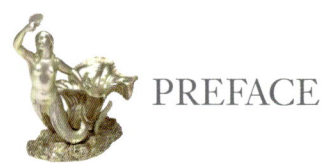

PREFACE

Collectors and museums often come in pairs. Rita Gans's involvement with the Virginia Museum of Fine Arts goes back to the 1980s, when she and her late husband, Jerome, visited Richmond for the first time. They were interested in the museum's holdings of Fabergé, and they thought perhaps the VMFA would like to exhibit their exceptional collection of English eighteenth- and nineteenth-century silver. The informal and spontaneous nature of this first encounter gave little indication of the long-term partnership that would eventually develop between them.

At the time, the museum's collection of English silver was very limited, and it was not an area that had been methodically cultivated. The exhibit of the Gans silver was well received, and in 1997, soon after Jerome's death, Rita Gans gave the museum the entire collection that she and her husband had formed. She continued her commitment by supporting an innovative study area in the galleries. This was particularly welcoming for children, and it furthered a long interest on her part to introduce antique silver to the broadest possible audience. In 2001 Rita presented to the museum the extraordinary pair of ewers and matching rosewater dish made in 1699 for Henry Grey, 12th Earl of Kent. This set was of unsurpassed importance; she had purchased it knowing that it belonged in a museum. Rita funded several scholarly undertakings in connection with the silver she had given: an initial catalogue by Joseph Bliss published in 1992; addenda by John Culme in 1999 and 2001; and finally, two volumes by Christopher Hartop, of which this is the second. She supported an international symposium in 2004 entitled "The Line of Beauty: Rococo Silver in England and Its Colonies," and underwrote the subsequent publication of scholarly papers. In 2006 she presented sixteen outstanding works to the museum, greatly increasing the scope and prominence of the collection.

This publication marks an exceptional gift of fifty additional pieces of silver to the museum. When her husband died, Rita anounced that she would never collect again. Only a few short months had passed, however, before she felt the siren call and bought a beautiful Paul de Lamerie basket. In New York, her home, and on her annual trips to London, she resumed the pursuit. Rita sought out pieces that spoke to her for their formal beauty, their ornament, or their sculptural presence.

The fifty pieces in this most recent gift reflect Rita's own taste, and there is a discernible difference between them and the earlier collection she had built with her husband. Often smaller in scale, with fine chased or engraved ornament, her more recent acquisitions sometimes make reference to earlier styles. The three standing cups (cat. nos. 42, 44, and 45) are refined and very early examples of Renaissance revival taste that was being explored by Rundell, Bridge & Rundell and other retailers in the 1820s. Though neither Rita nor Jerry intended to build a didactic collection, this group of three cups makes a perfect art-historical statement. Many of the pieces of silver in this "second" collection have a delicate intimacy or a surprising feature, like the Paul Storr teapot (cat. no. 31), which can be lifted from its neoclassical stand. "I was immediately drawn to it," Rita says, "because it was marvelous to hold in my hands." Like many collectors, Rita vividly remembers the first sight of an object that she loves, and her judgments about a purchase are famously quick and decisive. Above all, Rita enjoys the excitement of the art market, and for many years now she has been a familiar sight at antiques fairs or auctions. Deliberations about a purchase might take as long as a nice lunch or a walk around the block, but they are absolute, and there is never any ambivalence.

In choosing English silver as a focus for their interest, Jerome and Rita Gans were in good company: Americans have long been devoted collectors of English silver. In 1908 the *New York Times* called silver collecting "a modern craze," and pointed out, perhaps with a hint of *schadenfreude*, that "every year ... the palaces and chateaus of the continent are being almost denuded of their contents to furnish the homes of our wealthy citizens ..."[1] In 1928, the Secretary of the [British] Antique Dealers' Association issued a statement: "We do not mind the Americans having a certain number of our treasures, because we have so many, but things are going too far."[2] Resounding publicity

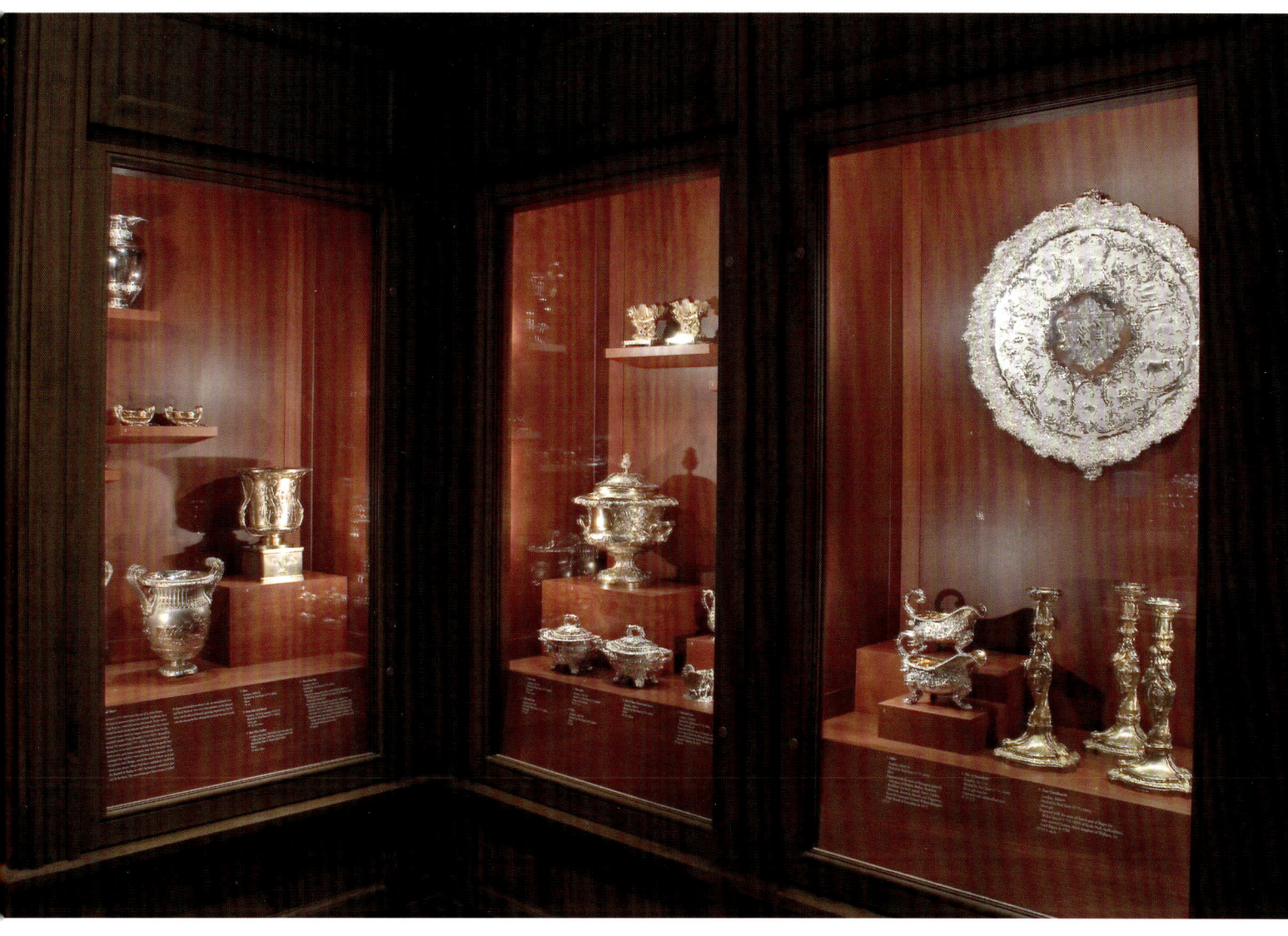

1. The Gans Gallery at the Virginia Museum of Fine Arts, Richmond.
Katherine Wetzel

surrounding several sales, like that of the collections of William Randolph Hearst in 1937, increased the American appetite for English silver. Even throughout the Second World War, shipments of silver to America continued.

Silver collectors in the early years of the twentieth century in America were particularly attracted to the patriotic associations of colonial American silver. English-made pieces that had been brought to the colonies before the Revolution were also of interest, though even rarer than colonial silver. On trips to London, New York, Chicago, or Boston, these collectors acquired what was more readily available in the thriving antiques market: English domestic pieces that were similar in form to colonial American classics such as cream jugs, tankards, or tea kettles. The taste for Colonial Revival furnishings, and the influence of Colonial Williamsburg, founded in 1926 by John D. Rockefeller Jr., offered a domestic context for these collections.

"Plain silver" was more widely appreciated, and more widely available, than the high-style mannerist pieces pursued by the ambitious financier J. Pierpont Morgan, who left his wide-ranging collections to the Wadsworth Atheneum in Hartford, Connecticut, and to the Metropolitan Museum of Art in New York. Though English silver was not his particular interest, his vast holdings included some outstanding examples. Morgan's bequest to the Metropolitan Museum was credited with "breath[ing] into the institution a new life, communicat[ing] to it a new and tremendous impulse."[3] American tastes soon expanded beyond modest domestic items. Hearst, who was credited with cornering twenty-five percent of the world's art market during his collecting heyday in the 1920s and 1930s, bought English treasury pieces to complement his pictures, tapestries, armor and sculpture. The sale of Hearst's collection attracted the attention of Robert Sterling Clark, among others. Clark had been buying silver for more than a decade, and when he opened the Clark Art Institute in Williamstown, Massachusetts, in 1955, he considered the silver a central element, to be shown with his American and European painting, sculpture, and works on paper.

Through their gifts, bequests, and endowments, this early generation of collectors made a lasting mark on American museums. In the 1930s the Museum of Fine Arts, Boston, received the English silver collections of Theodora Wilbour and Frank Brewer Bemis. Miss Wilbour's later bequest of an endowment to support acquisitions encouraged an institutional commitment to silver and to the decorative arts. Similarly, at the Portland (Oregon) Art Museum, William H. and Alice Nunn, Henry Failing Cabell, and Anna Wheeler Hayse entrusted the museum with their silver collections. Later purchases from a fund created by the Nunns have augmented that museum's holdings. Silver was among the most important components of Judge Irwin Untermyer's diverse collection of English seventeenth- and eighteenth-century decorative arts, now at the Metropolitan Museum of Art. Harvard University's Fogg Art Museum, the Minneapolis Institute of Arts, and the Birmingham (Alabama) Museum of Art house silver collections that were initiated by private collectors. At the Dallas Museum of Art, the Esther Hoblitzelle Collection includes outstanding examples of works by Paul de Lamerie and other Georgian silver. At the Museum of Fine Arts, Houston, George S. Heyer's refined taste is expressed in a distinguished silver collection.

Throughout the first half of the twentieth century, it was private collectors, not museum curators, who led collecting taste. Carefully cultivated by knowledgeable dealers, the collectors were the experienced connoisseurs who most closely followed the market. In the 1960s and 1970s, however, American museum curators came into their own in the marketplace and began to buy English silver privately and at auction. Robert Sterling Clark had not been impressed with curators, whom he called "archaeologists, not appreciative of art."[4] Yet museums would become serious competition for some English silver collectors, and several of the pieces in this catalogue were bought when Rita Gans successfully outbid museums.

With the presentation of this outstanding collection to the Virginia Museum of Fine Arts, those hotly contested acquisitions will come full circle. The fifty pieces collected by Rita Gans, on her own, will join the collection that she formed with her husband, Jerome. With this publication and the opening of a permanent gallery, the silver will be accessible to scholars, to collectors—both beginning and experienced—and to a broad general audience. Though literally dozens of American museums house collections of English silver, the Gans Collection will always maintain its prominence and its distinct character. "Purity of form, sense of proportion and perfection of line,"[5] the qualities that were admired in 1916 when Judge Clearwater's collection was exhibited at the Metropolitan Museum, are present in abundance. But also beautifully represented are ambitious sculptural pieces that celebrate the reflective qualities of the medium and the goldsmiths' inspiration. Among the great partnerings of museums and silver collectors are Robert Sterling Clark and the institution that bears his name, or Irwin Untermyer and the Metropolitan Museum. Rita Gans, in joining forces with the Virginia Museum of Fine Arts, has ensured that the silver she and her husband so lovingly and thoughtfully collected will be celebrated, studied, and cared for.

Ellenor Alcorn
Associate Curator of European Sculpture and Decorative Arts, Metropolitan Museum of Art, New York

Notes
1. "The Modern Craze for Very Old Silver," *New York Times*, January 5, 1908, p. 8.
2. "Expert Moves to Check Drain of Treasures to America, Increased since the War," *New York Times*, May 15, 1928.
3. "Museum's Tribute to late J.P. Morgan," *New York Times*, May 8, 1918.
4. Quoted in Wees, p. 16.
5. R.T.H. Halsey, "The Clearwater Collection of Colonial Silver," *Bulletin of the Metropolitan Museum of Art*, 11, no. 1 (January 1916).

2. A mid-eighteenth-century London silver shop, from Phillips Garden's trade card, 1749.
British Museum, London

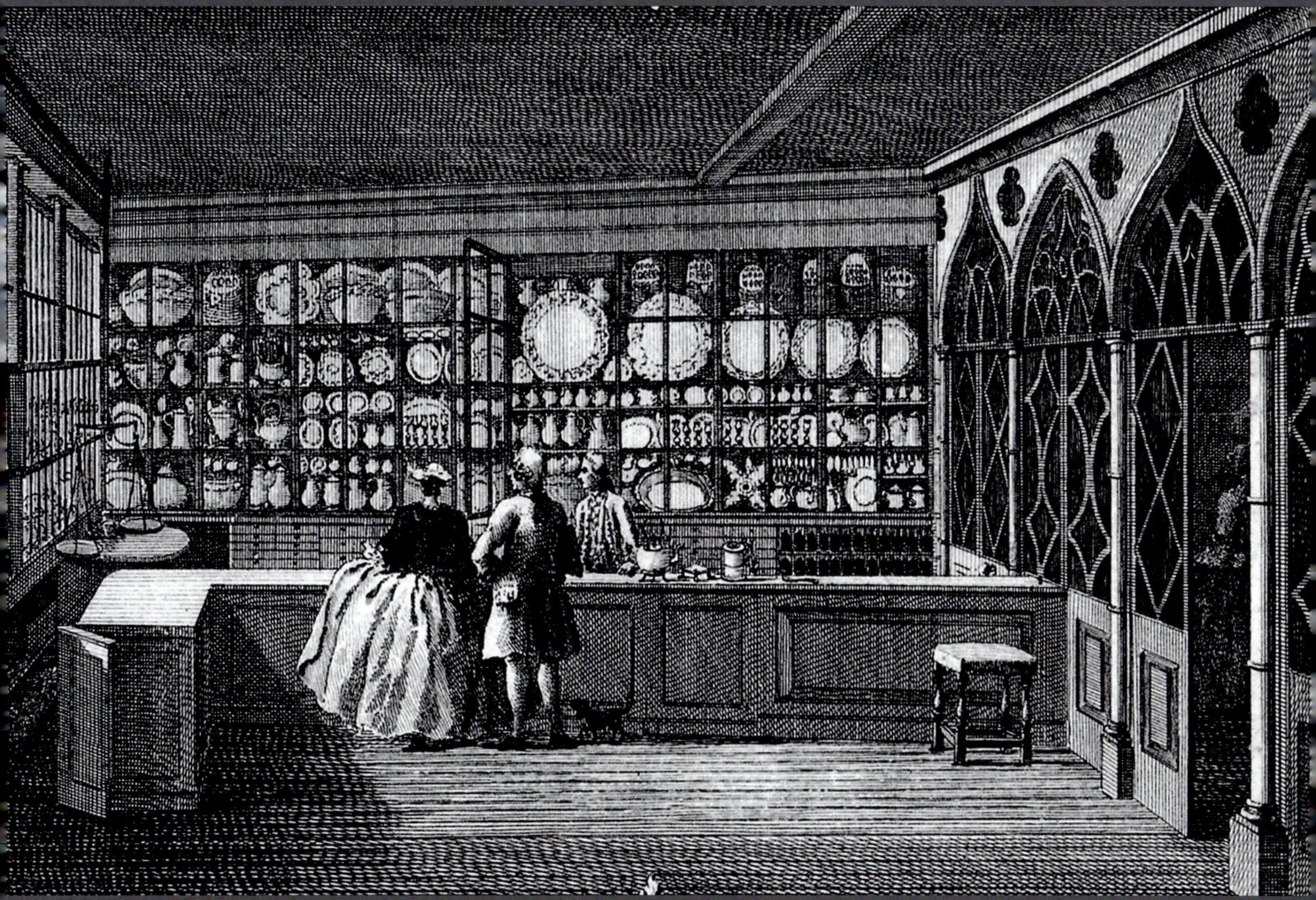

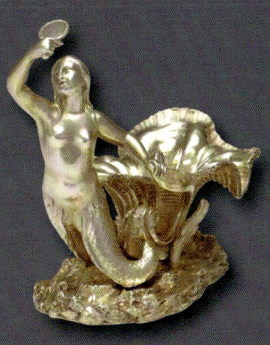

ACQUISITION AND USE

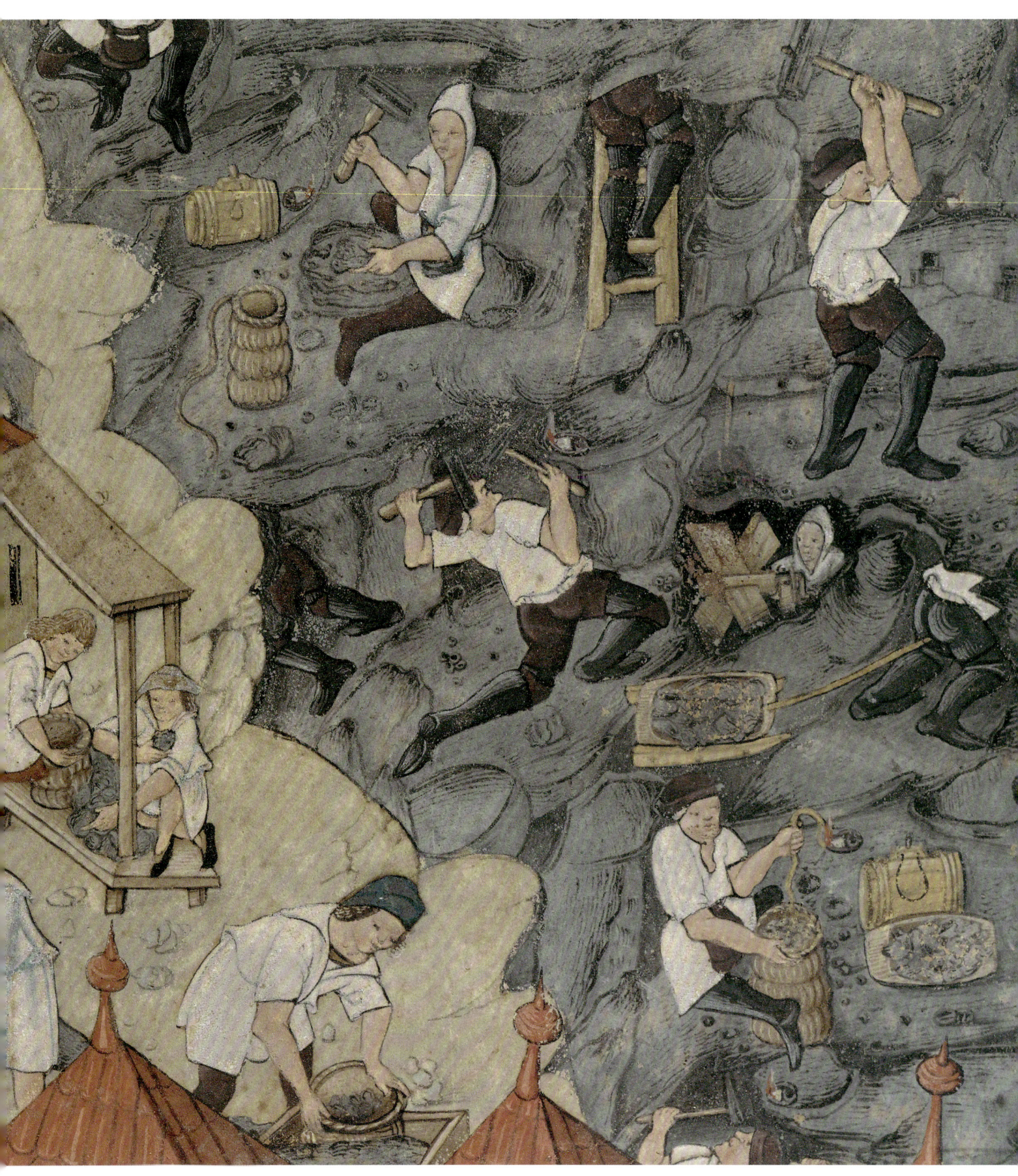

Chapter One

ACQUISITION AND USE

Over the past hundred years or so, authorities have written at length about antique silver, charting the development of styles, elucidating the lives of makers and designers of silver, and pronouncing on its hallmarks. Yet, rather surprisingly, few authors have asked the fundamental question—why have people down the ages acquired silver? What has been its attraction? When collecting old silver first became a widespread pastime in the nineteenth century, writers tended to take for granted the presence of silver in everyday life, at least for those who could afford it. But they were writing at the end of a long period, dating back to ancient times, during which silver was an integral part of existence for virtually everyone, for even if someone was not wealthy enough to own at least one silver spoon, coins made of silver passed through their hands nevertheless. In today's world, silver plays a much more modest role. Its industrial and medical uses aside, the presence of silver in the vast majority of homes today often does not stretch beyond some flatware or jewelry. So it is all too easy to forget how pivotal silver was in the households of the past.

In this book, the items collected by Rita Gans during the past thirteen years, recently given to the Virginia Museum of Fine Arts, provide a perfect vehicle for the study of the manifold reasons for silver's importance in history. In this chapter, we shall see how silver, although often decorative, was acquired first and foremost for use. Then, in Chapter Two, we shall see how, with the rise of the collector, there was a burgeoning interest in silver articles as much for their historical aspects as for their aesthetic appeal.

Throughout history, the beauty of silver has remained a constant. As one of the two "noble metals" of the ancient world (the other being gold), it has always been prized for its lustrous surface and the way it catches the light. Whether seen in daylight or by firelight, candlelight, or electric light, silver presents an ever-changing luminosity. Among metals it is second only to gold for its ductility, and can thus be worked by a number of methods to present a smooth surface, or low- or high-relief decoration. Plain pieces—where the appeal may lie as much in the outlines and surfaces as in the color and patina of the metal—have been made and used down the ages alongside intricately worked creations. Both styles today have their enthusiasts. But it is often the tension caused by juxtaposing areas of brightly polished plainness with elaborate decoration on the same piece that is most attractive. The assertion that silver has color often comes as a surprise to would-be collectors. When polished it always reflects the colors of the things around it, but every piece has a distinct color of its own. This is because no silver object is made of pure silver and the other elements used in the alloy impart their particular hue. The way the surface has been prepared or evolved over time through use or cleaning will also affect the color.

Perhaps these aesthetic attractions would have been justification enough for holding silver in such high regard. But there were other reasons for acquiring and using it. Its rarity and relative durability made it an ideal material for financial transactions in the shape of minted coins. Moreover, households knew that their silver could, at short notice, be melted down and converted back into currency. Its costliness, therefore, was also one of its attractions. Ownership of it was a way of proclaiming wealth. As one writer observed some years ago: "[T]he great cistern on the sideboard was the Bentley, the massive wine cooler the sable."[1] In a hierarchical age, silver was more than a useful denominator of status; it was also a convenient means of storing capital. In Joseph Addison's comedy *The Drummer, or, The Haunted-House*, first produced at Drury Lane in 1716, Lady Truman is visited by the fortune hunter Mr Tinsel, who sizes up the cash value of her silver:

Tinsel: I take notice thou hast a great deal of old plate here in the house, widow.

Lady T.: Mr Tinsel, you are a very observing man.

Tinsel: Thy large silver cistern would make a very good coach and half a dozen salvers that

3. Silver mining in Bohemia, a panoramic frontispiece from an illuminated manuscript choir book, paint on vellum, Prague, c. 1490. Acquired by the Galerie Středočeského kraje, Kutna Horá, Czech Republic, 2009.
GASK/Sotheby's Images

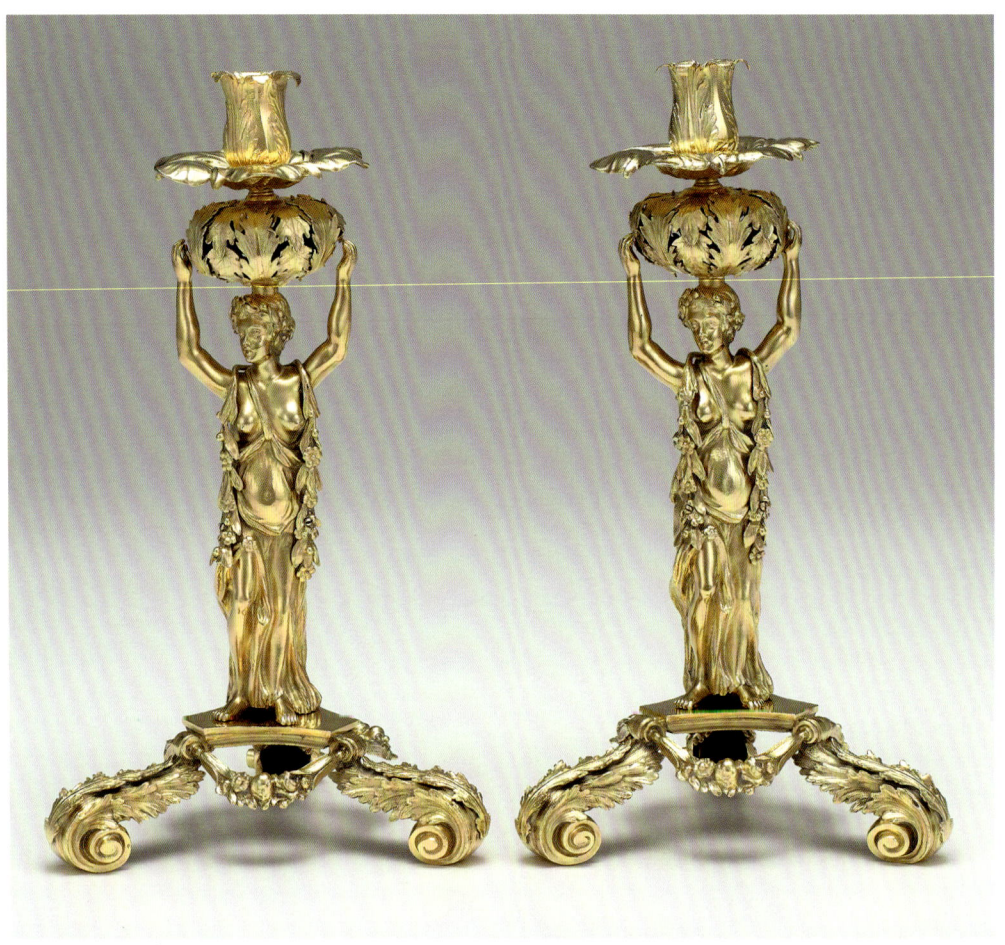

4. Pair of candlesticks, silver gilt, London, 1766/67, maker's mark of Thomas Heming. The caryatid form of candlestick of the 1690s was revived in Heming's workshop in the 1760s. This pair was supplied to Lord Bute, who served as British prime minister from 1762 to 1763. Cat. no. 28

I saw on the sideboard might be turned into six as pretty horses as any that appear in the ring.
Lady T.: You have a very good fancy, Mr Tinsel.[2]

Silver therefore had three great attributes: it was beautiful, precious, and it was recyclable. While newly mined silver, mostly from Eastern Europe —and after the European settlement of the Americas—from Mexico and Peru added to the existing stock of the metal, a significant proportion of the alloy of any new silver article could well have come from an ancient Greek dish, a Roman spoon, or a medieval chalice. But early writers on silver collecting perhaps laid too much emphasis on this constant recycling: true, it happened every now and again on a massive scale due to wars, or upheavals like the Reformation, but to have the silver of your ancestors melted down and refashioned in the latest style could become a costly business—you had to pay the "fashion" charge for the making. In the early eighteenth century that could range from a mere five pence per ounce for plain plates and dishes to many times that for elaborately decorated works involving technically advanced casting and a high degree of handwork. This could have meant a loss of as much as forty percent of the intrinsic value of the piece. As a result, a great deal of old silver from all periods, from the late seventeenth century onwards, survives from Britain. Wars and revolutions did not take their toll as they did in continental Europe, and the constant rise in prosperity as the country became an imperial power meant that silver remained a part of daily life in the British Isles until well into the twentieth century.

If the wine cistern was the Bentley automobile of former centuries and a token of wealth and status, the simple spoon, such as the rare fifteenth-century example illustrated in fig. 6, also represented, albeit at a more modest level, a capital investment. It too elevated its owner. As spoons were often the only silver articles in a prosperous artisan's or a yeoman's household,

5. Pieter Gerritsz. van Roestraeten: *Still life with candlestick, porringer and* mementi mori, c. 1690, oil on canvas. Roestraeten created various compositions using the same silver items, such as this caryatid candlestick. *Vanitas* still lifes incorporating silver objects and symbols of man's mortality enjoyed a vogue in the second half of the seventeenth century. *Collection of Neil Hamilton.*

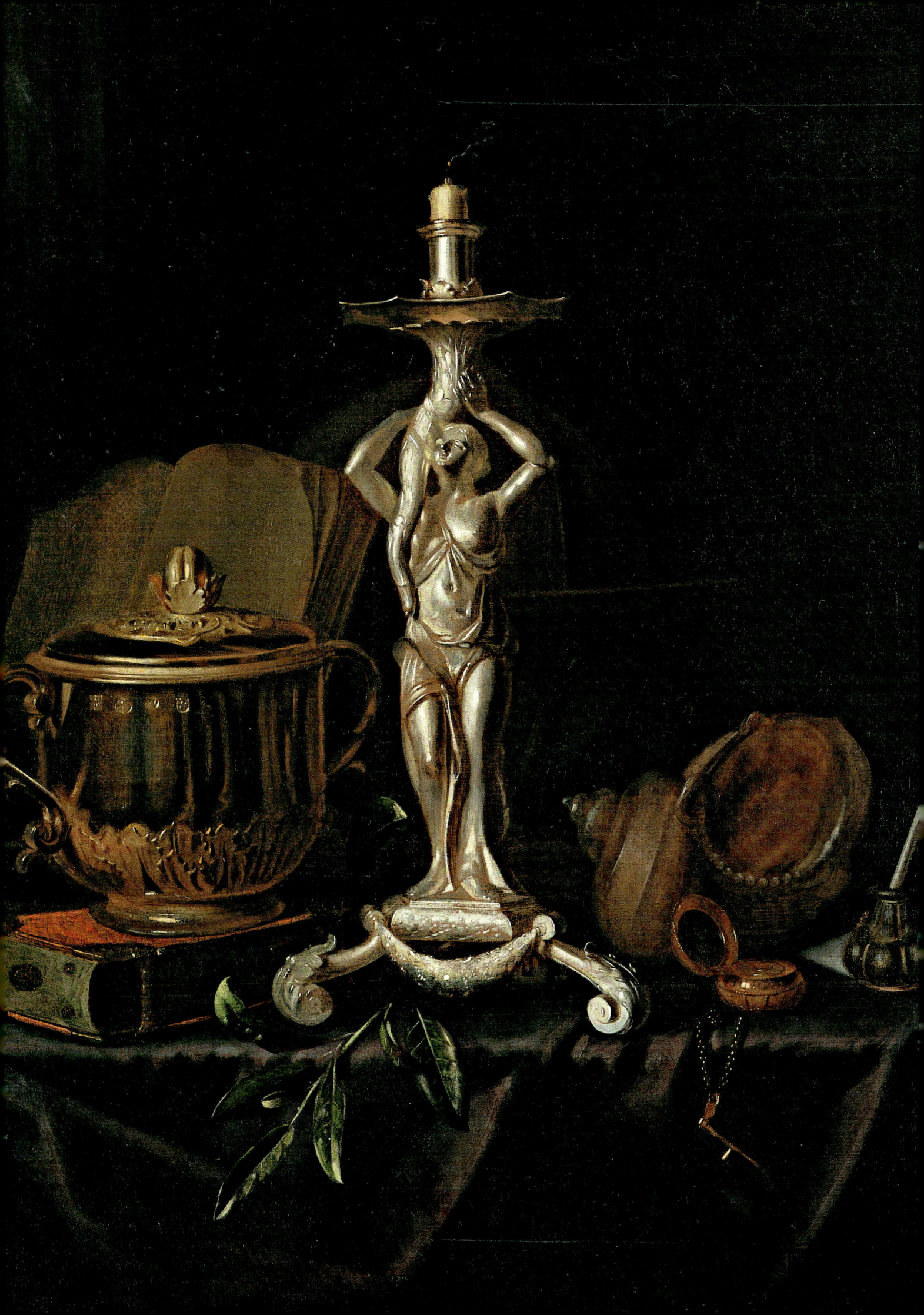

they acquired special status. We still speak of being born with a silver spoon in one's mouth, and the custom of presenting a spoon to a newborn infant dates from the Middle Ages. Spoons from the medieval period have often survived because they were hidden, perhaps in times of unrest, and later found buried or in a wall or the thatched roof of a house, or merely because being light in weight their intrinsic value was so small that they were overlooked. Some also survived for sentimental reasons, sometimes on account of inscriptions engraved on them recording birth dates or an event, and became heirlooms passed down from generation to generation.

Medieval spoons were often adorned with a cast finial in the form of an apostle—sets of thirteen, comprising the twelve apostles and one depicting Christ, were common. It is easy to forget how devout a Catholic country England was in the fifteenth century; all would change with the Reformation, but apostle spoons continued to be popular throughout the sixteenth century and well into the seventeenth. The upheavals of the Civil War in the 1640s, which fueled an iconooclastic attitude towards any religious depictions of the saints, makes it all the more surprising how many apostle spoons have survived to the present day. Other decorative finials, such as those in the form of a maiden's head, were much more rare. The Gans spoon, which dates from about 1440, has a finial in the shape of a mythical wild man known as a woodwose. He appears often as decoration in manuscript illumination and on stone carvings in churches, especially in East Anglia. In fact, it is from this region in the southeast of England that one of the few documentary references to these spoons comes. In Coggeshall, Essex, the Wardens of the Goldsmiths' Company, when carrying out an inspection of local craftsmen in 1468, found a dozen spoons "with woodwoses" in the possession of one Derek Knyff which were made of substandard alloy. The Gans example is one of only four woodwose spoons recorded.[3]

From the earliest times, silver has been recognized as the purest material with which to make spoons and other items for eating and drinking. Yet writers on its history have seldom discussed silver's important hygienic properties. In the past it was recognized that silver and gold were the purest materials, even though the scientific reasons behind it were unknown. Communal use of silver articles was widespread: large tankards such

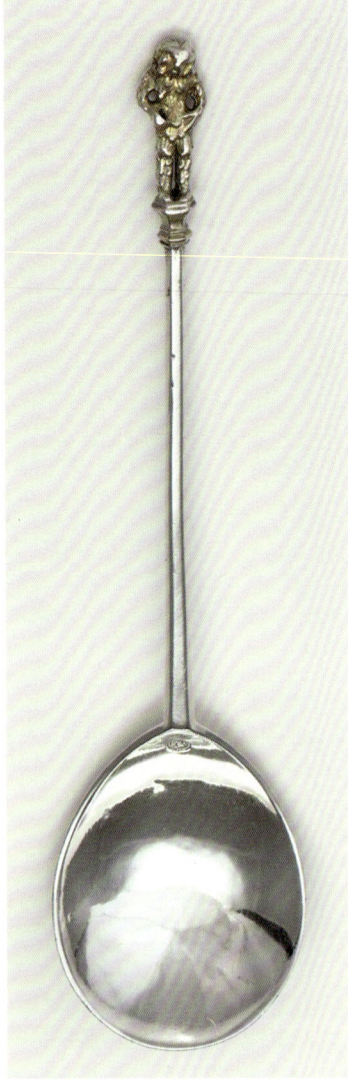

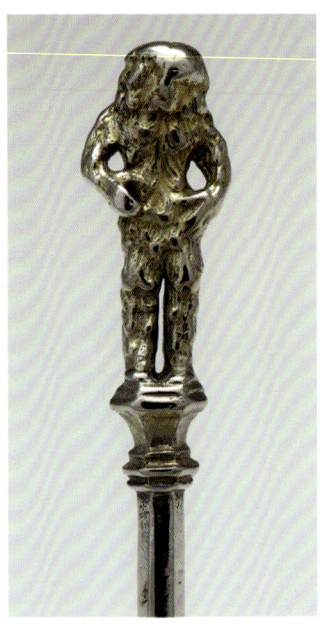

6. Spoon, silver, parcel gilt, c. 1440. The simplest, and perhaps most ancient, of silver articles, the spoon was often the only silver article in a modest household.
Cat. no. 1

7. Detail of the woodwose finial of the spoon in fig. 6. Medieval spoons were adorned with cast decorative finials. This one in the form of a mythical wild man, or woodwose, is extremely rare: only four examples are known.

as the magnificent example in fig. 8 were passed back and forth between drinkers; some English examples follow the Scandinavian practice of having a vertical line of pegs inside to ensure that each drinker took the same measure (hence the expression to take someone "down a peg"). In Henry Fielding's *Tom Jones*, published in 1729, Tom and his companion stop at a wayside inn and share a "loving cup." At church services, all of the Protestant congregation drank from shared communion cups.

In the early nineteenth century it was scientifically proved that silver was aseptic, but it was not until the beginning of the twenty-first century that it was proved that silver, unlike gold, is also antiseptic and will fight the growth of advanced colonies of bacteria. The medical uses of silver, for wound dressing and for surgical

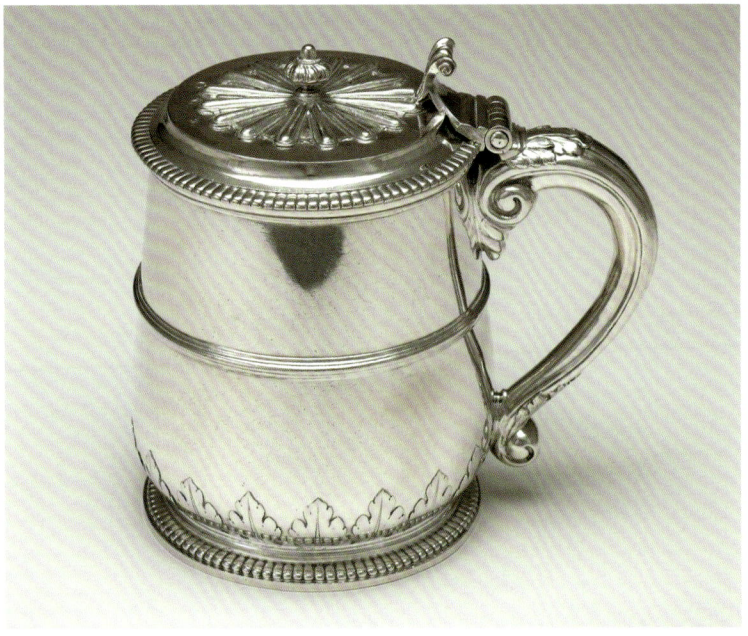

8. Tankard, silver, London, 1691/92, maker's mark of David Willaume. Many articles for eating and drinking were shared. This large-size tankard was probably passed back and forth between two drinkers. The antiseptic properties of silver made it the ideal material for such items. Cat. no. 7

9. Beaker, silver gilt, c. 1690. Like the spoon, the beaker was a very personal article, often kept in a fitted leather case and taken on the road. This example, plated with gold, is decorated with a mirrored cipher surmounted by a bridal wreath, suggesting it was a gift from groom to bride. As one of the "noble metals," gold, like silver, was thought to be hygienic. Cat. no. 6

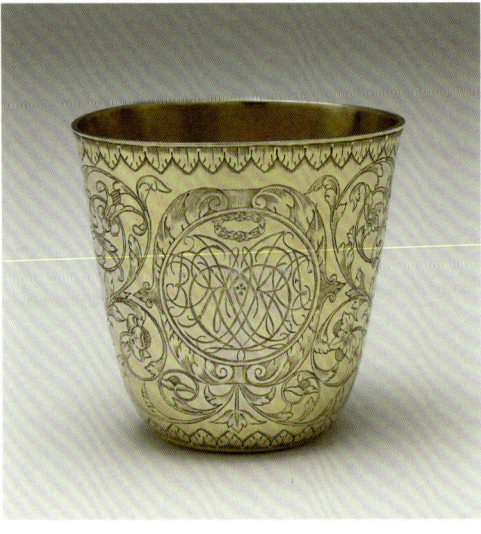

instruments, had all but died out with the rise of antibiotics during the twentieth century, but recent years have seen a resurgence of use of the metal, not only for bandages but also for items such as door handles in hospitals (a small amount of silver in the alloy will suffice to give it antiseptic properties). Hospital gowns are now sold with silver thread woven into them, to combat "super bugs."

Gilding silver, in other words plating it with gold, was popular from the earliest times, but because of the huge price differential between the two metals (in the Middle Ages to the beginning of the twentieth century it was a fairly constant ratio of 20 to 1) gilding was used only sparingly.[4] To combat the corrosive effects of the acid in fruit and wine, the interiors of bowls and cups were sometimes gilded, or the rim given a coating of gold. The gold was applied by a highly skilled and dangerous process in which the gold was melted with mercury and the amalgam applied to the surface of the silver. The mercury evaporated and the remaining gold could be burnished bright. Because alloyed gold could be used, the color could be varied, from pale yellow to deep red, and the rich patina was, and still is, highly prized. Electro-gilding, the method employed today, uses electricity to coat the silver with a thin layer of pure gold; the result lacks the warmth and richness of fire gilding. With the rise in prosperity in the early eighteenth century, and the fashion for silver services specifically for the "dessert" at the end of dinner, it became common to gild entire salvers and dishes to counter the effects of fruit juices and to give a magnificent effect on a sideboard. The fashion for gilding complete dinner services can be attributed to Napoleon Bonaparte at the beginning of the nineteenth century. He sought to recreate in France the splendor of Nero's *Domus Aurea*, to give his new regime legitimacy, and the English, led by the Prince Regent, enthusiastically followed suit (see the Paul Storr salvers, fig. 47).[5]

Whether it was a magnificent array of gold-plated silver on a tiered buffet, or merely a cup or a tankard on a sideboard, the English love of displaying silver, and thus their wealth and status, lived on well into the nineteenth century, long after the practice had all but died out on the continent. Eighteenth-century visitors to London remarked on the necessity of having a sideboard to display items of silver, even utilitarian objects such as spoons and spurs. Because of its intrinsic value, a piece of plate could be given as a thinly disguised bribe. In his diary Samuel Pepys (1633–1703) records with astonishing candor the gifts of silver he received from Admiralty contractors.

Inheritance, purchase, or bribes aside, there were other ways to acquire silver. One of these was to receive it from the crown. From the Middle Ages, the Jewel House was the office within the royal household that was responsible for providing silver for all official requirements. It was issued, in carefully regulated quantities, for use by household and government officials such as ambassadors while serving abroad, and also given as New Year's gifts or as payments, or "perquisites" (hence the term "perk of office"), to the hereditary officers of state such as those who assisted in the coronation of the monarch. During the Civil War, the Jewel House had been depleted of stock and it was not re-established until the Restoration of Charles II in 1660.[6] For his coronation, the new king wanted to revive many of the old customs of the ceremony. One of these was a canopy, last used at the coronation of Queen Elizabeth I, which was held over the monarch by his closest officers of state as he progressed to Westminster Abbey to be crowned (fig. 11). In May, 1660, the Lord Chamberlain issued a warrant to the Great Wardrobe (another office within the royal household) to provide "one Canopie wth Silver bells for the barons of the Cinque Ports after the Manner as it hath beene formerly accustomed."[7] "Fower Bells for the Canopie" (fig. 10) were ordered from Robert Vyner, the Royal Goldsmith, weighing just under 19 ounces in total. The silver needed cost 5 shillings an ounce and the "fashen" or making of them cost a further £4.[8]

Samuel Pepys recounts the comical fight that took place at the banquet in Westminster Hall following the coronation on April 23, 1661, when the king's footmen tried to snatch the canopy from its bearers and so claim the silver bells as "perks." But the king ordered the footmen to be arrested and gave one of the bells to General George Monck, 1st Duke of Albemarle, who had been instrumental in the king's restoration by staging what amounted to a military coup. Described by Pepys as a "dull, heavy man,"[9] he was recognized as being a shrewd "fixer." His son, Christopher, succeeded his father as second duke in 1670. Known as "liberal, loyal and a leading man among the friends of the King and Duke [of York],"[10] Christopher was sent to Jamaica as Governor in 1686, where he died two years later.

When the Gans bell appeared on the market in 1953 it was recognized as possibly being Monck's "perk." The vendor described to Arthur Grimwade, Christie's silver expert, how his ancestor had purchased the bell in the 1850s in the West Indies from a "Miss Monck"—presumably she had been a descendant of an illegitimate child the duke had fathered on the island.

Other officers of state to receive perquisites included those who held the two silver matrices of the royal seal used on official documents. Hot wax was impressed between these two halves to make a

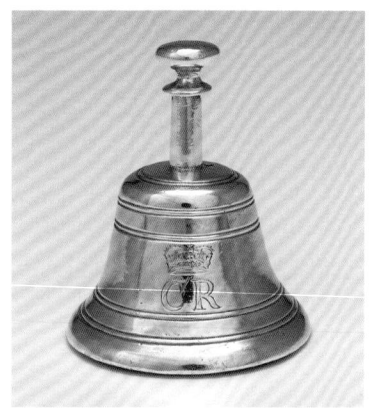

10. Bell, silver, c. 1660. This bell is probably one of those hung from the canopy which covered Charles II in his coronation procession in 1661, and was apparently given to the Duke of Albemarle, as a perquisite after the ceremony.
Cat. no. 3

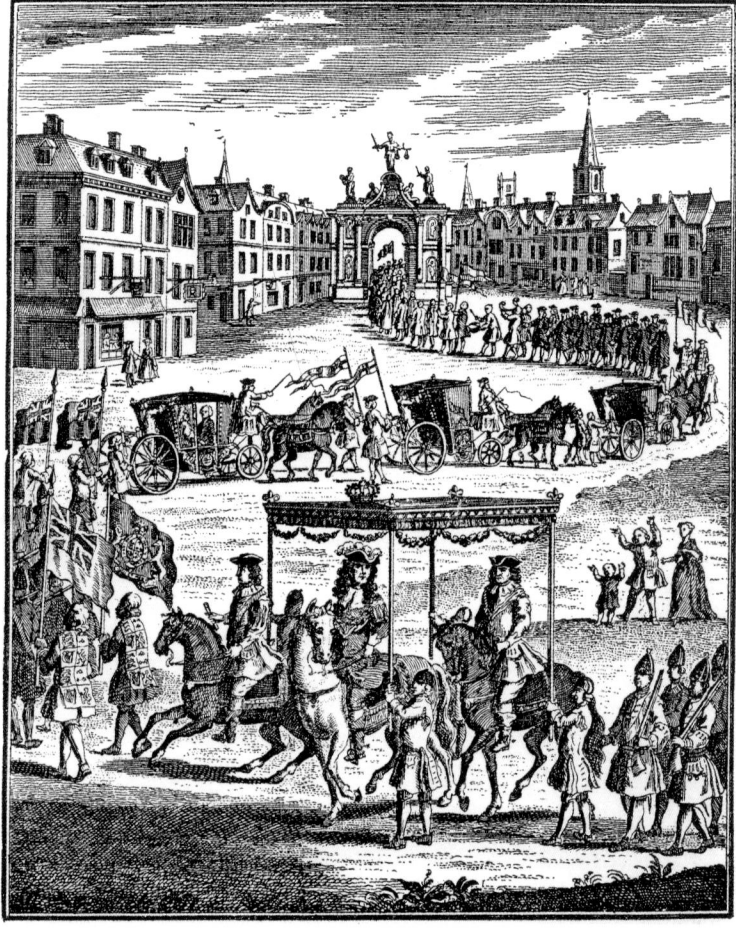

11. The coronation procession of King Charles II, April 22, 1661. Engraving after Dirk Stoop.

seal. With a new monarch, the old matrices which bore the previous monarch's armorials were defaced and given to the new holder of the office. A rare pair of these silver matrices, dating from 1878, is illustrated in *A Noble Feast*, cat. no. 101. Instead of melting down the matrices for cash, the recipient often chose to commemorate his appointment by using the silver to have a cup or other piece of silver made. The earliest of

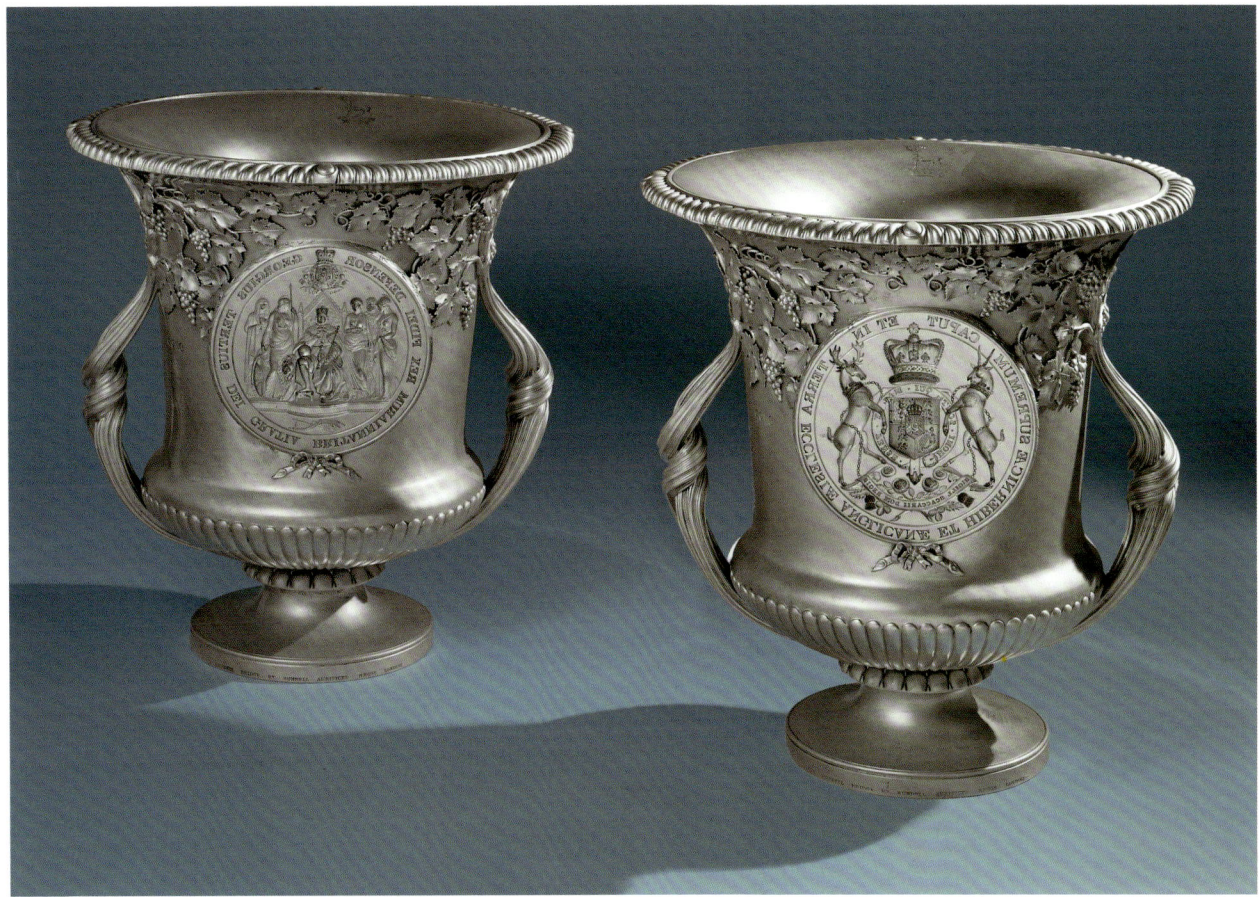

12. Pair of wine coolers, silver, London, 1823/24, maker's mark of John Bridge for Rundell, Bridge & Rundell. Set into these vases are the defaced matrices of the obsolete seal of the Chancellor of the Exchequer, received by Lord Goderich as a "perk" of office when he became Chancellor in 1823. As they are molds, the depictions of the seal are reversed. Cat. no. 40

13. Frederick Robinson, Viscount Goderich, subsequently 1st Earl of Ripon (1782–1859) by Sir Thomas Lawrence, oil on canvas. *National Portrait Gallery, London*

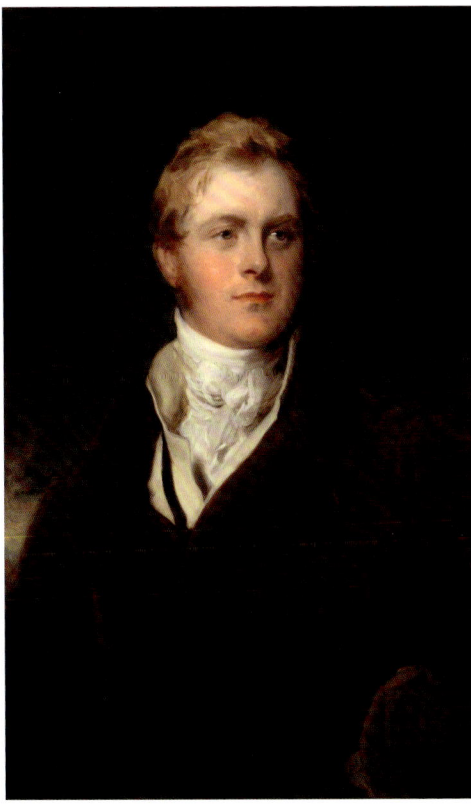

these are the two surviving Bacon cups of 1574, ordered by Sir Nicholas Bacon to be made from the seal of the previous reign.[11] Toward the end of the seventeenth century, salvers engraved with the royal arms from the seal superseded the cups. In the early nineteenth century, a handful of vases and wine coolers, such as the pair made for Frederick Robinson (figs. 12 and 13), were made with the matrices themselves set into the bodies as part of the heraldic decoration. Because they are molds, however, the carved design of each side of the seal is in reverse. Made in 1823/24, the Gans wine coolers commemorate Robinson's appointment as Chancellor of the Exchequer.

Robinson's contemporaries agreed that he was not equipped for leadership in turbulent times; his term of office as Chancellor coincided with economic depression and he was given the nickname "Prosperity Robinson." In September 1827 he became Prime Minister, lasting in office only until the following January, when his Cabinet fell apart. Robinson is unique among British Prime Ministers in never having faced Parliament. After his death in 1859, the *Annual*

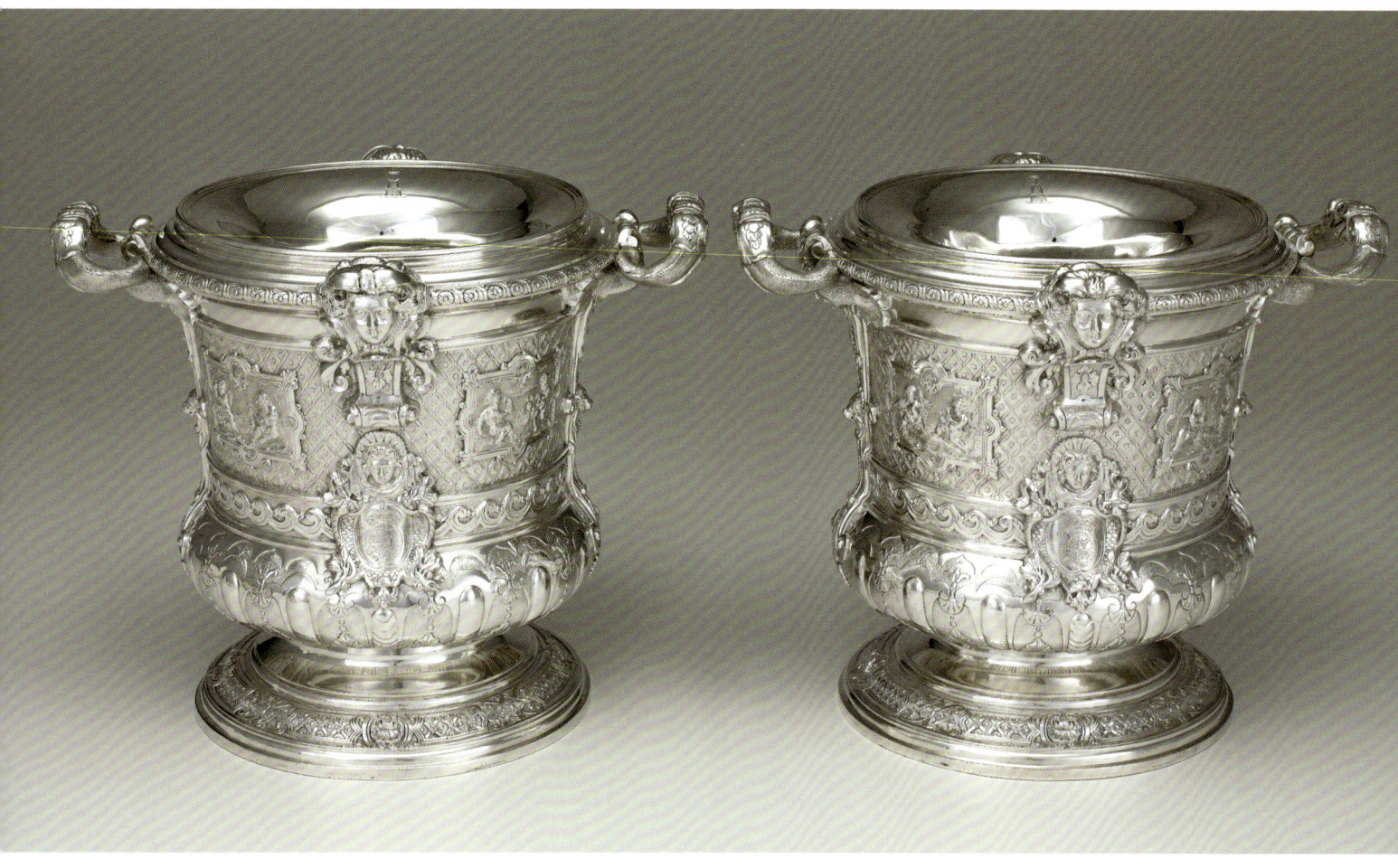

14. Pair of wine coolers, silver, London, 1826/27, maker's mark of Robert Garrard II for Garrard & Co., engraved with the arms of George Stanhope, 6th Earl of Chesterfield (1805–1866). The 4th Earl of Chesterfield had received a pair of wine coolers identical to this pair as part of a grant of silver on his appointment as ambassador to the court in The Hague in 1728. A hundred years later, to mark his coming of age, the sixth earl added to the service by ordering these copies from Garrard's.
Cat. no. 41

Register observed that "… as a statesman he was perhaps the weakest Premier to whom a Sovereign of England ever entrusted the seals of office."[12]

A further pair of wine coolers in the Gans Collection represents not only another means of acquiring silver but also shows how the pull of ancestral silver could triumph over the attractions of new fashions. Ordered from Garrard's in 1826/27 by the 6th Earl of Chesterfield as part of an order of plate to mark his coming-of-age, the coolers are exact copies of ones issued by the Jewel House to his predecessor, the fourth earl, almost exactly a hundred years before. Interestingly, the date of the copies coincides with the enthusiastic revival of many earlier styles in decorative arts.

The 4th Earl of Chesterfield's coolers had formed part of his ambassadorial issue of plate when he was posted to The Hague in 1728. The warrant authorized 5,893 ounces of white plate (for a dinner service) as well as a further 1,066 of gilt plate for a dessert service. Ambassadors, as

personal representatives of the monarch, were expected to entertain lavishly. Chesterfield's longstanding feuds with Sir Robert Walpole, the Prime Minister, and with George II damaged his political career, but as an envoy he came into his own. An obsessive Francophile, the earl cleverly exploited the fact that the Jewel House placed no limit on the amount that could be charged for "fashioning" the allowance of silver. He therefore ordered an elaborate service in the latest French taste, with many of the components, such as these wine coolers, probably directly copying contemporary Paris-made pieces. The great amount of modeling and casting required to make them incurred considerable expense over and above the cost of the raw material. It appears that John Tysoe, the Royal Goldsmith, turned the Chesterfield order over to the Huguenot silversmith Paul Crespin, who in turn bought the finished wine coolers from a colleague, the celebrated Paul de Lamerie. The Royal Goldsmith was not usually a maker of plate himself but sub-contracted the manufacturing to various specialist suppliers. Such a large and ambitious order could not be fulfilled by one silversmith and de Lamerie's mark on the coolers was overstruck with Crespin's before delivery.[13]

Even though the original warrant of 1728 had specified that the silver was "to be return'd into the Jewell office upon demand," the Chesterfield ambassadorial service appears to have been retained by the fourth earl. The entry in the Delivery Book of the Jewel House accounts has been struck through and an annotation in the margin records that it was "discharged" in 1768, meaning no doubt that Chesterfield paid a cash equivalent (forty years later)![14] Sixty years after that the sixth earl paid homage to his predecessor by adding to the service. In similar vein, in 1807/8 the 4th Duke of Newcastle commissioned eight sauce tureens matching a pair of soup tureens made to a design by William Kent that had been purchased by his father in 1757 (fig. 76).

Ambassadorial services cannot of course be classified as royal gifts, as they were supposed to be returned, and those that were retained by the recipient were often paid for by cash or in lieu of the ambassador's out-of-pocket expenses. The giving of gifts, however, oiled the wheels of government and commerce. A piece of plate could be converted to cash, but bestowing a cup or tankard on a government official was not as blatant as handing over a bag of coins. English embassies, such as the ones sent to Russia in the seventeenth century in an attempt to forge trading agreements, took silverware (usually outmoded objects from the Jewel House), but such gifts cannot have been regarded as glamorous as the French wine and majestic horses that the Dutch embassy took with them. "Douceurs" (literally, sweeteners) in the form of silver salvers on which were placed expensive sweetmeats and, later, a bag of coins, were given annually from 1679 onwards to the Lord Mayor by the Jewish community of London who were appreciative of his protection. A piece of silver was usually given by grateful investors to the captain of a merchantman for

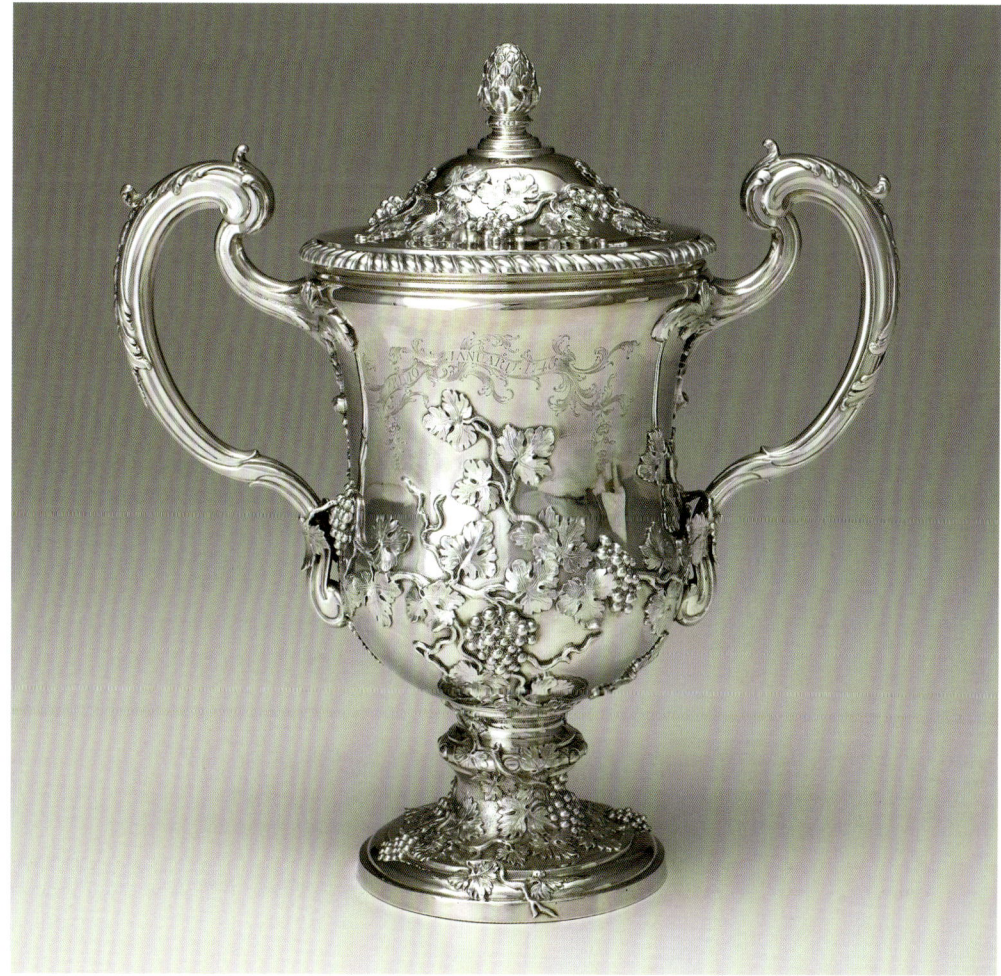

15. Cup and cover, silver, London, 1746/47, maker's mark of George Wickes, engraved with the inscription: *EX DONO CAROLI HALE AR & PRIMO JANUARI 1746*, **recording the gift of this cup.**
Cat. no. 25

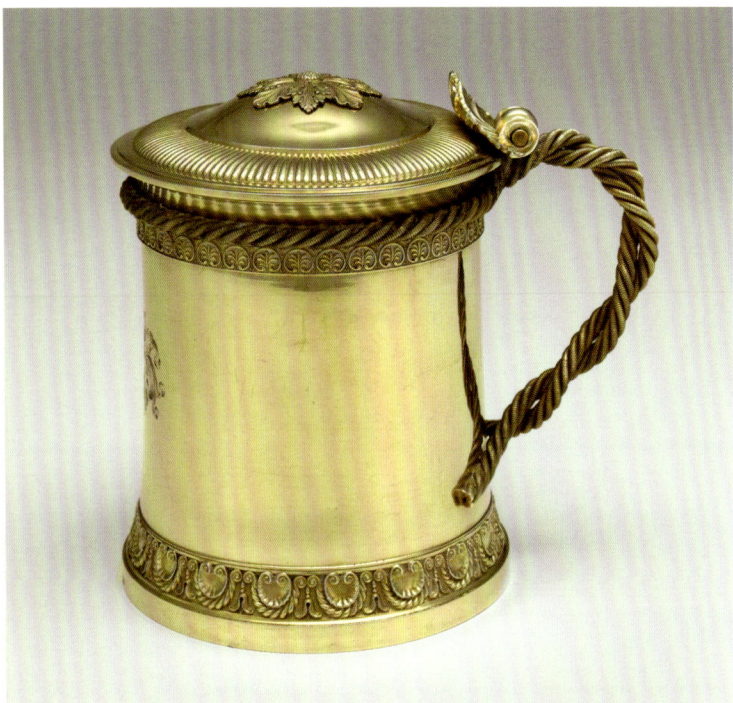

16. Tankard, silver gilt, London, 1811/12, maker's mark of Benjamin Smith II & James Smith II for Rundell, Bridge & Rundell, engraved: *This TANKARD was presented by DECIMA BARBER to her excellent friend HENRY NUNN ESQR. as a small token of GRATITUDE & ESTEEM.* Cat. no. 35

salvaging a cargo, or just for completing a successful voyage. The custom of giving race prizes in the form of a silver, or even gold, cup or porringer dates from the time of Charles II and has continued to the present day. Gifts of plate to military or naval heroes started in the eighteenth century but it was the Napoleonic Wars at the end of the century and Britain's emergence as an imperial power that gave great impetus to the custom of giving not only silver but also costly jewelled snuffboxes and swords. Committees and civic bodies such as the Corporation of London commissioned presentation pieces and even complete dinner services from the 1790s onwards, with most of the orders going to Rundell & Bridge, who in 1797 became Royal Goldsmiths. By the middle of the nineteenth century, these silver testimonials had moved down the social scale and had become so common that a writer in the *Illuminated Magazine* of September 1844 lampooned them with an article entitled "The Mutual Piece-of-Plate Presentation Club."[15]

To bestow silver on another person could also be an act of friendship. Wills in the eighteenth century often specify bequests of money "to buy a piece of plate." In 1794 Lord Dacre left his cousin Thomas Chute of the Vyne "twenty guineas to buy a Ring as a token of my regard for him."[16] Rather than purchase a ring, it seems that Chute turned his twenty guineas into a silver inkstand

which he had embellished with his and Dacre's coats of arms. An inscription records that it was "From Thomas Lord Dacre by Will." The inkstand has recently returned to the Vyne, Hampshire, now a National Trust property. The handsome cup and cover of 1746/47 (fig. 15) were given by Charles Hale as a New Year's gift in 1746, but the identity of the recipient is unknown. The tradition of giving gifts on New Year's Day dated back to the Middle Ages and the custom was not moved to Christmas Day until the nineteenth century.

During the Regency period, Henry Nunn and John Barber were partners in a successful haberdasher's business in Covent Garden, London. Nunn's sister Decima had married Barber, and the silver-gilt tankard in fig. 16 was given by her to Nunn. Later, in 1839, a widow and childless, she made her brother her sole legatee.

Nunn's tankard is engraved on the side with his coat of arms within a decorative cartouche that is part of the tankard's decoration. The practice of engraving or even stamping one's initials on silver dates back to the later Middle Ages: spoons given as baptismal or wedding gifts are often adorned with the recipient's initials. Heraldry had begun simply as a means of identification with a composition of animals, flora, or inanimate objects painted onto a knight's shield,

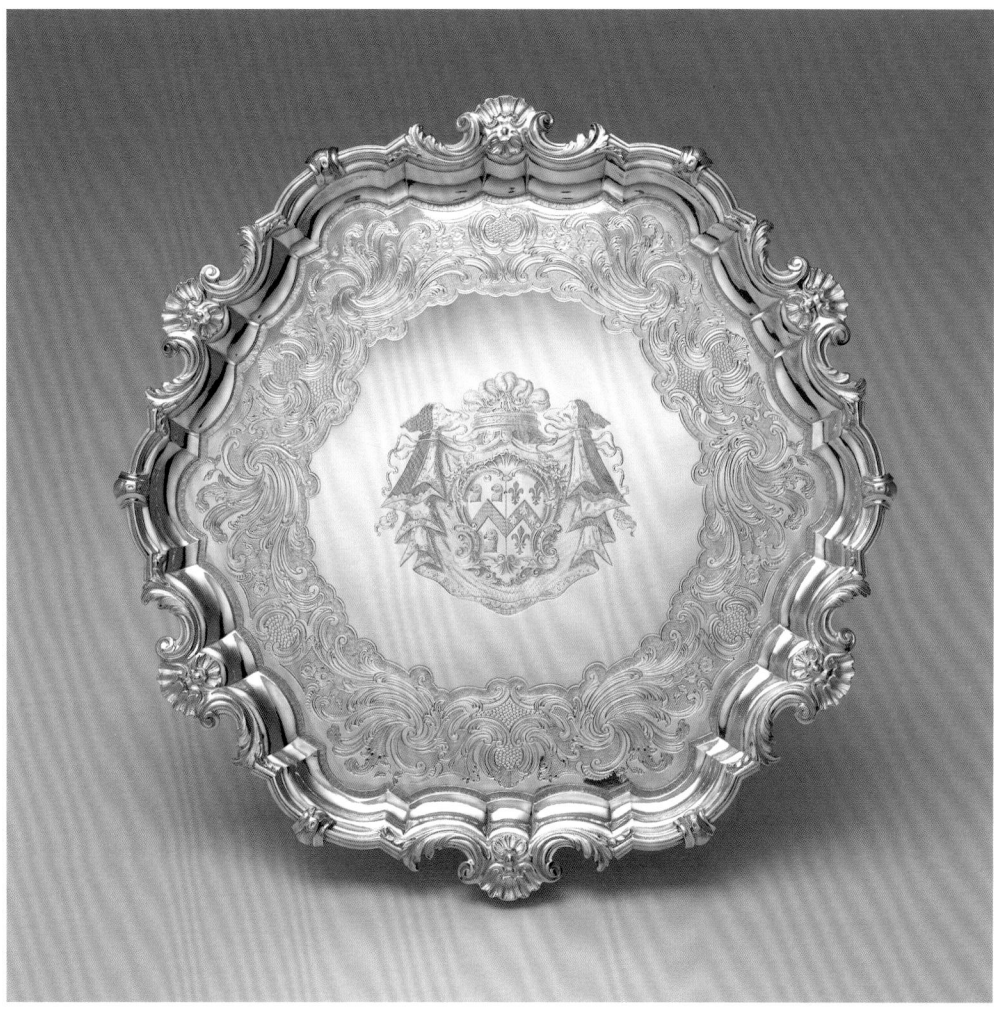

17. Salver, silver, London, 1742/43, maker's mark of George Wickes, engraved with the arms of Manning Lethieullier, a London merchant of Huguenot descent. The flat surface of this salver acts as a perfect canvas for the decorative heraldic engraving. Cat. no. 23

while his helmet was surmounted by a three-dimensional symbol known as a crest. In time, a system of rules developed which dictated how the symbols should be arranged and what colors could be combined. The heralds, appointed by the crown, kept records of armorials and ensured there were no duplications, as a coat of arms is unique to an individual. From being an efficient means of identification in case of theft, heraldry on silver had, by the end of the seventeenth century, become a part of its decoration—as well as a means to advertise genteel status. Large ewers and basins, such as the set made in 1699/1700 for the Earl of Kent (illustrated in *A Noble Feast*, fig. 4, p. 17), were essentially display pieces with no function: the large circular charger is almost completely flat and would be useless to catch the liquid poured from one of the ewers, but it acts as a canvas for the splendid armorial composition engraved on it. The poet Thomas Gray reminds us in his *Elegy Written in a Country Churchyard*,

1751, that "The boast of heraldry, the pomp of power" are as mortal as the grandee who enjoys them.

To be able to display your coat of arms on the sideboard was an important reason for acquiring silver, and if you had made an impressive marriage to an heiress with longer lineage than yourself, what better reason could there be to acquire new silver and have it engraved with your arms combined with hers?

While a great nobleman such as the Earl of Kent was readily recognizable as such by his deportment, dress, retainers, and houses, those further down the social scale welcomed the possibility of advertising their genteel status with heraldry, and here was ground enough for acquiring new silver. The salver in fig. 17, dating from 1742/43, is engraved with the arms borne by Manning Lethieullier against an ornamental background depicted as rich fabric. The effect is almost three-dimensional. Like the much larger

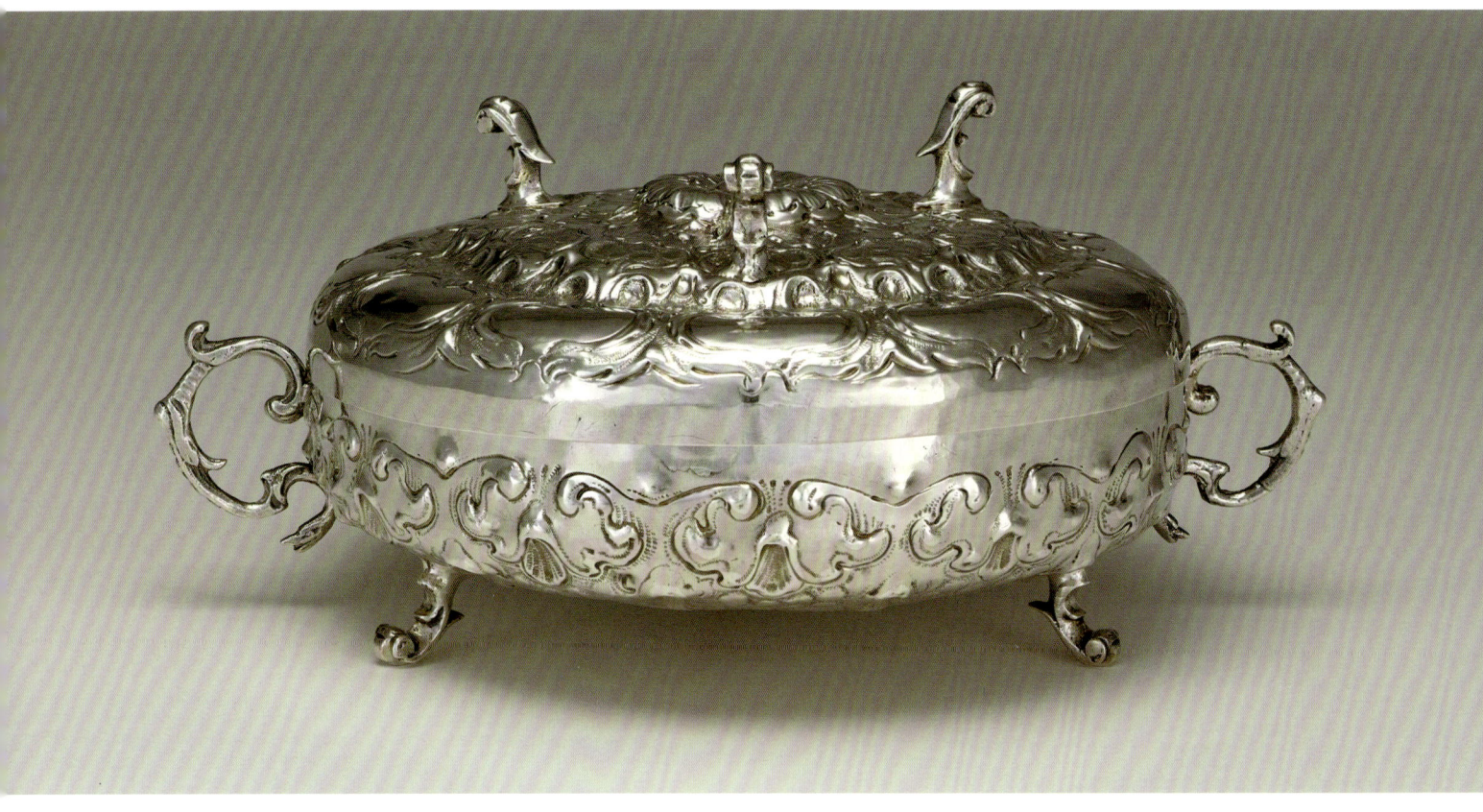

charger made for the Earl of Kent, this salver was probably intended to be propped up on a sideboard for display. A merchant trading with India and the Far East, Lethieullier was descended from a Huguenot immigrant who had come to England fifty years before and acquired a coat of arms, and he was no doubt keen to demonstrate his gentility. Following the rules of heraldry, his coat of arms is displayed on the left side of the shield, which has been divided down the middle with a vertical line. On the right side he displays the arms of his wife's father, Edmund Green, of a Yorkshire family with a much longer lineage than his own.

Heraldic engraving was often retained even after the object had become worn out or obsolete. Organizations such as livery companies (trade guilds) and even individuals would preserve the memory of a donation or inheritance by having the same arms or inscription engraved on a new piece of silver made from the old. Much as the 6th Earl of Chesterfield, having just attained his majority, sought to honor his predecessor by adding to the ancestral dinner service with pieces in the same style, so beneficiaries of legacies of silver would strive to retain the armorial engraving on the plate they inherited. In 1766, the Countess of Mountrath, leaving her husband's Paul de Lamerie silver to a friend, Lady Milton, in her will, specified that the silver should be used by Lady Milton and her children "with the same arms and crests as are now engraved thereon without being erased or altered."[17]

It was the fickleness of fashion, however, that was perhaps the most significant contributor to the coffers of the goldsmiths and silversmiths. Notwithstanding familial piety, or friendship, the lure of something new was irresistible in all periods. With improved roads and increasing prosperity, the seventeenth century saw the emergence of London as the social centre of England. Families spent a "season" in the capital and shopped for items in the latest taste. Moreover, for much of the period between the Restoration and the death of George IV, France was the dominant influence not only in fashions of the table but also in clothes and the decorative arts, including silver. The English ruling elite frequently spoke and corresponded in French; they also sought to eat French dishes presented in the latest French style.

The old notion that it was the artists and craftsmen who drove prevailing taste has long

18. Three-legged bowl and cover, silver, London, 1671/72, maker's mark *WW*. A utilitarian piece for serving a hot alcoholic drink, such as posset. Cat. no. 5

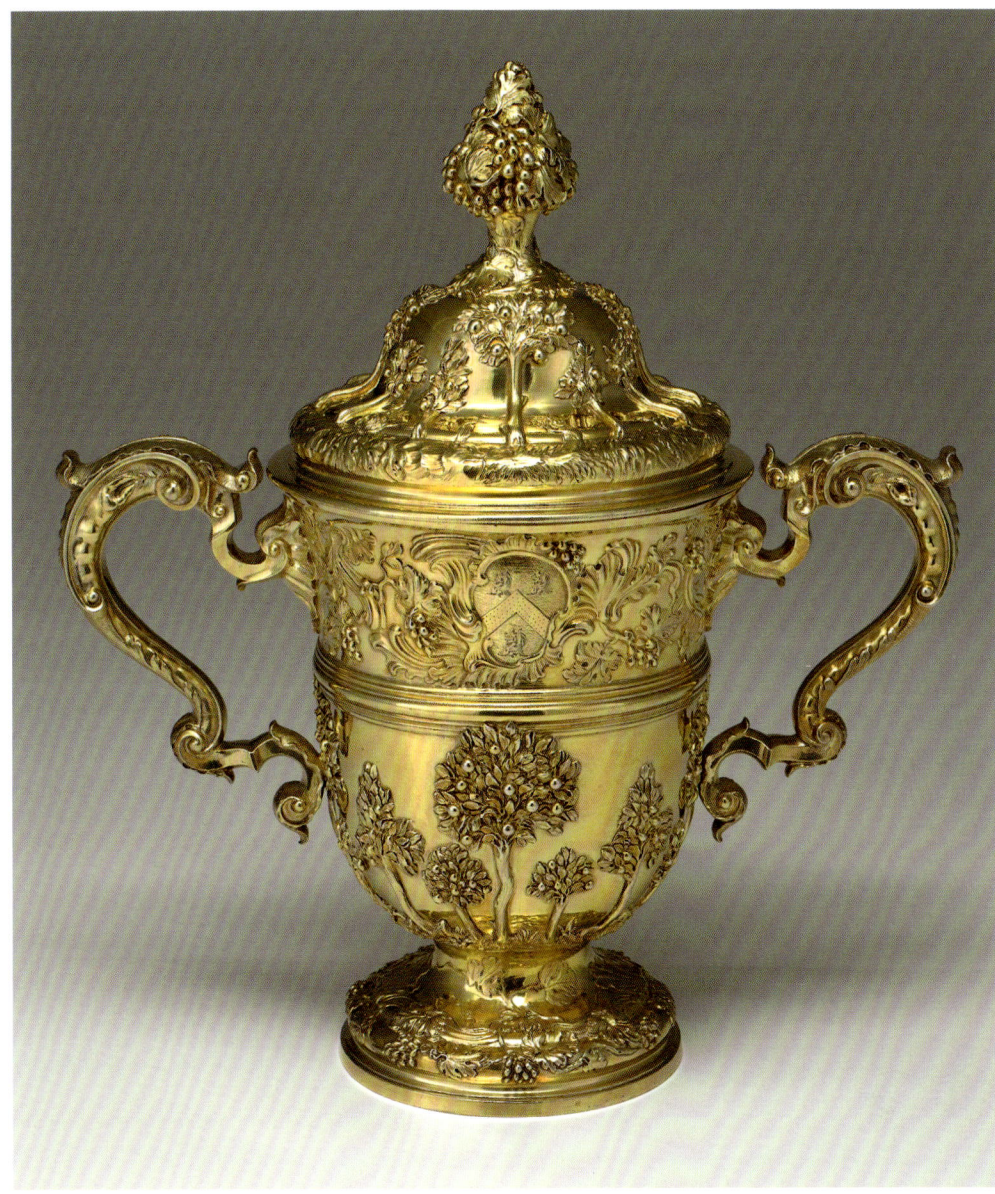

19. Cup and cover, silver gilt, London, 1740/41, maker's mark of Frederick Kandler. The form of the two-handled cup developed in the middle of the seventeenth century and continued to be popular in Britain until well into the nineteenth century. Cat. no. 20

been revised to acknowledge the fact that it was the customer who was proactive in the adoption of new styles. The modern view of the artist introducing startling and revolutionary ideas with each new work cannot be applied to Europe before the nineteenth century. Traditional workshops of masters, apprentices and journeymen were part of a continuous tradition of handing down skills from one generation to the next, and changes in styles or techniques could only be done slowly.[18] Often the first step towards the adoption of a new vessel or style was to copy an example from abroad, usually from France.

Curiously, vessels used for drinking tended to be the most slowly affected by the waves of fashion. The tankard enjoyed popularity from the middle of the sixteenth century until well into the nineteenth century, and the uniquely English vessel, the two-handled cup, with or without a cover, was in vogue from the middle of the seventeenth century until the beginning of the nineteenth. During the Restoration period, influence from the Dutch republic and northern Germany led to the introduction of the shallow covered vessel on three feet, often with auricular (or "ear-like") decoration (fig. 18). Known in Germany as a *Wöchnerinnenschüssel*, it was used to serve brandy punch, usually hot and heavily spiced. The Gans example is one of just a handful of English examples, and by the 1680s the form had passed

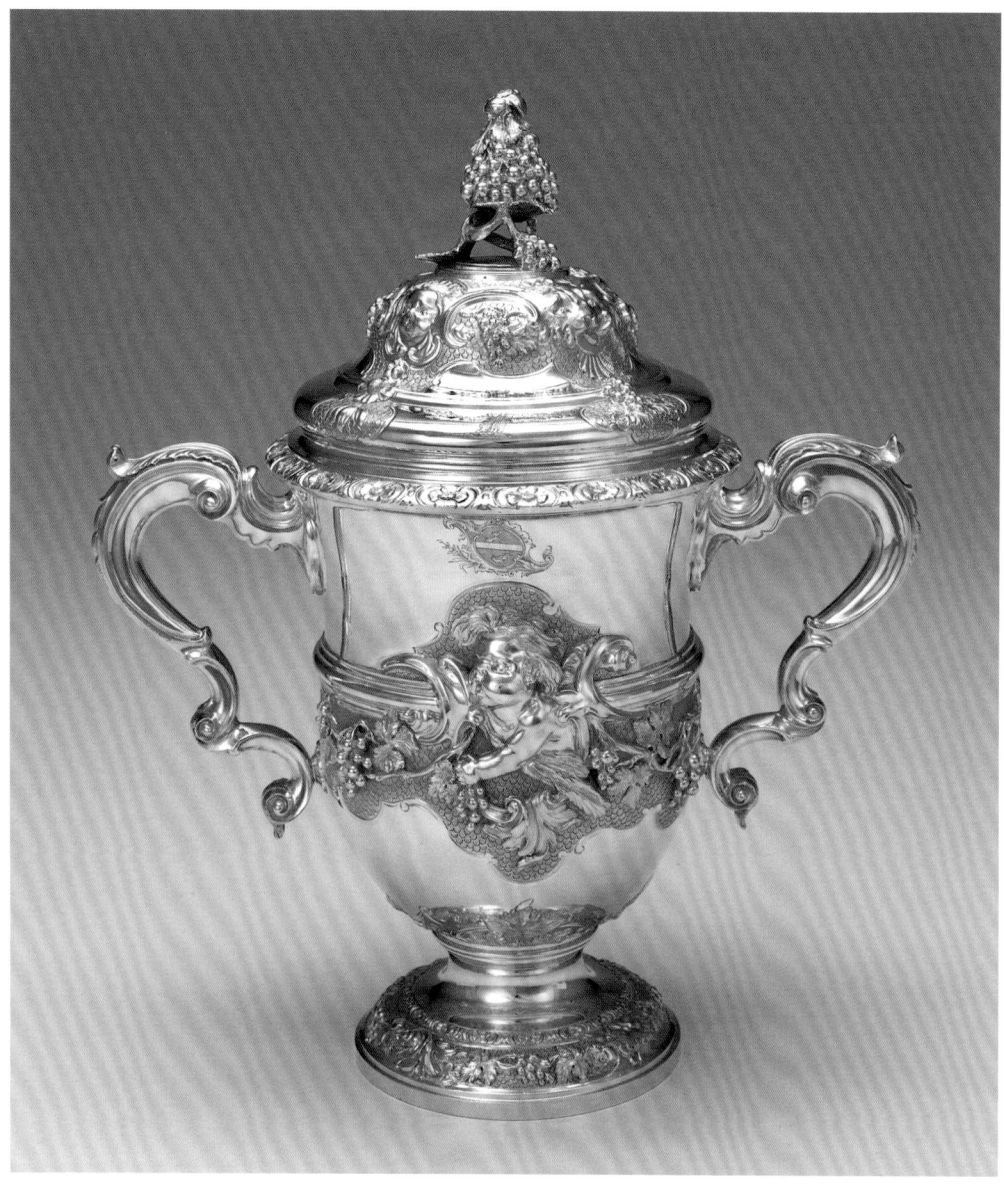

20. Cup and cover, silver, London, 1750/51, maker's mark of Paul de Lamerie. Another example of the popular cup-and-cover form, this example is a late product of de Lamerie's workshop and well illustrates the advanced rococo decoration that developed in the 1740s.
Cat. no. 26

from the fashionable scene. The two-handled bowl, such as fig. 54, known in England as a "porringer," continued to be the commonest hollowware vessel sold by silversmiths. The more modest of these were no doubt used for communal drinking, but at the top end of the scale, the dearest examples, usually in the forefront of the prevailing taste, were works of art in themselves and without doubt part of the display of plate on the sideboard. Two such examples are those illustrated as figs. 19 and 20. The first, of 1740/41, is from the workshop of Frederick Kandler. A few years before, he had taken it over from his putative father, Charles Kandler, who had returned to Germany, where his uncle, Joachim, was the chief modeler at the Meissen porcelain factory. The

Kandlers produced an idiosyncratic form of baroque which paid only lip service to the rococo with some of its surface decoration and, on this cup, the naturalism of its grape-cluster finial. In contrast, the cup in fig. 20, from the workshop of Paul de Lamerie in 1750/51, is not merely composed of rococo decoration grafted onto the baroque form of cup, but it flows with subtle curves and becomes a piece of sculpture in its own right. The contrasting surfaces of plain silver and fish-scale ornament, together with the *putto* emerging as if from water, are typical of the work of the modeler/chaser who has been dubbed the "Maynard Master." His identity is unknown, but he appears to have worked for de Lamerie and a few others between about 1736 and 1745. By the

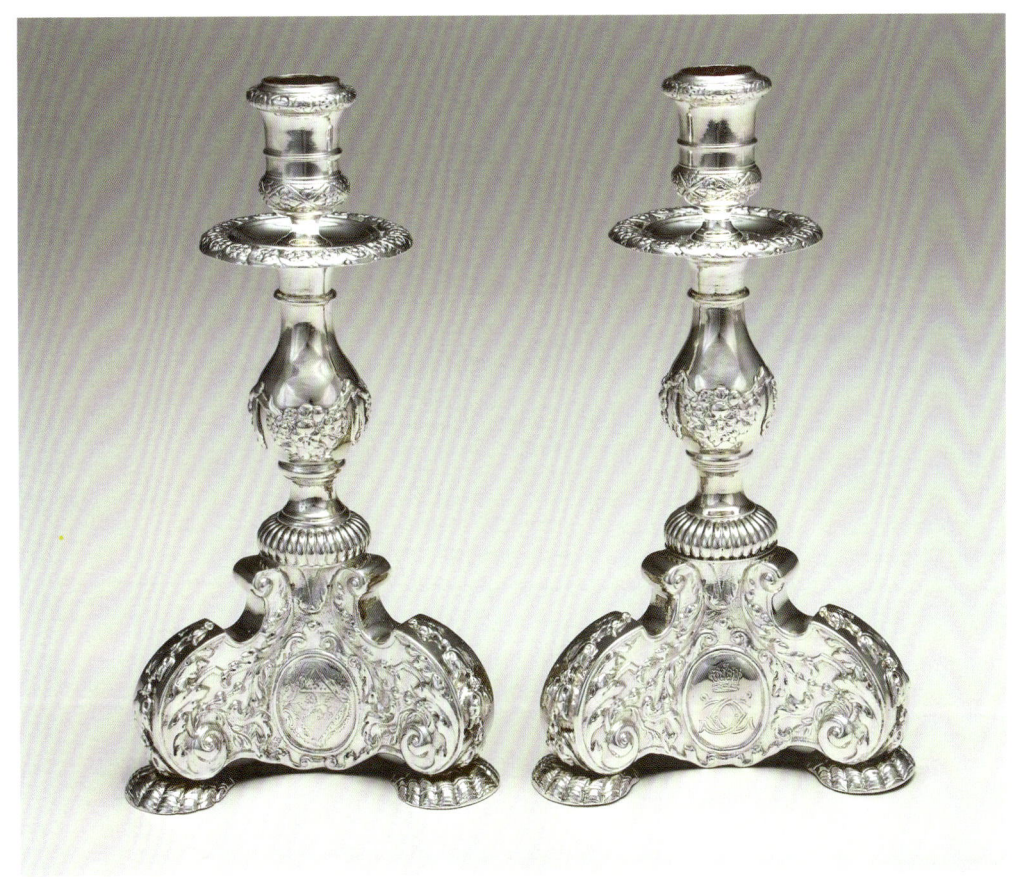

21. Pair of candlesticks, silver, London, 1700/1, maker's mark of Joseph Bird.
Cat. no. 9

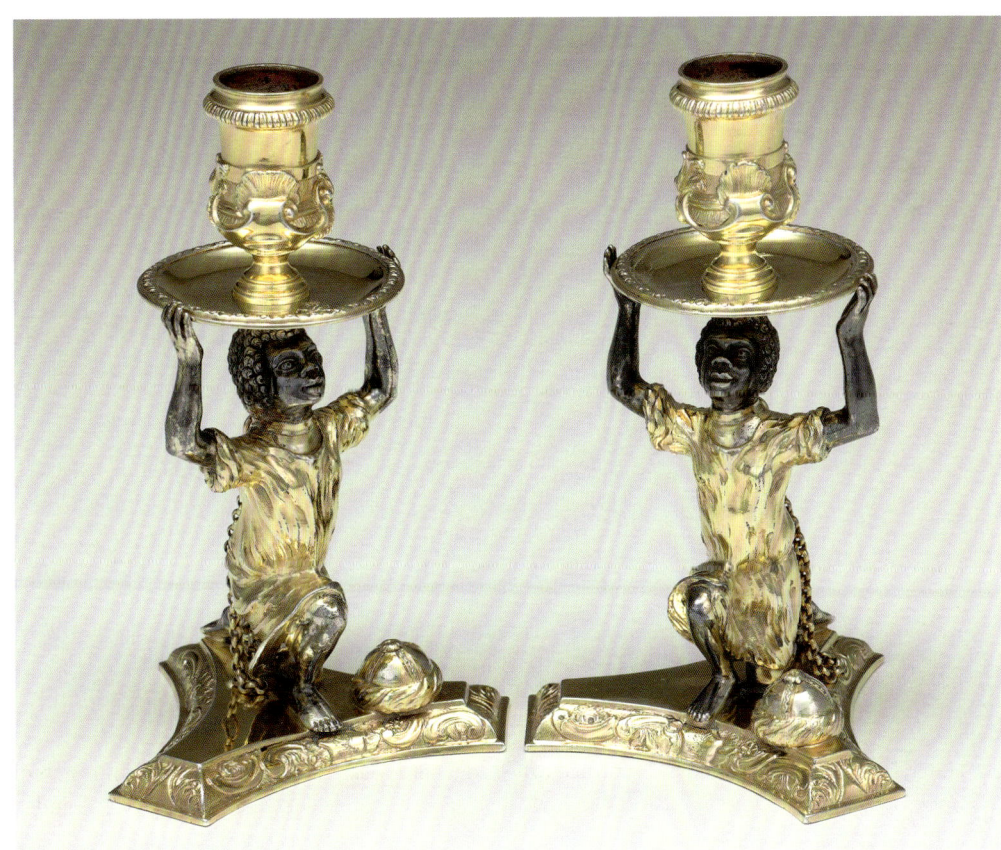

22. Pair of candlesticks, silver, parcel gilt and partially oxidized, London, 1745/46, maker's mark of Isaac Duke.
Cat. no. 24

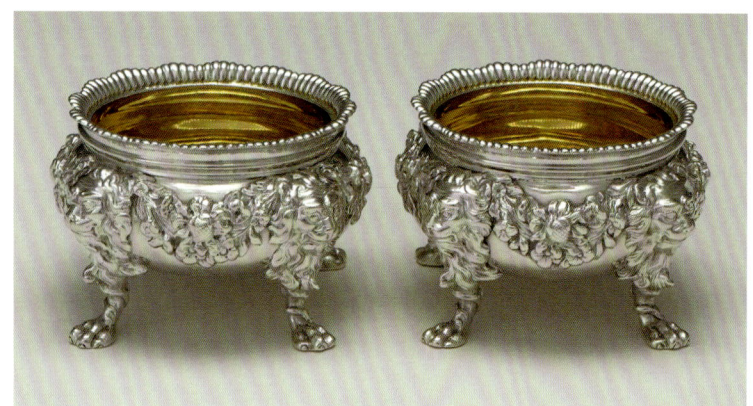

23. Pair of salts, silver, interiors gilt, London, 1734/35, maker's mark of Paul de Lamerie.
Cat. no. 18

time this cup was made, it is very likely that there were several imitators of his unique style in London. In fact, Paul de Lamerie died in 1751; his will, made in May of that year, speaks of a "long and tedious illness" and directs that Samuel Collins, his journeyman and former apprentice, should finish the remaining stock in his workshop.[19]

The tension between function and decoration was always present. We have seen how vital silver was as a material, but what of objects that were more decorative than functional? The candlesticks of 1700/1 by Joseph Bird, illustrated in fig. 21, which may have been part of a set for an altar, are eminently practical. Their strong outline and restrained surface decoration do not interfere with their ability to reflect the maxi-

mum amount of light. The heavy bases make them extremely stable. In contrast, the pair of silver-gilt candlesticks in fig. 22, made in 1745/46, is entirely decorative. The gilding and the patination of the boys' faces, arms, and legs would have reflected little light compared to the surface of the Bird examples. Candlesticks in the shape of enslaved black Africans first appeared in the 1680s and the form was revived from time to time during the eighteenth century.

Silver for dining, like that for lighting, was extremely susceptible to the whims and influences of fashion. The way in which changing fashions in eating and drinking influenced silver design has been explored in the companion volume to this guide, *A Noble Feast*. Dining plate was by far the greatest portion of a person's

24. Pair of sauceboats, silver, London, 1755/56, maker's mark of Thomas Gilpin.
Cat. no. 27

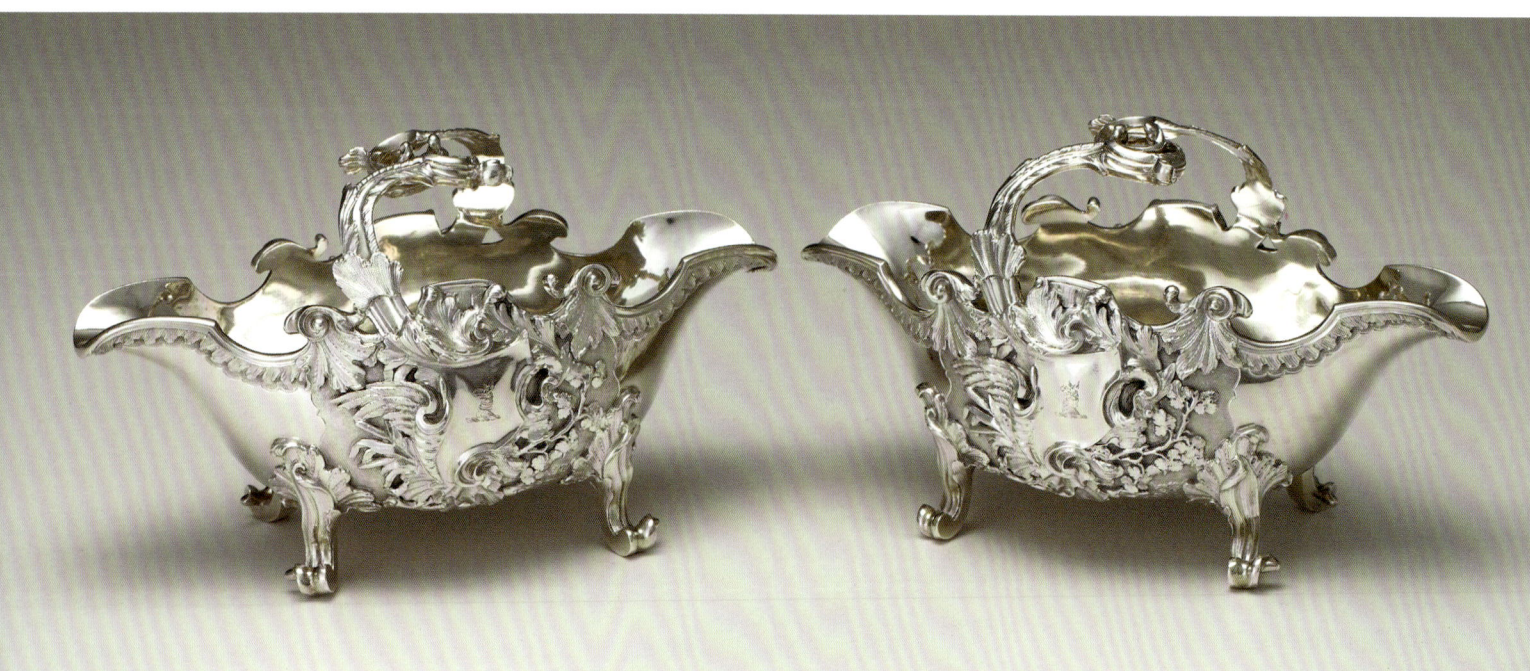

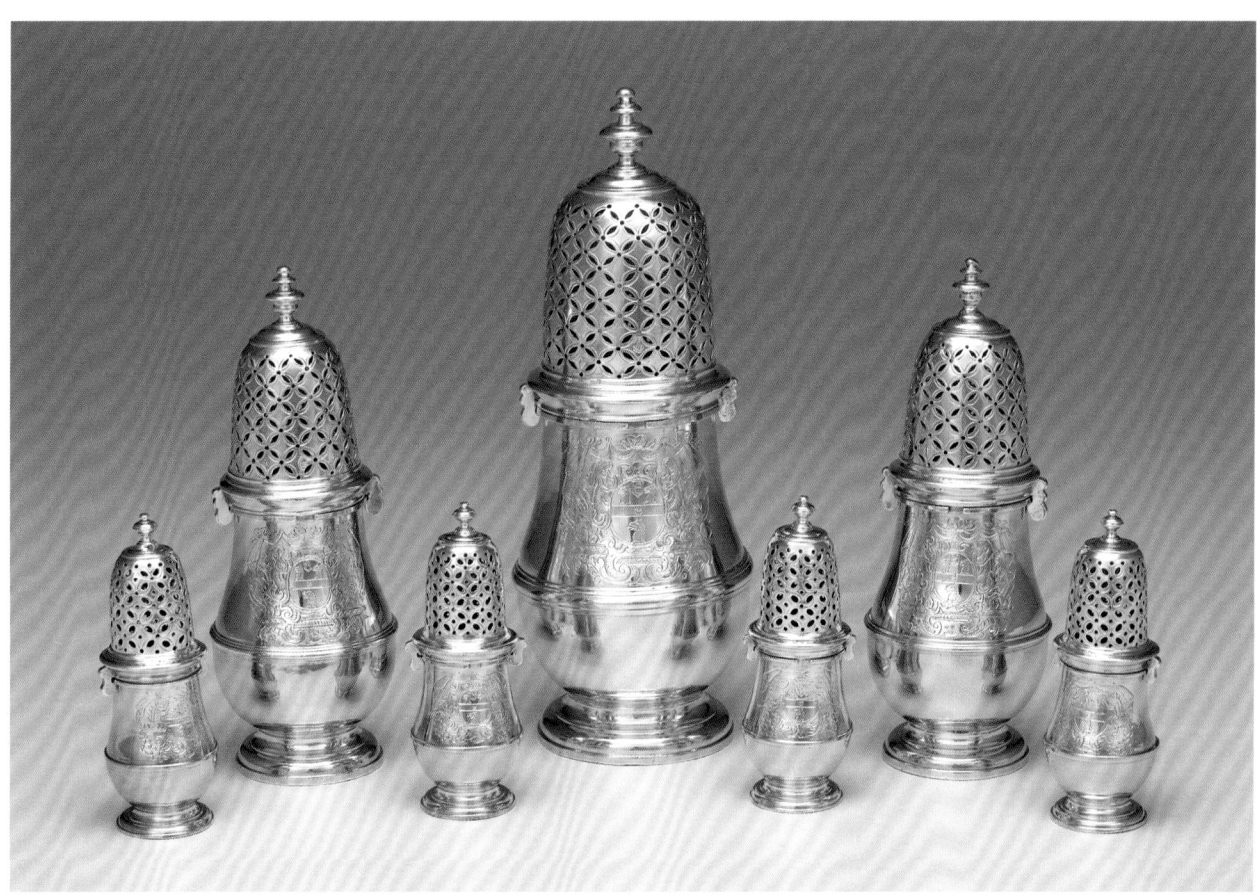

25. Seven casters, silver, London, 1705/6, maker's mark of Joseph Ward.
Cat. no. 10

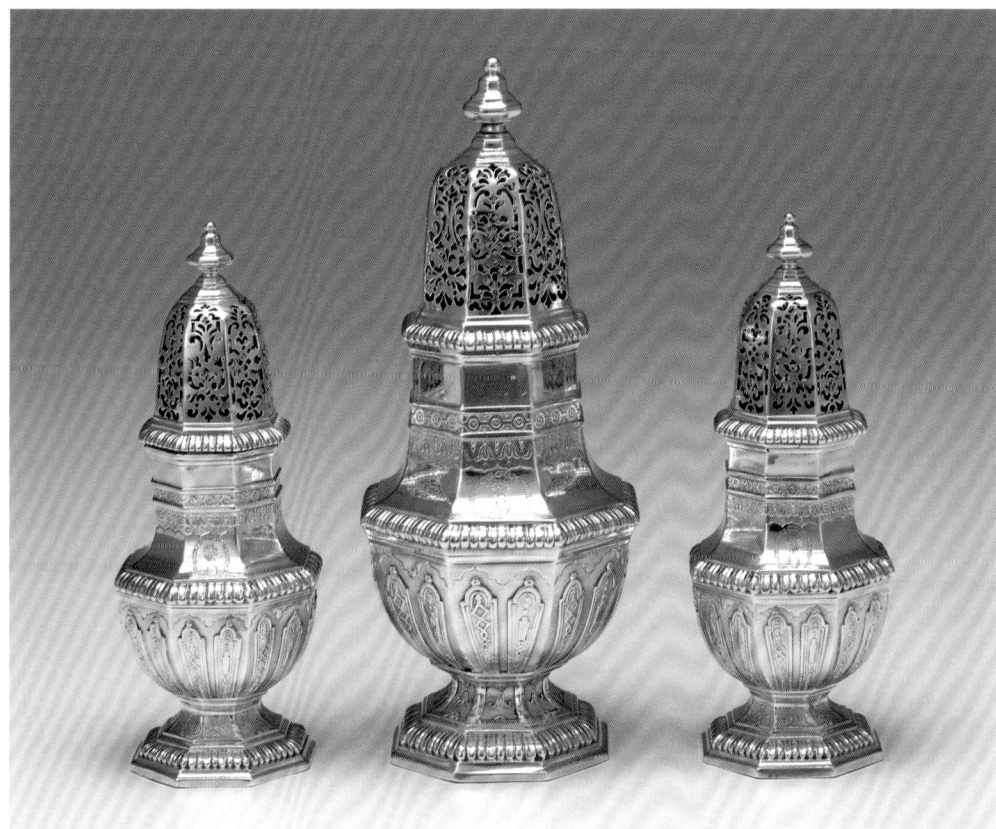

26. Three casters, silver, c. 1705, the smaller pair with maker's mark of William Fleming.
Cat. no. 8

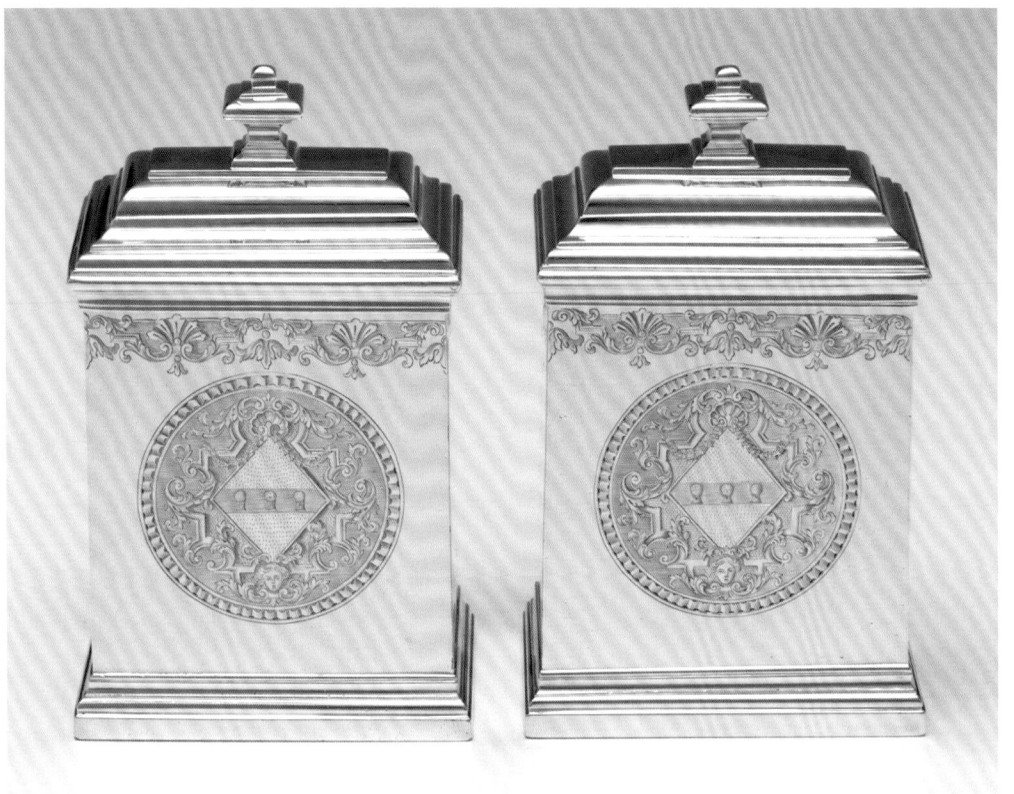

27. Pair of tea caddies, silver, lead, iron, London, 1724/25, maker's mark of Paul Crespin. Engraved with the arms of a lady of the Vernon family, the caddies were probably kept under lock and key in her parlour (owing to the high price of tea at the beginning of the eighteenth century). Cat. no. 14

expenditure on silver, not only because of the large numbers of plates and dishes required for the prevailing custom of *service à la française*, in which all the dishes of a particular course were placed on the table at once, but also because of the myriad of vessels and implements required for the many things offered on a Georgian table.

Salts (fig. 23), a feature of the table since the earliest times, tended to be large, and came in sets, often of six or more, while new items such as sauceboats (fig. 24) appeared as the English enthusiastically adopted French cooking. Such light rococo creations must have caused a stir when they appeared on the dining table. More traditional items such as casters for various condiments give us only an inkling of the scale of a nobleman's dining plate—they are now usually the sole survivors of a massive *surtout de table*, the centerpiece having been long consigned to the melting pot as fashions changed yet again. The set of casters illustrated in fig. 25 is unusual in being so extensive: the trio of larger examples would have been used to hold sugar, pepper, and mustard, but we can only guess at the ground spices contained in the smaller ones. The monumental set of three in fig. 26, copies of contemporary French examples, was made for a Scottish patron,

George Baillie, and shows how the pervasive influence of France reached the north of Britain. If silver for dining was the province of the husband, articles for the new fads of coffee, tea, and chocolate were often ordered by the lady of the house.

Whether the province of the man or the lady of the house, silver remained an extremely personal accompaniment to daily life. There were also some who sought to surround themselves with startlingly innovative silver to adorn the interiors they were creating. Among these were William Beckford and George IV, discussed at length in the Interludes which follow.

Notes
1 Henderson, p. 40.
2 *The Drummer, or, the Haunted-House, A Comedy As it is Acted at the Theatre-Royal in Drury-Lane by His Majesty's Servants*, London, 1716, Act IV, Scene 1; quoted in John Culme's essay on the Wentworth Cistern in Sotheby's auction catalogue, *Treasures: Aristocratic Heirlooms*, July 4, 2010.
3 Gask, p. 55; How, 1952, vol. I, chap. 1, section IV, plate 16, and vol. II, chap. III, plate 1. Dating such spoons is not easy, for before 1478 only one hallmark was used, that of a leopard's head. The late Commander How and his wife Jane Penrice How (see fig. 58) categorized the small number of surviving examples of these marks in their landmark publication on early marks in 1952, dividing them into seven variations; the mark struck on the Gans spoon, designated an "Arabian" leopard's head, was dated by them

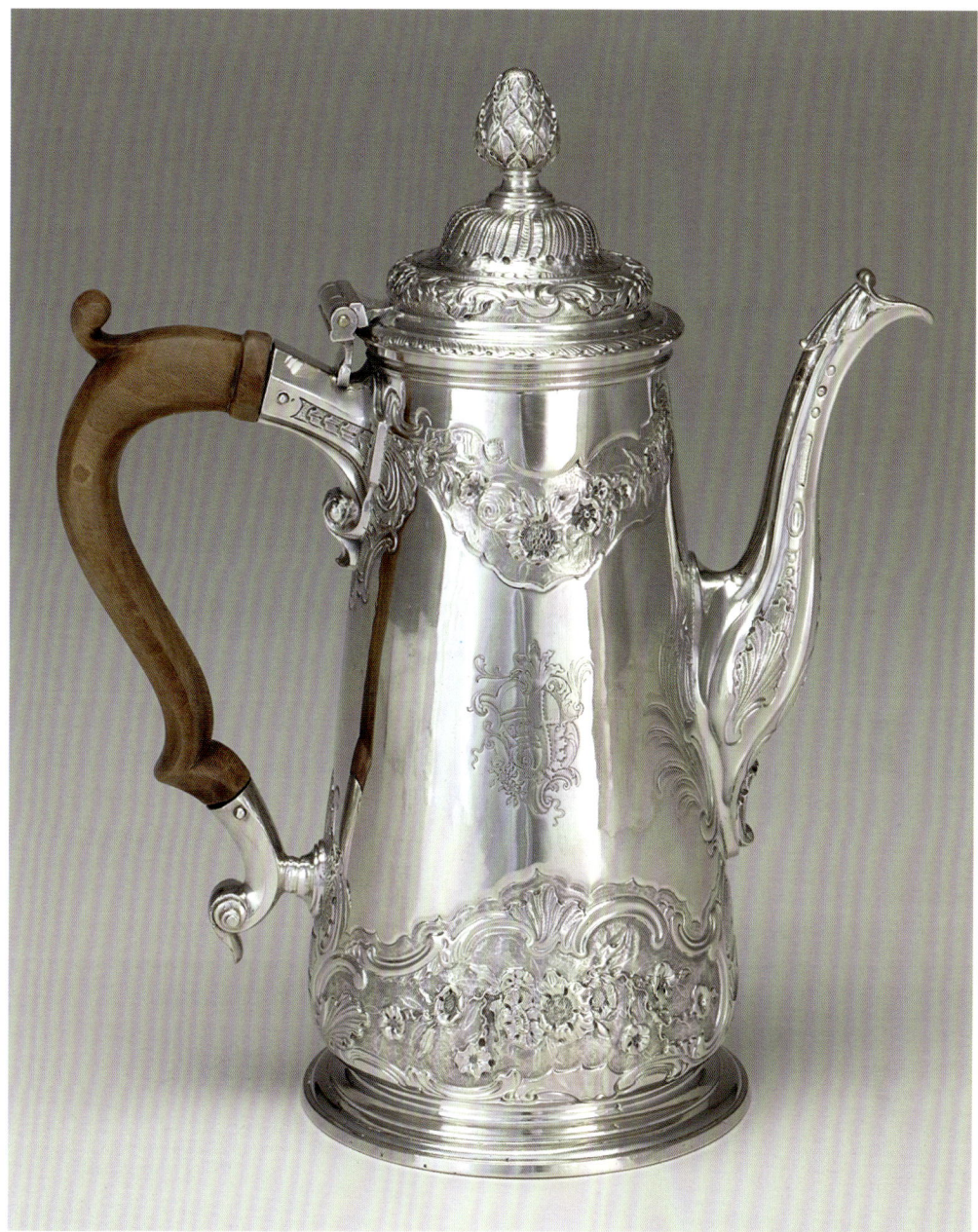

28. Coffee pot, silver, fruitwood, London 1739/40, maker's mark of George Wickes. With the arrival of the rococo, coffee pots and teapots provided the opportunity for elaborate chased or engraved decoration. Cat. no. 19

to the first half of the fifteenth century. The date letter first appeared in1478.

4 By the 1960s it was approximately 27 to 1; in 2010 it is 66 to 1.

5 See Vitali, pp. 17–21.

6 Sitwell, pp. 137–8.

7 National Archives [PRO], LC5/60, p. 133, I am grateful to Anna Keay for giving me her transcript of the relevant entries; see also Keay, pp. 3–8.

8 National Archives [PRO], LC2/8. The Gans bell weighs just over 4 ¼ ounces.

9 March 14, 1660, Latham and Matthews, vol. I, p. 87.

10 Lord Aylesbury, *Memoirs*, London, 1729, vol. 1, p. 89.

11 One of these, engraved "an heyrelome to his howse of Redgrave," is in the British Museum; another "to his howse of Stewkey" is now in the Ashmolean Museum. Banister, p. 278.

12 Quoted in *Complete Peerage*, vol. XI, p. 3.

13 Hartop, 1996, pp. 98–109; Lomax, p. 135. The coolers stamped by de Lamerie and Crespin were sold along with the Gans examples by Chesterfield descendants at auction in 1988. The originals are now divided between the Victoria and Albert Museum and the Royal Scottish Museum. A soup tureen of 1736/37, which probably also belonged to the 4th Earl of Chesterfield, forms part of the Jerome and Rita Gans Collection and is illustrated in *A Noble Feast*, fig. 13, p. 27; its mate appears to be the one in the Metropolitan Museum of Art, possibly presented as a "perk" after the coronation of George IV in 1821 to John Dymoke, King's Champion (see *A Noble Feast*, p. 28).

14 National Archives [PRO], LC/5 and LC/9/44, f. 297.

15 *Illuminated Magazine*, vol. III, pp. 261–6, quoted in Culme, 1977, p. 150.

16 National Archives [PRO], PROB 11/1247.

17 Hartop, 1996, p. 203.

18 See Hartop, 2007.

19 Hare, p. 13.

WILLIAM BECKFORD, 1760–1844

The Pursuit of Perfection

Born to great wealth, William Beckford seemed destined for the life of a Whig grandee. But posterity was to remember him not as a landowner or politician but as a collector of the most refined taste. Early in life a sexual scandal made him a social outcast and he filled the void created by his lack of social contacts with amassing collections of both old and new treasures. Beckford's father, known as Alderman Beckford, had been a bluff, outspoken figure who, at his death when William was nine years old, was said to have left thirty illegitimate children. The alderman had served twice as Lord Mayor of London, and as a Whig MP he had been notorious for his radical politics. But he was also an enthusiastic art patron. He rebuilt the family seat at Fonthill in Wiltshire in the Palladian style, and filled the house with classical art and Old Masters. A contemporary observer, Mrs. Lybbe Powys, spoke of its "utmost profusion of magnificence" and hinted at its vulgarity. It was popularly known as "Fonthill Splendens."

In the midst of all this splendor the young Beckford was brought up by his mother, whose Hamilton lineage (she was a granddaughter of the Duke of Abercorn) was to be a source of obsessive pride for him. His mother refused to send the boy to school and, lacking the company of children his own age, Beckford grew up to be petulant and utterly egocentric. In his teens he began to show an artistic sensibility. Sent to Switzerland to study at the age of seventeen, he also acquired a love of travel which, together with a flare for writing with immediacy and what James Lees-Milne described as "astonishing ebullience," was to produce some of the best travel writing of the period. In his early twenties Beckford also wrote *Vathek*, a romantic novel set in a fantastical Arabia. A best-seller in its day, it is now one of those influential books which are seldom read but often cited. As Roger Lonsdale observed, "Perverse and grotesque comedy alternates with scenes of 'oriental' magnificence and evocative beauty."[1]

While Beckford's early start as a Whig grandee appeared on the surface, at any rate, to be conventional, it was soon clear that his life would follow a most unconventional path. His romantic inclinations led him to a passion for the exotic and the rich. He loved gold and silver gilt, and as soon as he had reached his majority in 1781 he set about making alterations to Fonthill and ordering a considerable quantity of opulent silver from the leading suppliers of the day. Beckford was a perfectionist and an exacting patron. Although in the conventional neoclassical style then in vogue, his early silver purchases are characterized by their high quality, especially in the faultless burnishing of the gilding. This was to be true of his silver commissions for the rest of his life.

In 1784 a scandal threatened to destroy everything. A series of romantic attachments with young boys had induced his mother to push Beckford into a marriage with Lady Margaret Gordon, daughter of the Earl of Aboyne. She was pretty and vivacious and became devoted to him. Six months after the marriage, however, Beckford was said to have been seen *in flagrante* with "Kitty" Courtenay, the sixteen-year-old son of Lord Courtenay of Powderham Castle in Devon. A prosecution was threatened and although no charges were made against him, Beckford thought it prudent to leave the country. At Dover he turned back, however, and went back to his pregnant wife, who remained fiercely loyal to him. The Beckfords left the following year for Switzerland, but nonetheless despite the scandal and subsequent ostracism, Beckford continued to buy works of art and to patronize the silver trade. He even ordered a neoclassical teapot in gold to use on his travels. Now in the Barber Institute in Birmingham, England, it is struck with London gold hallmarks for 1784/85 and the rare "duty drawback" mark that signified that the tax had been refunded at the port of export.

Beckford's woes were not over. Shortly after arriving in Switzerland, Lady Margaret died of puerperal fever after giving birth to their second daughter. Beckford was heart-broken and returned to England where he remained for a short time before setting out again, with his huge entourage of servants, with the intention of visiting his West Indian plantations. The prospect of a long sea voyage, however, drove him to alter his plans and he set sail instead for Portugal, where he remained for two

29. William Beckford (1760–1844) by Sir Joshua Reynolds, oil on canvas. Aesthete and collector, Beckford enthusiastically patronized the leading silversmiths of the day. *National Portrait Gallery, London*

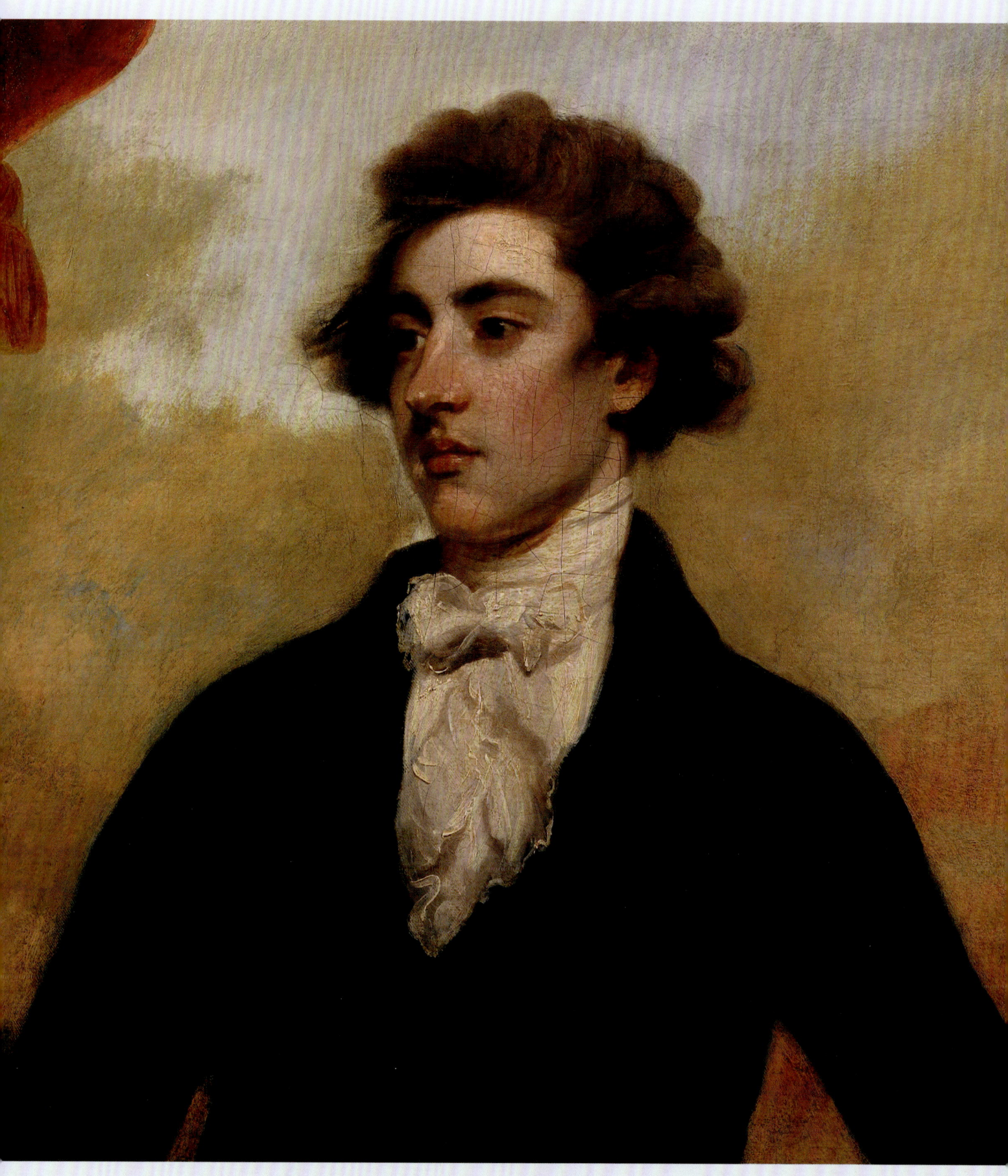

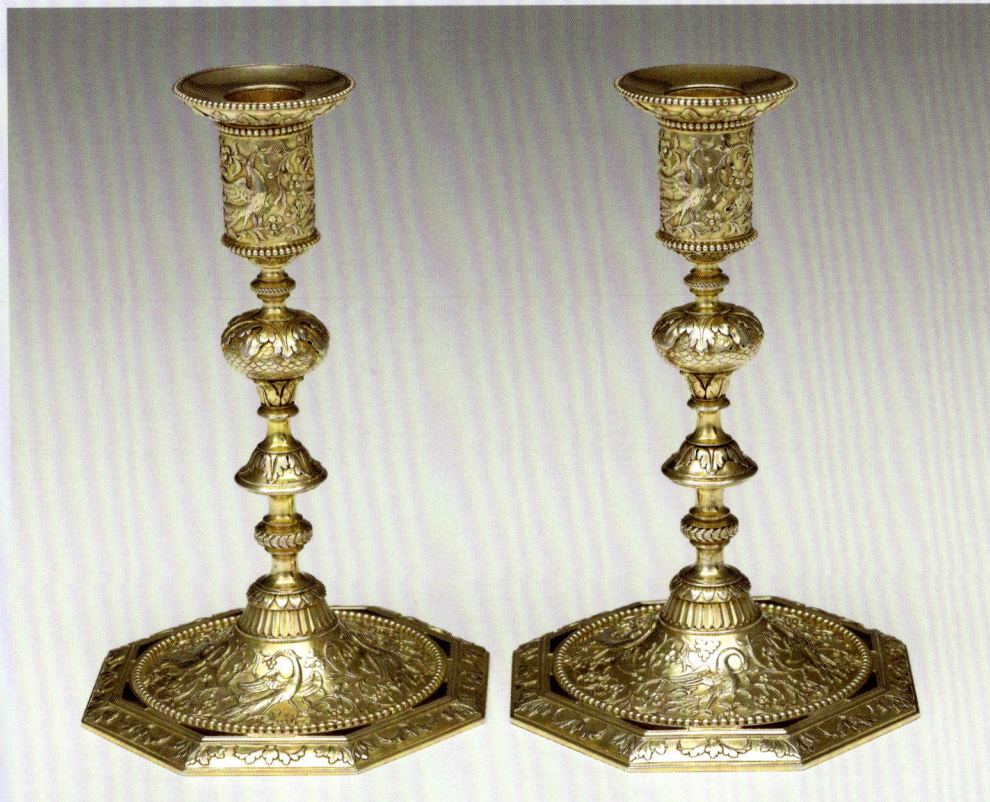

30. Pair of candlesticks, silver gilt, London, 1800/1, maker's mark of Paul Storr. Beckford's first purchases had been of neoclassical silverware but with the commissioning of these unique candlesticks from Vulliamy's, based on French seventeenth-century wooden examples, he began a collection of highly eclectic silver—all of it, like these candlesticks, of the highest quality. Cat. no. 32

years before moving on to Spain and then to Paris. Interspersed with brief visits to Fonthill to see how his redecorations were proceeding, Beckford spent the next ten years on long sojourns in France and Portugal. He was in Paris at the start of the Terror and managed to acquire many art works at knock-down prices, such as the magnificent desk that Jean-Henri Riesener made for Stanislaus of Poland and a number of pieces of silver gilt from the great Paris goldsmith Henry Auguste "in the true spirit of Corinth and Athens."[2] Also acquired at this time was a gold ewer from the Auguste workshop. In a restrained yet monumental classicism, the Auguste pieces were designed by the neoclassical artist Jean-Guillaume Moitte (1746–1810).[3] Unusually for the times, Beckford regarded the designer as important as the goldsmith, and subsequent catalogues listed them as "after the antique, by the celebrated French sculptor Moiette [sic] and executed by H. Auguste."[4]

Yet toward the end of the 1790s Beckford was growing bored with neoclassicism, although he was to come back to it at intervals throughout his long life. His visits to Portuguese monasteries, with their combination of incense and decay, had sparked his romantic nature and he was being drawn toward Gothic ruins. With the deaths of both Kitty Courtenay's father and Lord Loughborough (the Lord Chief Justice of the Court of Common Pleas who had been married to Kitty's aunt), Beckford felt safe enough to return to England permanently and at once set about planning a Gothic ruin in the grounds of Fonthill. The idea for a ruin was soon transformed into a plan for a monumental Gothic edifice which in time was to eclipse the Palladian mansion nearby. Fonthill Abbey, as conceived by Beckford and executed by the architect James Wyatt (1746–1813), was vast and unlike anything that had been built in Britain since the Middle Ages. Its octagonal tower, some 276 feet high, was at the axis of four wings; from north to south the overall length of the house was more than 300 feet.

By Christmas 1800, enough of one wing had been completed for a visit by Admiral Nelson and Emma Hamilton; their *ménage à trois* with Emma's husband, Sir William Hamilton, a distant kinsman of Beckford's, had made them as socially undesirable as Beckford. The party stayed in Fonthill Splendens and visited the abbey by torchlight for a medieval banquet. Afterwards, "a collation was provided in the library, consisting of various sorts of confectionery, served in gold baskets." These were

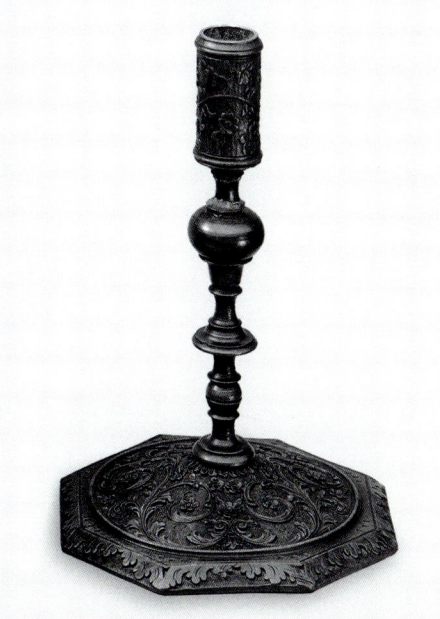

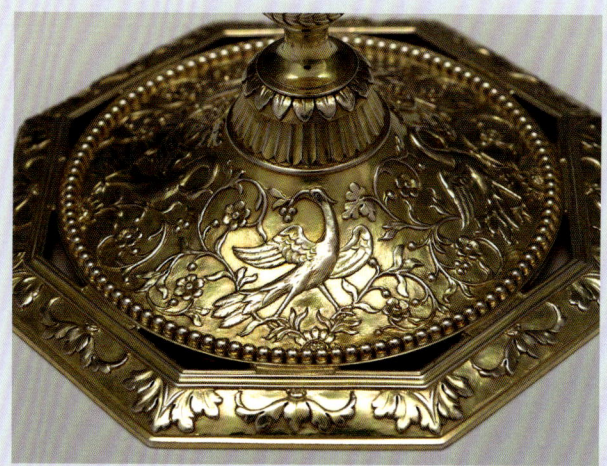

32. Detail of one of the
candlesticks in fig. 30. The
exotic birds seen here amid the
scrolling foliage could allude to
the Beckford crest of a heron.

**31. Candlestick,
walnut, c. 1690,
attributed to the
workshop of
Nicholas-François
Foulon, Nancy. A
small carved
candlestick like this
from a French
specialist workshop
provided the model
for Beckford's silver-
gilt candlesticks,
although Beckford
thought the design
was much earlier and
referred to them as
his "Holbein"
candlesticks.**
*Metropolitan Museum
of Art, New York*

presumably the massive silver-gilt baskets in pure neoclassical style which Beckford had had made by Paul Storr three years before.[5] But Beckford had already ordered much more eclectic silverware for the abbey. The pair of silver-gilt candlesticks in the Gans Collection (fig. 30) was supplied to him by Vulliamy & Son, a leading firm of decorators and suppliers of works of art, but were also made in the Storr workshop. They are hallmarked for 1800/1, so it is possible that they were already in the abbey when England's greatest naval hero visited Fonthill.

One of the problems facing those who wanted to create a Gothic environment was the dearth of surviving dining silver from the Middle Ages which could be copied. At Beckford's medieval banquet for the Nelson party, it was reported that the food was "served up in a long single line of enormous silver dishes … wholly in the massy style and fashion of the ancient abbeys."[6] What these dishes looked like is not known. But Beckford's skill in decoration was never constrained by strict historical authenticity. He mixed objects of different periods and different styles; for him the sum was greater than the parts. Even so, the individual objects he had made were very much works of art in their own right, such as the Gans candlesticks. These candlesticks are not medieval, however. They are not even of the sixteenth century, even though Beckford referred to them as his "Holbein" candlesticks. They are in the style of French late seventeenth-century carved walnut or boxwood examples which modern scholars now attribute to the workshops of Nicolas-François Foulon and others in Nancy (fig. 31).[7] Most of the surviving Nancy examples are components of toilet services, such as candlesticks and boxes, and it may be that they are copying silver originals destroyed when Louis XIV ordered the wholesale melting down of his and his subjects' silverware in 1689. Indeed it is possible that Beckford's candle-sticks are cast directly from one of the wooden examples which has not been traced. The decoration on the wooden examples tends to contain varying combinations of foliage and scrolling in an all-over pattern, but a unique feature of Beckford's silver-gilt examples is the exotic birds that inhabit the foliage (fig. 32). The birds could allude to the Beckford crest of a heron. On the other hand, they have similarities with pelicans as depicted in heraldic art (heraldic animals often having little resemblance to real ones). Traditionally, the pelican was a symbol of piety and self-sacrifice and in times of shortage was thought to feed its own flesh to its young.

Beckford's love of heraldry and of his own ancestry was well known. The undersides of the candle-sticks are engraved with the crest of Beckford as well as the crest of his mother's family, the Hamiltons, which he had recently been granted the right to use in conjunction with his own crest by the College of Arms. Through his mother, Beckford was, as he described himself, "a man who, by infinitely rare co-incidence, is without exception descended from all the barons—yes, all—who signed the Magna

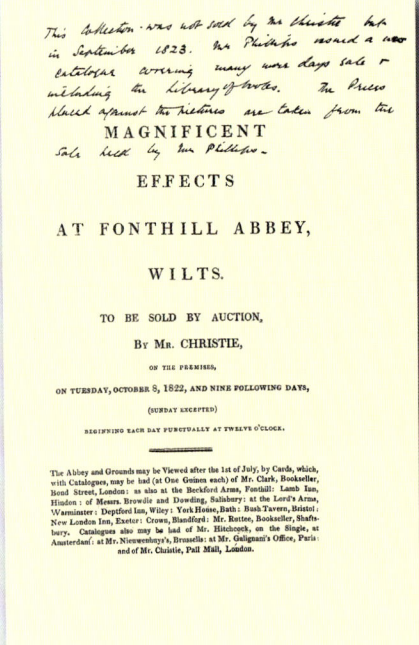

33. Title page of James Christie the Younger's abortive sale on the premises at Fonthill Abbey. In 1822 Beckford ordered an auction of the collections at Fonthill Abbey, but shortly before the sale was to take place he sold the house and estate together with the contents to John Farquhar, a gunpowder millionaire. Although they were included in Christie's catalogue, the "Holbein" candlesticks appear to have been held back from the sale to Farquhar by Beckford and taken by him to Bath.

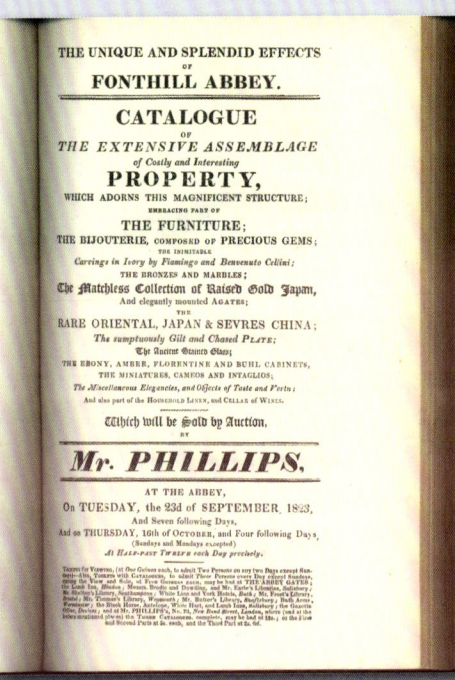

34. Title page of Harry Philips's sale at Fonthill Abbey. Shortly after his purchase of Fonthill, John Farquhar commissioned Harry Phillips, another London auctioneer who had been James Christie's chief clerk, to hold a sale of its contents. Phillips merely reprinted most of the Christie catalogue entries and added some lots which had not belonged to Beckford.

Carta."[8] Beckford extensively used heraldry, in the form of crests or heraldic badges, in the decoration of the abbey.

Vulliamy's bill describes the candlesticks as being "… Gilt and finished in so perfect a manner as exactly to resemble a pair of highly-finished Gold Chased Candlesticks."[9] Not only is the relief decoration on these candlesticks exceptionally well delineated, but the richness and quality of the burnishing of the gilding are exceptional. The use of the word "gold" in Vulliamy's bill is interesting, for writers on Beckford's collection continually described the candlesticks as being of gold, and Beckford appears to have done nothing to correct them.[10] Underneath each of the two crests is engraved an inscription: "Made for the Abbey at Fonthill by Vulliamy & Son 1800." Both the supplier and the patron had good reason to be proud of them.

As we have seen, Beckford had purchased gilt baskets made in Paul Storr's workshop in 1797/98. For these candlesticks he went to Vulliamy's, who in turn farmed the order out to Storr, who was then building a reputation for highly finished silver in the refined neoclassical taste. The quality of his output would lead to his appointment as manager of the Dean Street workshops of the retailers Rundell, Bridge & Rundell in 1808. Which retailer Beckford used before Vulliamy is not known, although his earliest purchases of conventional neoclassical silver, bearing the marks of specialist manufacturers such as John Scofield and Smith & Sharp, may have been from Rundell's, then known as Pickett & Rundell. For example, the large set of candlesticks he ordered between 1781 and 1783 is identical to a set purchased by Thomas William Coke of Holkham in 1776, probably from Pickett & Rundell.[11]

The so-called Holbein candlesticks are among the first of a series of unique silver commissions which Beckford was to make during the next forty years. In each case he, or rather his assistant, Gregorio Franchi, appears to have provided a drawing or drawings, and to have closely supervised the work, demanding endless revisions and ensuring that the quality was of the highest order. The luxury trade in London, however, had developed into a small group of powerful retailers, such as Rundell's, who used a network of specialist workshops, making it impossible for the client to have direct contact with the men and women themselves who modeled or made the item. In 1816 Beckford wrote to Franchi, "Advise Fiume [Beckford's nickname for one of the partners at Rundell, probably John Bridge], or rather Mr Storr, not to let the candelabra languish too long." Beckford was notoriously difficult with tradesmen. John Bridge visited Fonthill in 1794 and much to his chagrin was made to eat in the servants' hall. The other chief partner in the firm, Philip Rundell, himself known for his irascibility, in fact refused to deal with Beckford and left him to the other partners. This may be because Beckford, through Franchi, had managed to make contact with some of the firm's best craftsmen, such as Edward Aldrich, and was dealing directly with them. But Beckford continued to buy new and antique silver from Rundell's right into the 1830s; indeed his routine when in town was to pay a daily visit to their shop in Ludgate Hill after visiting Jennings's bookshop in Cheapside.

In time Beckford moved into the abbey and in 1806 he decided to demolish his father's house, Fonthill Splendens, an act that seemed to put the seal on Beckford's rejection of the neoclassical. But the tremendous rise in sugar prices during the Napoleonic Wars, which had paid for Fonthill Abbey and enabled Beckford to fill it with old and new treasures, was followed by a crash after the peace of 1816. In addition, he had so neglected his affairs that his employees and agents had secured fortunes for themselves from their management of his estates. By 1820 his financial affairs were in such dire straits that he took the painful decision to sell Fonthill. James Christie the younger, son of the founder of the firm of auctioneers, was called in to prepare an auction sale to be held on the premises. Everything was to go, including the Holbein candlesticks which were described in the catalogue as "A pair of beautiful silver gilt candlesticks, executed by Vulliamy, *from an original design by Holbein.*" Seventy-two thousand copies of the auction catalogue were sold within a few days. The rich, the fashionable, and the merely curious flocked to what was to be the sale of the century. But on the last day of the public viewing, a sign on the locked gate announced that the sale had been cancelled. Beckford had pulled off an astonishing coup. Harry Phillips, Christie's former chief clerk and now a rival auctioneer, had introduced him to John Farquhar, a millionaire who had made a fortune in selling gunpowder to the army. Farquhar was well into his seventies and lived in squalid rooms in Baker Street. His appearance was so grubby that on meeting him, Beckford thought he was a tramp. But Farquhar, seemingly as a speculation, bought the estate and the abbey, and most of its contents, from Beckford for £300,000.

Beckford removed to Bath where he began to decorate and fill an elegant stone row house on a hill overlooking the city. But there were to be more surprises. Less than a year later, a new sale of the contents of Fonthill Abbey was announced, with Phillips as the auctioneer. Most of the descriptions in the catalogue were merely copied from the Christie's one, but Phillips also cleverly added to the sale a number of additional lots which would benefit from a Beckford provenance. Beckford was even able to buy back some of his works of art, at greatly reduced prices. Then, in 1825, the great tower of the abbey collapsed, destroying much of the rest of the house. In time the estate was sold but the abbey was never rebuilt and eventually became a romantic ruin.

Beckford evidently decided to keep the Holbein candlesticks after all, for they do not feature in the second Fonthill sale catalogue. They joined a smaller, but in many ways choicer, collection in Beckford's new house in Bath. Soon the collection had grown to necessitate the acquisition of the house next door, separated from Beckford's by a narrow lane. He built a corridor at second floor level connecting the two houses. A few years later, the house on the other side was also purchased, enabling Beckford to create an *enfilade* at second floor level some 120 feet in length. But the urge to build returned. Farmland at the rear of the row was purchased to create a private landscape stretching a mile up to the summit of Lansdown Hill, which afforded a

35. Kettle, silver gilt, velvet, sequins, gold thread, London, 1822/23, maker's mark of Philip Rundell for Rundell, Bridge & Rundell. Now ensconced in Bath, Beckford continued to commission highly individual silver such as this kettle inspired by Persian decorative work.
Cat. no. 38

panoramic view of the surrounding countryside. Here, Beckford engaged a young and unknown architect, Henry Edmund Goodridge, to construct a tower some 150 feet in height. For the design, Beckford rejected the Gothic and returned instead to a classical idiom, which has variously been described as Tuscan, Greek, and Byzantine. The sumptuously fitted-out interiors of Lansdown Tower were filled with the best of Beckford's works of art.

Beckford started on a new round of silver commissions, ordering conventionally neoclassical silver from Rundell's, presumably for use, as well as eclectic mounted Asian porcelain and exotic pieces of his own design, sometimes from Rundell's and sometimes directly from a small group of specialist craftsmen. The silver-gilt kettle (fig. 35), supplied to him by Rundell's in 1822/23, incorporates meandering scroll decoration derived from Islamic ceramics with bands of Mughal stylized foliage. As always, the finish is superb and the overall effect is clearly the result of close supervision by the client through all stages of design and manufacture.

36. Title page from the Christie's sale of silver for the 13th Duke of Hamilton in 1919. At Beckford's death in 1844, his collections in Bath were inherited by his favorite daughter, Euphemia, who had married the 10th Duke of Hamilton; much of Beckford's silver, including the "Holbein" candlesticks, was sold by the family in 1919.

It was in Bath that Beckford died in 1844. Most of his collections passed to his favorite daughter, Euphemia, who had, much to Beckford's delight, married the 10th Duke of Hamilton. Silver and gold neoclassical silver and gold items originally purchased for Splendens, together with precious mounted hardstones and porcelains ordered for Fonthill Abbey and for Lansdown Tower, made their way northward to Hamilton Palace in Scotland.

The two Beckford/Gans pieces show Beckford's genius at combining works and motifs from different periods to create a stunning whole. But what was Beckford's legacy? As a patron he was virtually unique in the degree of control he sought over design and manufacture of the objects he commissioned. As a patron many of his commissions are a foretaste of the eclecticism of the Victorian era, but Beckford's earlier exclusion from society, which in later life he turned into total reclusiveness, meant that very few people saw his works of art. As a collection, it was a completely private one. But it is perhaps easy to overemphasize this aspect: the retailers he dealt with, such as Rundell's, and the craftsmen who made the items to his, and Franchi's designs, were inspired to continue to experiment in these new styles. During the 1820s, Rundell's in particular were at the forefront of creating works in precious metal in a new, exotic blending of Gothic, Asian and Byzantine motifs, a style clearly influenced by Beckford (figs. 38–9).

Notes

1 Lees-Milne, p. 8; Lonsdale, p. ix; for Beckford's life see Ostergard, Mowl, and Lees-Milne.
2 William Beckford to Sir William Hamilton, February 27, 1792, reproduced in *The Hamilton and Nelson Papers, The Collection of Autograph Letters and Historical Documents formed by Alfred Morrison*, 2nd series, vol. I, 1756–1797, London, 1893, p. 165.
3 For a discussion of some of these pieces, and their possible dating, see my catalogue entries in Ostergard, pp. 161–70.
4 Rutter, 1823, p. 11; similar descriptions are in the 1822 Christie's sale (fig. 33) and the 1823 Phillips sale (fig. 34).
5 W. Gregory, *The Beckford Family: Reminiscences of Fonthill Abbey and Lansdown Tower*, London, 1898, p. 38.
6 Redding, 1859, p. 123.
7 In this essay I have drawn heavily on Ellenor Alcorn's catalogue entry for the candlesticks in Ostergard, pp. 377–8. Regarding the wooden prototypes, traditionally but erroneously attributed to César Bagard (1620–1709), a figural sculptor in stone, see Pinto, pp. 365–7 and Hélène Demoraine, "Bois de Bagard," *Connaissance des Arts*, 191, January, 1968, pp. 90–3.
8 Boyd Alexander, *Life at Fonthill*, London, 1957, p. 180.
9 NA [PRO], C.104/57.
10 Redding, vol. II, p. 274; Snodin and Baker, part I, p. 743.
11 Hartop, 2010, p. 45.

37. George IV (1762–1830) by Sir Thomas Lawrence, oil on canvas, 1822. Unlike William Beckford, whose collections were intensely private, the king's silver purchases from Rundell, Bridge & Rundell, the Royal Goldsmiths, were extremely influential in setting the taste of the first three decades of the nineteenth century. *The Wallace Collection, London.*

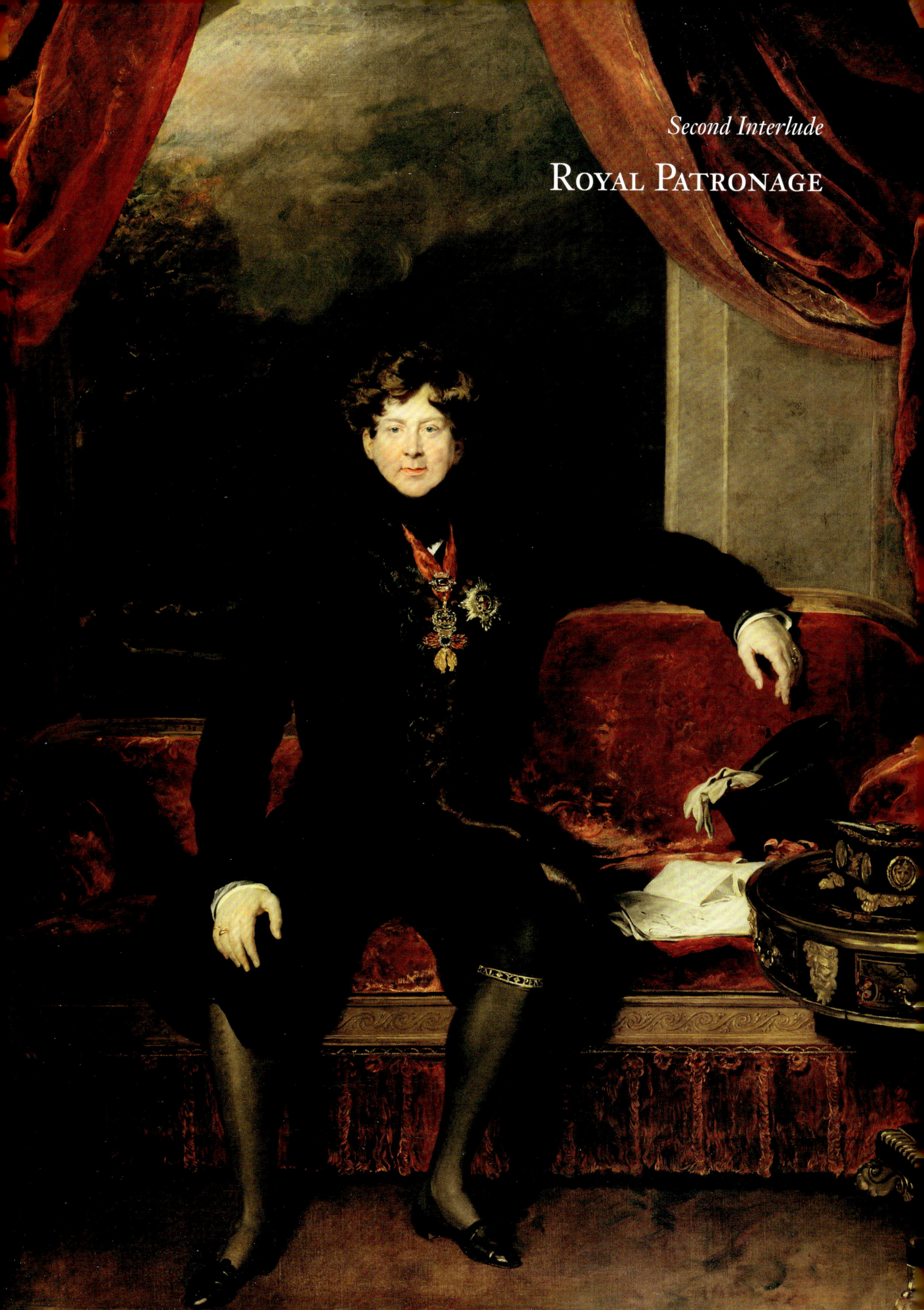

GEORGE IV AND WILLIAM IV

The history of royal patronage of goldsmiths in England is a long and rich one, although virtually no English royal silver or gold objects survive from the Middle Ages. The two exceptions are the gold ampula, or decanter, in the form of an eagle, which dates from the fourteenth century, and the gold spoon into which oil from the ampula is poured to anoint the head of the new sovereign. The spoon is believed to have been first used at the coronation of King John in 1200. These two items form part of the Crown Jewels on display in the Tower of London. But they give only a hint of the richness of the medieval king's plate on his table and altar. Stored in the Jewel House in the Tower until required, much of this silver had an itinerant life, accompanying the king as he ceaselessly traveled the roads of the kingdom to govern, mete out justice, or fight his rivals. At the beginning of the thirteenth century, King John lost a good deal of his household plate when the baggage wagons were overtaken by the tide as they crossed the marshes around the Wash that connect Norfolk with Lincolnshire.

The King's Lynn Cup, dating from the fourteenth century and still the most prized possession of that town, is a rare surviving piece of enameled English domestic silver. It may or may not have a royal provenance. To this very small group we must add a handful of foreign pieces that came to England as diplomatic gifts, such as the enameled gold cup made in France in 1380/81 and given to King Henry VI by Charles V of France. Now in the British Museum, it speaks of the power of medieval kingship and the sophistication of life at court. From the inventory made of Henry VIII's possessions after his death in 1547, and from one made of Queen Elizabeth's gold and silver in 1574, we can get an idea of the tremendous variety of objects that lined the shelves of the Jewel House. Cups are listed in the form of humans, monsters, and animals. Just a handful of surviving objects can be identified from these listings, such as Henry VIII's silver-gilt and enameled rock-crystal cup of 1511/12, which owes its survival to having been given as a diplomatic gift to one of the popes. It is now in the Church of San Lorenzo in Florence, where it was discovered by the silver scholar Timothy Schroder in 1994.[1]

With a few exceptions, usually for religious reasons, there was little sentiment for old plate in the Middle Ages, and wholesale melting down of outmoded items was common. But the most devastating instance was the destruction of virtually all of the royal plate to finance the Civil War in the 1640s. Charles I stripped the Jewel House, and it was not until after the Restoration in 1660 that stocks were replenished. This makes the display of early seventeenth-century English silver in the Kremlin, also diplomatic gifts, so precious.

The loss of Charles I's silver is doubly distressing, for he, together with George IV, was the most discerning of collectors and the silver he commissioned, glimpsed sometimes as "props" in contemporary portraits, was clearly of far superior quality to the light and insignificant domestic articles that have come down to us from the period.

The Hanoverian monarchs were no patrons of the arts. Indeed George II (reigned 1727–1760) remarked, when shown a picture by Hogarth, "I hate *bainting*, and *boetry* too!"[2] The silver that flowed through the Jewel House was only occasionally enlivened by the appearance of an elegant French piece or two acquired second-hand, or when the Earl of Chesterfield ordered copies of high-fashion Paris silver for his embassy in 1727 (see pp. 20–1). But the silver used on the royal table, or given as gifts or "perks," was always of the highest quality if not in the vanguard of fashion.

All this changed with the accession of George III in 1760. Thanks largely to the influence of his Prime Minister and mentor, Lord Bute, and to the Francophile design studio and workshops of the Royal Goldsmith, Thomas Heming, the young king purchased pieces in the extravagant naturalism that marked the last phase of the rococo. Then, in the 1770s, the king ordered an extensive dinner service in the neoclassical style from the workshop of the Paris goldsmith Robert-Joseph Auguste. Used in the royal palaces in Hanover, the service was split up in the 1920s and much of it is now divided between the Louvre and Waddesdon Manor in Buckinghamshire. Neoclassicism of a more ponderous

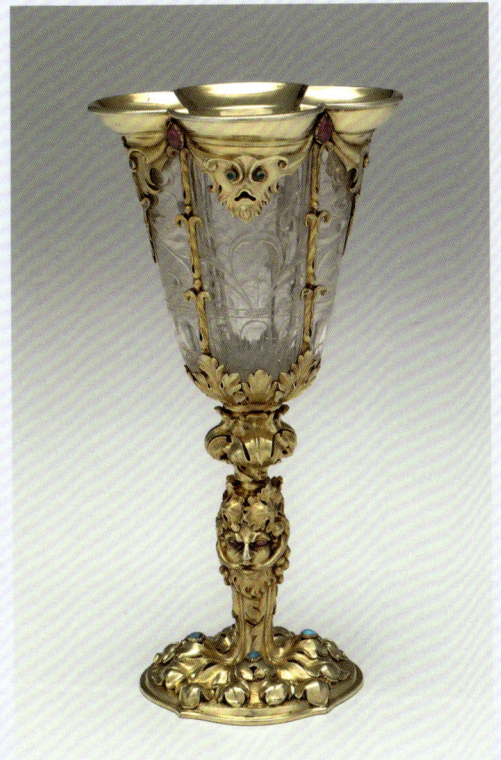

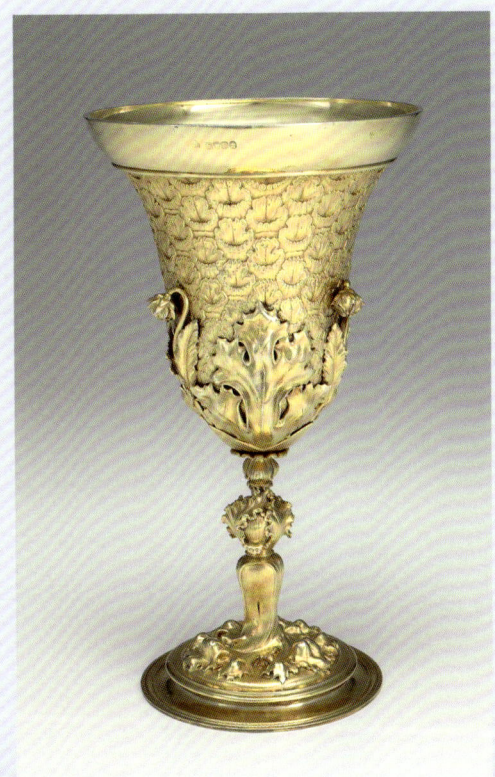

39. Goblet, silver gilt, London, 1830/31, maker's mark of John Bridge for Rundell, Bridge & Rundell. Augustus Welby Northmore Pugin, the Gothic Revivalist, may have designed this cup for Rundell's. Cat. no. 45

38. Goblet, silver gilt, rock crystal, semi-precious stones, London, 1827/28, maker's mark of John Bridge for Rundell, Bridge & Rundell. An exquisite example of the eclectic taste promoted by Rundell's during the 1830s, with a mixture of naturalistic and medieval motifs. Cat. no. 44

sort, largely due to the influence of the king's architect Sir William Chambers, was purchased from London makers.

The king's silver commissions soon proved paltry compared to the purchases made by his sons. As soon as he attained his majority and work had begun on his own palace, Carlton House, in the 1780s, the eldest, the Prince of Wales, who was destined to become Prince Regent when his father finally became incapable of ruling in 1811, set about ordering silver in the most eclectic blend of the neo-classical (including works by the Moitte/Auguste collaboration, discussed in the First Interlude) and copies of baroque originals. It was clear that here was a patron of great discernment who was not constrained by the narrowness of mainstream taste. In this he affords comparison with William Beckford. Both men, one a king and the other "England's richest son," had grown up to be self-indulgent and egocentric. But while Beckford led the life of a recluse, his royal contemporary lived the most public of lives. Beckford's silver was seen by few outside his very small circle of artists and servants and can be said to have had limited influence on the decorative arts of the day, although much of what he commissioned anticipated artistic trends that were to come. In contrast, the royal collection and the palaces that the prince built or remodeled and filled with treasures exerted tremendous influence on the taste of the time. While the silver and silver gilt on the royal table was seen at one time or another by virtually everyone in the fashionable world, the prince's collection of newly commissioned exotic pieces and antique plate was by no means a private *Kunstkammer*.

In the development of the royal silver collection, the role of the Royal Goldsmiths, Rundell, Bridge & Rundell, was pivotal.[3] Never before had a commercial firm exerted such influence over the fashions of the day. The size of their business and their product range, extending beyond silver to jewelry, snuffboxes, medals, presentation swords, and antiques, had much to do with it. But much of their success stemmed from their very forward-looking business policy. Already in the 1760s and 1770s Robert Adam had been one of the first designers to turn the tables and adopt a proactive role with the client. Noblemen turned to the Adam studio for guidance and to commission designs in what was an established house style. No longer were they going to artists or craftsmen merely to have them draw or execute an idea or design that they had conceived from their experiences on the Grand Tour or from the books in their library. Philip Rundell and John Bridge were shrewd enough to realize that the future

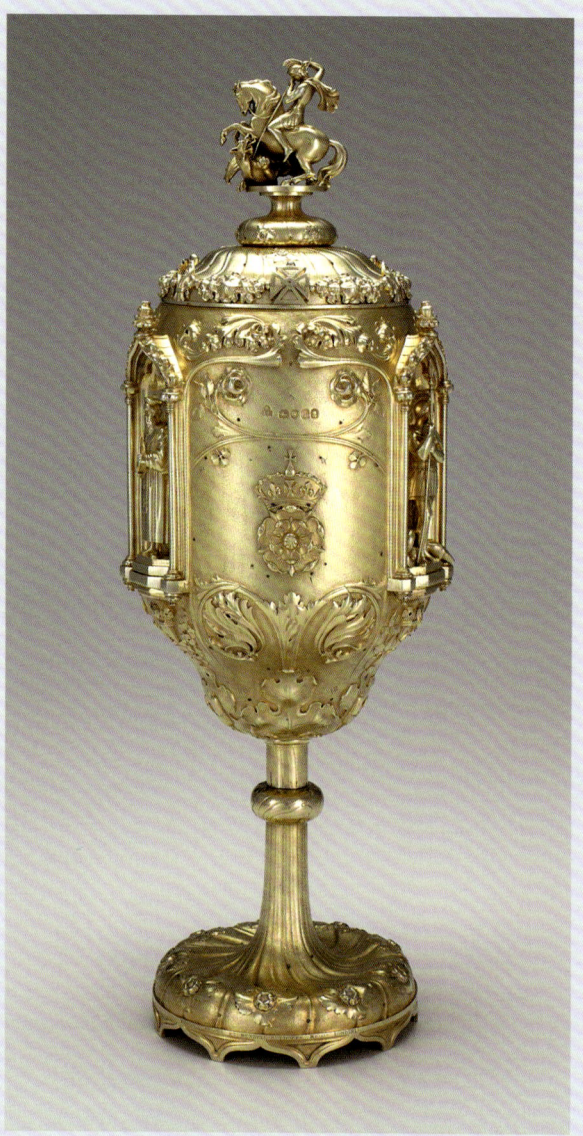

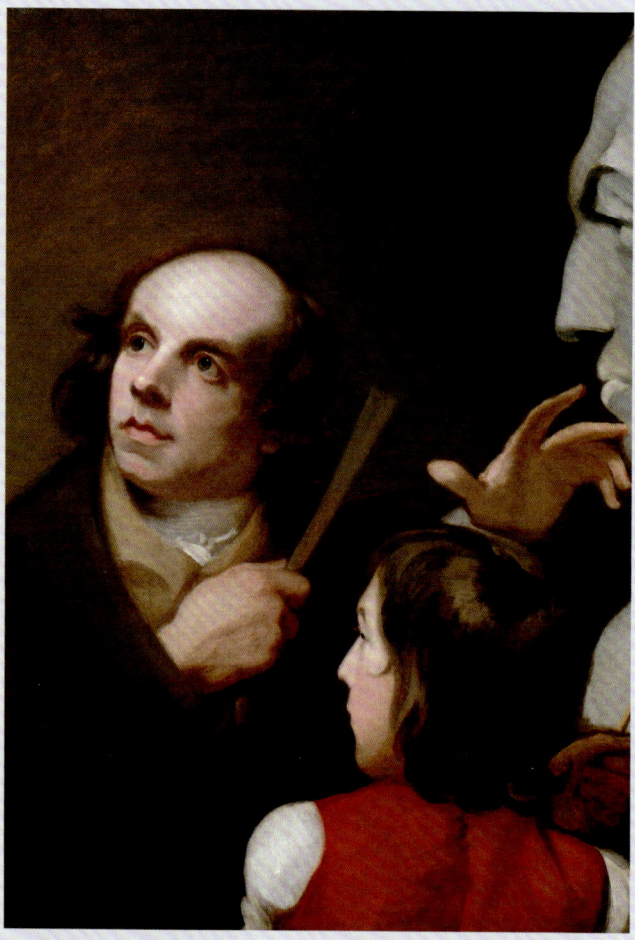

41. John Flaxman (1755–1826) and Thomas Alphonso Hayley by George Romney, oil on canvas, 1795. Flaxman was one of a number of distinguished artists who worked for Rundell's as designers.
National Portrait Gallery, London

40. The National Cup, silver gilt, London, 1826/27, maker's mark of John Bridge for Rundell, Bridge & Rundell. George IV collected not only modern silver in the "imperial" style, but also commissioned innovative items in naturalistic taste as well as antiquarian. This cup, boasting the emblems of England, Scotland, Wales and Ireland, was designed for Rundell's by the sculptor John Flaxman.
Cat. no. 42

lay in the response of the fashionable public to these brand-name designers and makers. Cleverly they established their own design studio and staffed it with a host of distinguished artists, some of whom were members of the Royal Academy. They could also call upon the talents of truly world-famous artists such as the sculptor John Flaxman (1755–1826) for special commissions. More than that, they established not only their own gem-cutting and jewelry workshops, but set up their own silver manufactories, the first in Greenwich under the direction of Digby Scott (active 1802–1811) as chief designer and Benjamin Smith (active 1802–1824) as silversmith, and then, in 1808, a much larger establishment in Soho under the management of Paul Storr, already well known as a maker of plate of the highest quality. Besides achieving great efficiency and control over production by bringing the processes of design, modeling, and manufacture in-house, Rundell's were also able to prevent outworkers from re-using the designs they had paid for so dearly on behalf of other clients.

This new approach led to the birth of a singular style which dominated English silver for the first quarter of the nineteenth century. This so-called imperial style was both confident and massive and commingled a broad range of motifs taken from classical architecture with a strong element of vegetal naturalism. Owing to the scale of Rundell's operations, no rival could successfully challenge their supremacy until the 1820s. The partner John Bridge was in daily attendance on the prince and, as the acquisition of antique pieces became one of his passions, he doubtless experienced a vicarious thrill of the chase as he anticipated what new discovery would be shown to him by Bridge.

The Prince of Wales was key to the success of the firm. But, curiously, he often purchased silver *after* the firm had already sold identical pieces to other clients. Not only did the prince spend hundreds of thousands of pounds with the firm, his taste for *objets de luxe* set a fashion for the rest of British society, and foreign courts, to emulate. Perceiving himself as the vanquisher of Napoleon and creator of a new European order, the Regent led society in its taste for this new era of golden richness.

This patriotism is well expressed in the National Cup, first designed for Rundell's by John Flaxman in 1819. It was not until 1825 that the Regent, now King, purchased a version from the firm. The Gans example is hallmarked for the following year (fig. 40). Decorated with symbols of England, Scotland, and Ireland, the cups are embellished with the figures of the respective patron saints George, Andrew, and Patrick. Flaxman, always thought of as the neoclassical sculptor *par excellence*, was also at the forefront in experimenting with an eclectic mixture of naturalism and sinuous Gothic foliage which the firm used for a series of cups in the 1820s. Often using hardstones or rock crystal, like the example in fig. 38, these cups are characterized by their exquisite workmanship and should be compared with the exotic creations that William Beckford was commissioning around the same time (fig. 35). In 1827 John Gawler Bridge, nephew of John Bridge, discovered the adolescent Augustus Welby Northmore Pugin copying medieval drawings in the British Museum and hired him for the firm. The cup of 1830/31 in fig. 39 is very likely to have been designed by him. Beckford's objects of *vertu*, however, often retain a distinctively Eastern flavor through their use of Mughal and Persian motifs.

42. Ewer and basin, silver gilt, London, 1734/35, maker's mark of John White, engraved with the monogram of Queen Adelaide. Old silver also formed part of Queen Adelaide's own silver collection. Cat. no. 17

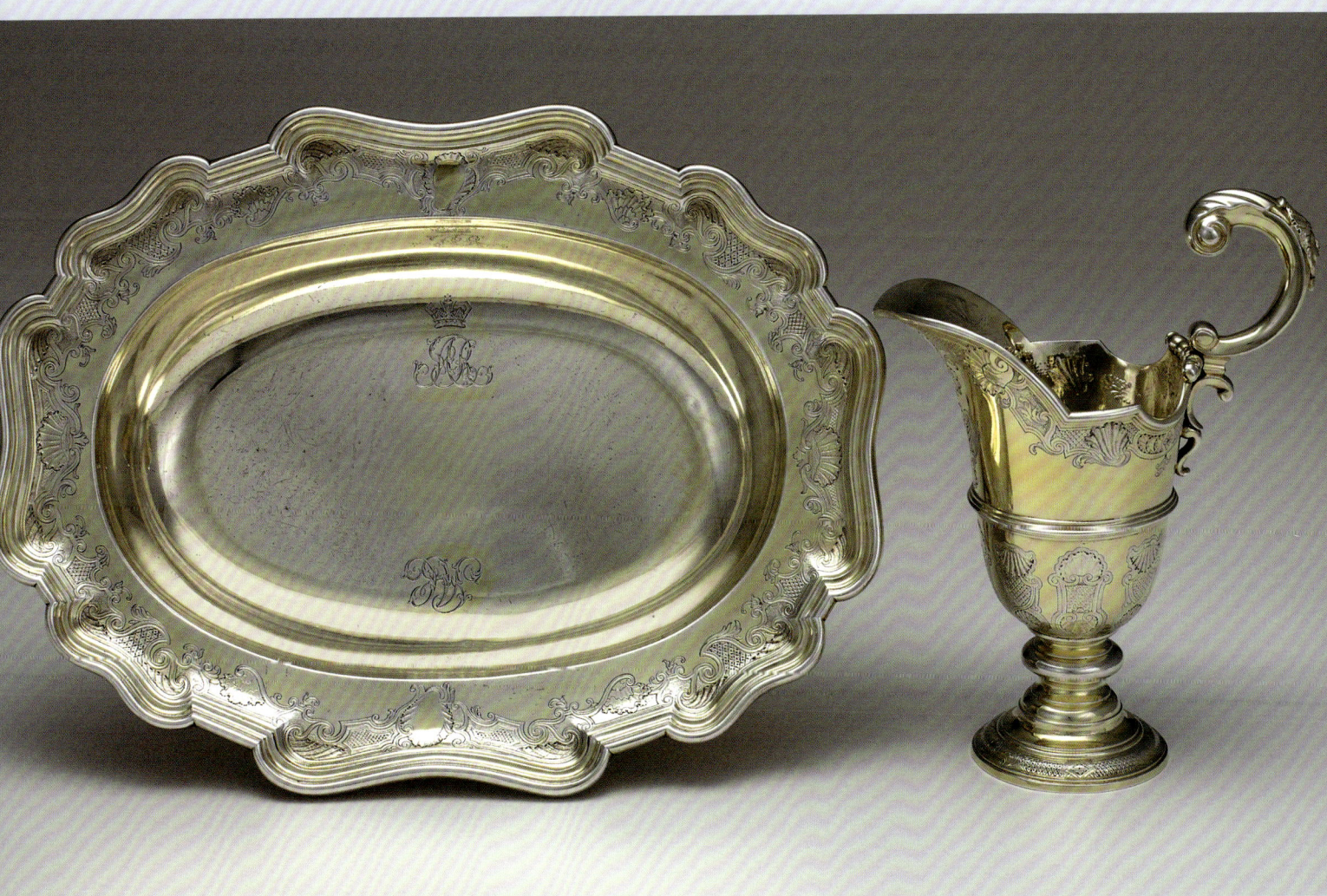

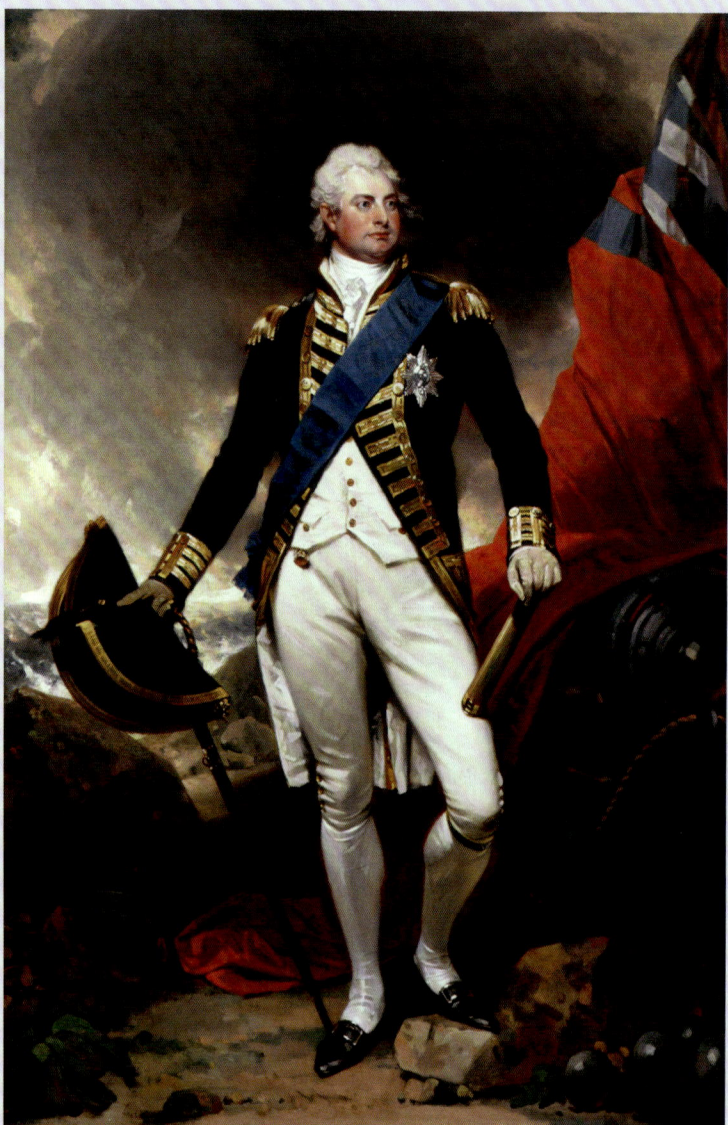

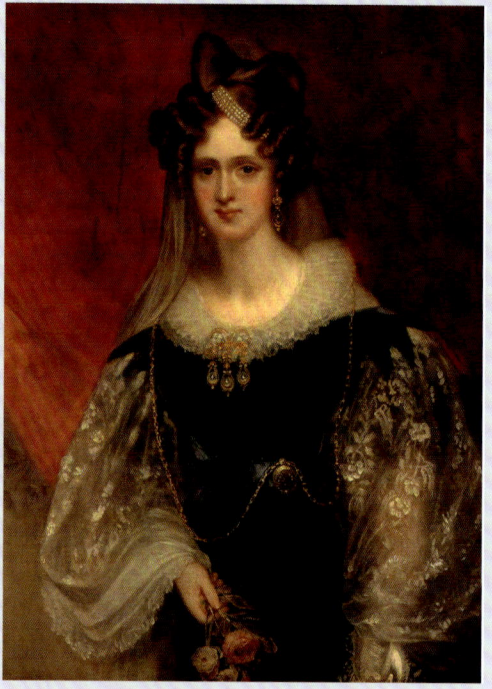

44. Queen Adelaide (1792–1849), consort of William IV, by Sir William Beechey, oil on canvas, c. 1831. William IV married Adelaide, a princess of a minor German royal house, late in life in the race between the royal brothers to produce an heir to the throne. *National Portrait Gallery, London.*

43. William IV (1765–1837) by Sir Martin Archer Shee, oil on canvas, 1800. William IV was not a connoisseur and collector as his brother George IV had been, but during his life he amassed considerable quantities of silver. *National Portrait Gallery, London*

George IV was not the only member of the royal family to collect silver at that time. His mother, Queen Charlotte, amassed a mixture of the exotic and antique as well as modern silver during her lifetime, much of which was sold at public auction after her death in 1818. Her other sons, the Royal Dukes, did not approach their eldest brother in connoisseurship, and some of them were accumulators rather than collectors of silver and silver gilt. The second son, the Duke of York, who in his youth had also bought neoclassical works by Henry Auguste, acquired some silver in Rundell's imperial style. But the duke also patronized another retailer, Kensington Lewis, who utilized a workshop headed by Edward Farrell (died 1850). Their output was quite different from the majority of Rundell's in that they gave emphasis to a rich naturalism bordering on the rococo. They also produced for the duke a set of massive silver-gilt candelabra in the best baroque tradition depicting Hercules.

Of the other dukes, only the Duke of Sussex, George III's sixth son, can be said to have had any discernment as a collector. He amassed a collection of antique silver which included Renaissance pieces. But the third son, William, Duke of Clarence, is of interest not only because he succeeded George IV as King William IV in 1830, but because of the silver he used during his lifetime. Like all the royal dukes, he had been chronically short of money and for many years was supported financially by his mistress, the successful actress Mrs. Jordan. She bore him ten children, but with the death of the Prince Regent's only child, Princess Charlotte, in 1817, a marriage race began between the royal brothers to

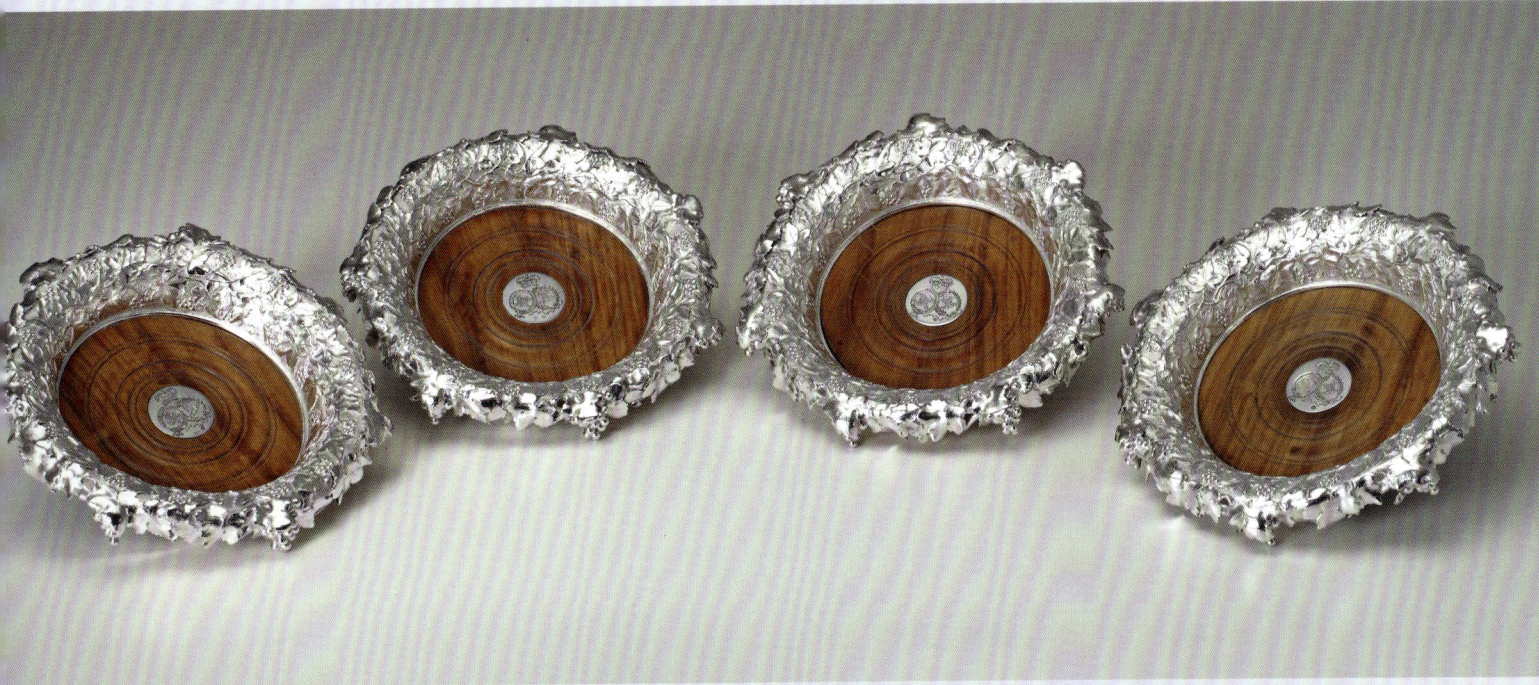

45. Four wine coasters, silver, wood, London, 1836/37, maker's mark of John Tapley for Rundell, Bridge & Rundell. Part of a large order of plate made by Rundell's for the king and queen shortly before the king's death. Cat. no. 47

forsake their mistresses (none of them had been financially stable enough to wed) and find a suitable princess to marry and produce an heir to the throne. Yet the problem for all of them was the dearth of suitable candidates, as the Royal Marriage Act precluded their marrying a Catholic, and the pool of marriageable Protestant princesses was very small. The Duke of Clarence found a congenial companion in Adelaide, a princess of Saxe-Meiningen whom he married in 1818. But the couple's relative impecuniousness meant that for silver they had to rely on old items from the Jewel House, or buy second-hand plate such as the ewer and basin in fig. 42, embellished with Adelaide's monogram.

With William's accession to the throne, economy continued to be a byword. The excesses of the previous reign, the building and remodeling of the royal palaces, and the late king's purchases of costly art objects and silver gilt, had brought about a backlash to curtail royal spending. William's own coronation, in contrast to his predecessor's, was a modest affair without the traditional banquet to follow—it was dubbed the "half crownation." But towards the end of his short reign, in 1835, William IV went on a spending spree accumulating modern silver, largely through Rundell's. By then though, with the original partners long gone and its bustling workshops disbanded, the firm had settled back onto its laurels. In short they were winding down and were eventually to close their doors for good in 1843. Yet in their final years, they could still rely on a skilled network of outworkers when the need arose. William

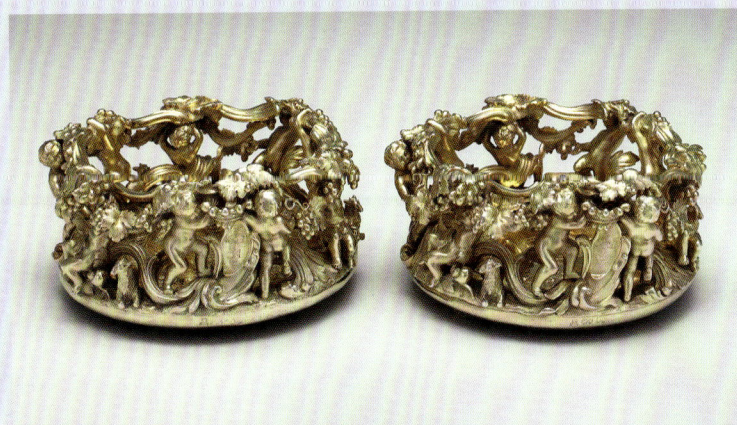

46. Pair of wine coasters, silver gilt, wood, ivory, London, 1837/38, maker's mark of Robert Garrard II for Garrard & Co. Like their rivals Rundell's, Garrard's were at the forefront in the fashion for sculptural, massive silver in the 1830s. Cat. no. 48

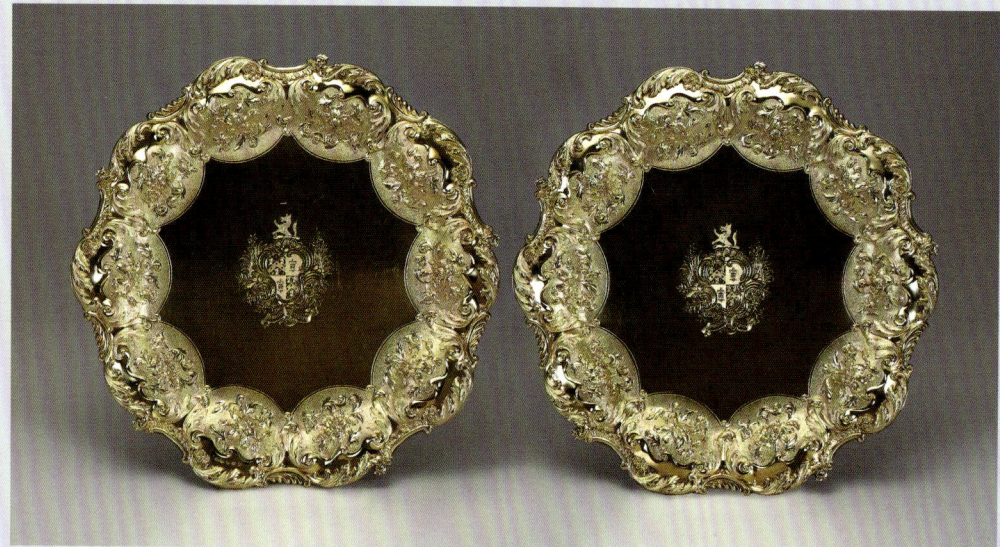

47. Pair of sideboard dishes, silver gilt, London, 1826/27, maker's mark of Paul Storr. The fashion for large display pieces in silver gilt started with the Prince Regent, later George IV, during the Napoleonic Wars and continued into the 1830s.
Cat. no. 43

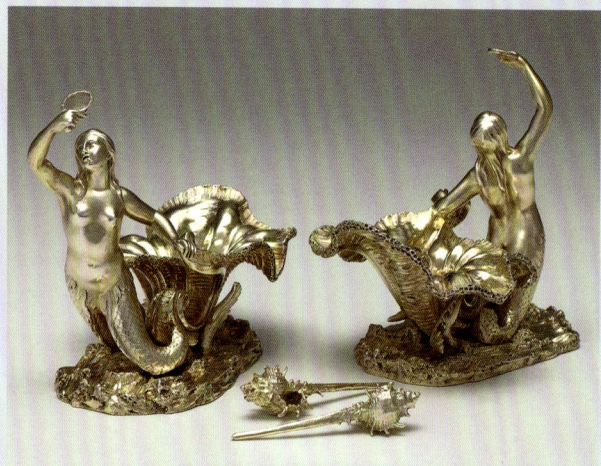

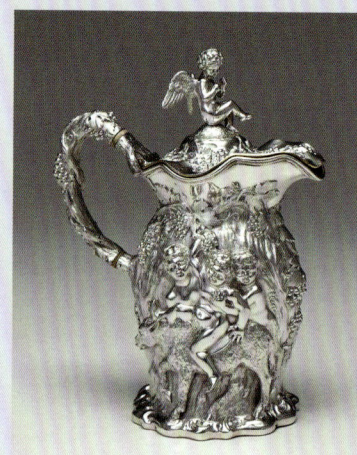

49. Jug, silver, ivory, gilt interior, London, 1833/34, maker's mark of Paul Storr. By the 1830s many different styles commingled on the dining table, and the growing consumer base meant that demand for innovative silverware was increasing.
Cat. no. 46

48. Pair of salts with spoons, silver gilt, London, 1840/41, maker's mark of John Mortimer & John Hunt; the spoons 1871/72, maker's mark of Charles Stuart Harris.
Cat. no. 49

and Adelaide's dinner service was monumental and in the latest naturalistic taste. The set of wine coasters in fig. 45 was made in the workshop of John Tapley, close by Rundell's shop near St. Paul's. Engraved with the monograms of the king and queen, the coasters are every bit as good in execution as the best work of Storr.

Unlike William Beckford's, the legacy of George IV and his brothers was far-reaching. Their passion for silver gilt, in large part emulating Napoleon's love of it, influenced virtually every great household in the land. Indeed, large display salvers embellished with armorials such as the pair in fig. 47, from the workshop of the now-independent Paul Storr in 1826/27, were an essential feature not only of aristocratic sideboards, but also those of the new mercantile elite. Sculptural silver like the wine coasters in fig. 46 and the salts, fig. 48, crowded the vast dining tables of the early Victorian period. Such exuberance was a far cry from William Beckford's rich yet mannered interiors.

Notes
1 Schroder, 1995.
2 John Ireland, illus., *Hogarth Illustrated*, London, 1791, vol. I, pp. 291–2.
3 For accounts of the firm, see Lovett, passim; Bury, 1966; Culme, 1977, pp. 57–65; Culme, 1999, pp. 18–25; Hartop, 2005.

50. Arthur Grimwade, the noted silver expert of Christie's, examines a hallmark, c. 1962.

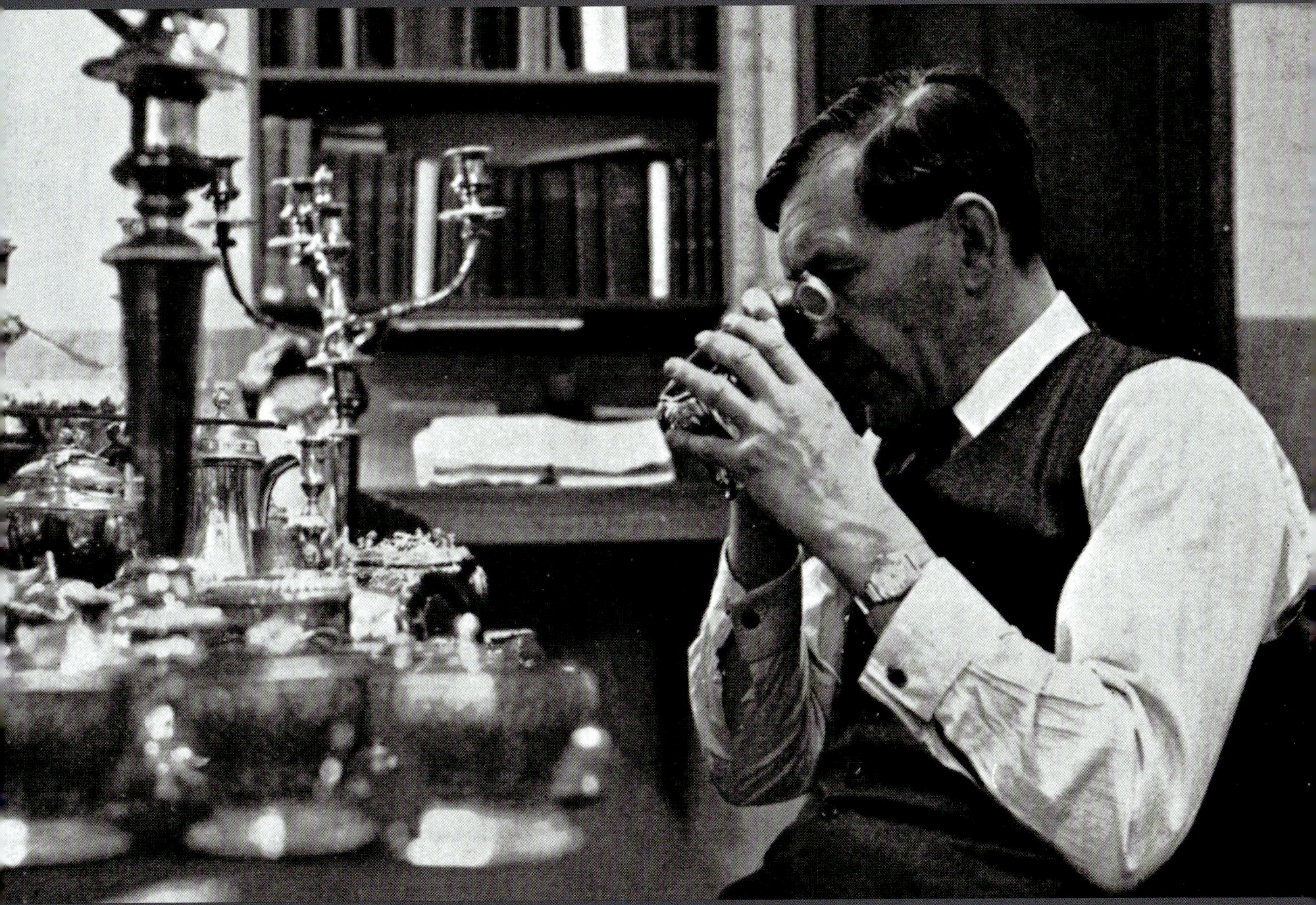

COLLECTING AND CONNOISSEURSHIP

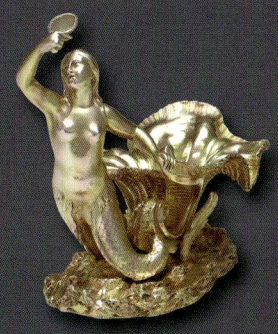

Chapter Two
COLLECTING AND CONNOISSEURSHIP

Old things have long held the West in their thrall. Well before the Renaissance, Greek and Roman artifacts were already being noticed and remarked upon, and by the sixteenth century archaeological remains were being studied and imitated. In the seventeenth century antiquity started to be sought after for its own sake. Deemed a link with an idealized glorious past, whether the classical world or ancient Britain, it brought echoes of former times that seemed nobler and better than the present. A parallel might be drawn with the relics in a medieval church treasury. There, too, is a tangible link with a lost inspirational past, in this instance with saints. Yet there was more to the increased interest in antiquities than mere escapism, there was also an earnest wish to understand the past, to find an answer to the eternal question of "Where do we come from?"

The first "antiquaries" were often lampooned for living in the past, which they did, in Thomas Fuller's famous phrase, not so much to "adore the Ancients, as to despise the Moderns."[1] As early as 1628, John Earle, Bishop of Salisbury, had described an antiquary as "one that hath an unnatural disease to be enamoured of old age and wrinkles, and loves all things—as a Dutchman do cheese—the better for being mouldy and worm-eaten ..."[2]

The Society of Antiquaries of London was founded in 1717, although informal meetings had begun in 1707. At each meeting, objects were brought for examination, and before long a journal was published leading to the development of analytical study of artifacts.[3] Concurrently with this grew up a market for antiques. A satirical essay of 1796 by Francis Grose, supposedly written by the concerned wife of an antiquary, captures the fervor of the times: "Before this unhappy period [her husband's election to the Society of Antiquaries], when he received his dividends at the Bank, or India-house, he would bring me home some little piece of plate or ornamental china, for my mantel-piece or buffet. Alas! Those times are no more; all the plate and china are removed, and in their room the shelves are stuffed full of broken pans, brazen lamps, copper chizzels, bell metal milk-pots, and a parcel of outlandish halfpence eat up with canker. For one of these pieces, I am told he actually gave a guinea."[4]

In time, antique silver too was to become collectable. So to silver's original threefold purpose of use, hygiene, and display was added a fourth. It was now perceived as something steeped in history or aesthetically appealing, and therefore worthy of pursuit.

There had always been a market for second-hand silver, which developed considerably during the early Georgian period when the cost of "fashioning" the more elaborate creations became so expensive. Many silversmiths' trade cards advertise second-hand plate as well as new. Admiral George Anson (1697–1762) bought second-hand Paul de Lamerie silver after returning from his celebrated circumnavigation of the globe in 1744 (see *A Noble Feast*, pp. 30–3), while George I's Vice-Chamberlain, Thomas Coke, purchased a "kitchen" (probably an epergne, or centerpiece), at an auction of the Duke of Shrewsbury's silver held at Covent Garden, London, in 1725. He paid 5 shillings an ounce for it (for silver, like flour or nails, was always sold, either at auction or from a dealer, by the ounce), a price which would have compared favorably with the 8 shillings or so an ounce he would have had to pay for a new piece.[5] An exception to this were the "certain Pieces of Plate sold being the Workmanship of Veanna, the most celebrated Silversmith of his Age," which fetched astonishing prices of between 20 and 26 shillings an ounce in the Arundel Collection sale in 1720.[6] The van Vianen family were Dutch silversmiths who specialized in virtuoso chasing in the auricular style. Christian van Vianen (1600–1667) had come to work in London in the 1630s at the behest of Charles I.

However, the pursuit of silver for its antiquity, rather than because of its association with a celebrated name, is an idea that only dates from the second half of the eighteenth century. A diary entry from 1786 by a young visitor to London, Sophie von de la Roche, is well known: "We visited Messrs Jeffries' silver store ... whose stock must be worth millions … [;] antique, well-preserved pieces, so Mr Jeffries said, often finding a purchaser more readily than the modern. This is because the English are fond of constructing and decorating whole portions of their country houses, or at least one apartment, in old Gothic style, and are glad to purchase any accessories dating from the same or a similar period …"[7]

The Gothic style had been revived as early as the 1630s in architecture and church plate, and William Kent had carried out some "Gothick" buildings in the 1730s as well as designing "Gothick" silver. For most people today, however, the beginnings of the Gothic Revival are synonymous with Horace Walpole (1717–1797), who created Strawberry Hill, a romantic environment filled with artifacts and curiosities that harked back to the cabinet of curiosities, or *Wunderkammer*. Unlike Beckford, his interest in antiques was primarily archaeological, or because of their historical associations (he owned, for example, Cardinal Wolsey's hat).[8] But Walpole also collected for aesthetic reasons: it cannot be merely that they came from the *Kunstkammer* of the Paston family in Norfolk that he acquired two pieces of exquisite goldsmiths' work, an Elizabethan silver-gilt mounted rock crystal tankard and a Dutch early seventeenth-century silver-gilt mounted nautilus shell.[9] We have already seen how difficult it was for the determined creator of a Gothic interior to find surviving dining plate from the medieval period (p. 35), but gaps in utilitarian plate could be made up with new.

Auctions were frequently attended by gentlemen and ladies in the latter half of the eighteenth century. James Christie, a former naval officer who founded his auction firm in 1766, was particularly adept at attracting the fashionable to his sales. At the end of the century, however, the antiques trade, a complex network of suppliers and retailers, gradually came to dominate the auction scene. Collecting old silver was by then a well-established pastime. Rundell, Bridge & Rundell and, to a lesser extent, Garrard's, sold antique silver alongside their new creations, very

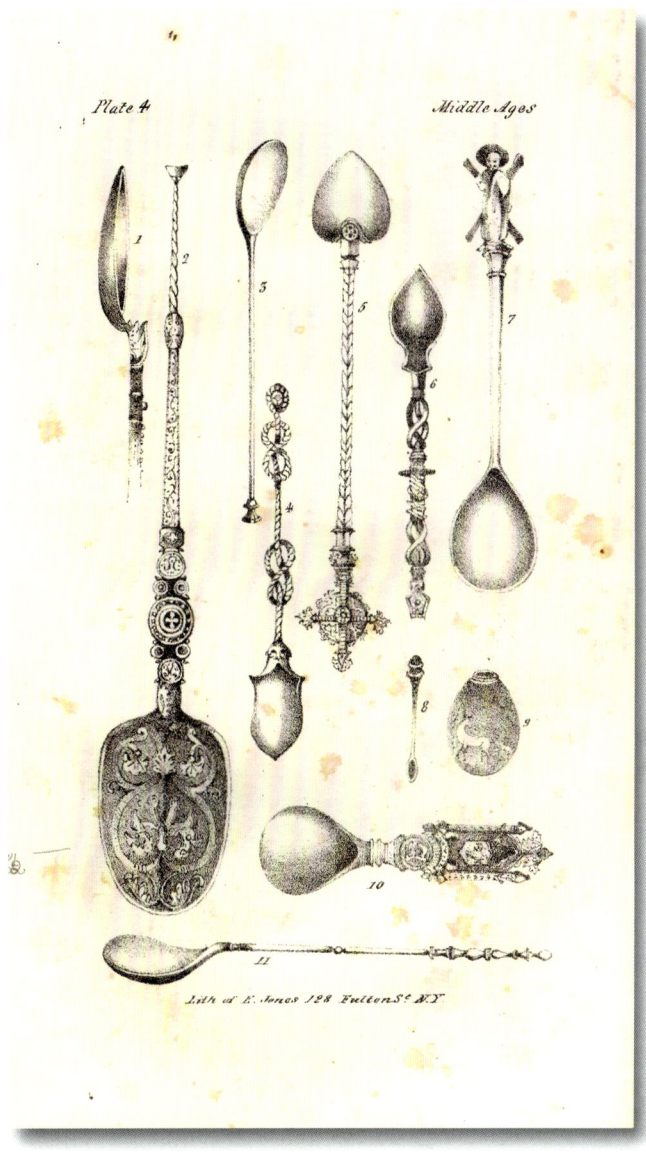

often to the same clients. In 1808 Rundell's were sold a considerable quantity of royal plate, as scrap, to finance the setting up of a separate establishment for Princess Caroline, the estranged wife of the Prince of Wales. Instead of melting it down, however, they sold it as antiques to their best customers, establishing a market for royal silver that has never since faltered.

The leading figure in the market, for both antique and modern plate, was George IV. Rundell's even went so far as to sell him some of the royal plate they had purchased in 1808, as well as such pieces as the early seventeenth-century Nuremberg nautilus cup by Nikolaus Schmidt, which is still at Windsor.[10] This cup cost them just over £150 at the Wanstead House auction in 1822; the following year, after restoration, they

51. Plate 4 showing the Anointing Spoon from the royal regalia and other early and exotic spoons, from Habbakuk O. Westman, *The Spoon … Primitive, Egyptian, Roman, Mediæval, and Modern*, London, 1845. Ancient curiosities had long attracted the attention of "antiquaries" from the mid-seventeenth century onwards. Systematic analysis of material culture began in the nineteenth century.

DATE	MAKER'S MARK		ARTICLE AND OWNER.
1652	(KF)	. . . .	Salt, gift of Wrightington, 1653. Trin. House, Hull.
1653	(IV)	. . . .	Frosted cup on baluster stem, *ex dono* Bloodworth. Vintners' Company.
Do.	(ET)	. . . .	Small cup with punched ornament. Earl Amherst.
Do.	WM	As in 1648 . .	Dish deep like soup plate. Lord Harlech.
Do.	(Ꜵ)	Hound sejant . .	Set of communion and altar plate. Rochester Cathedral.
1654	(SV)	. . . .	Seal-headed spoon. Rev. T. Staniforth.
Do.	. .	. . . .	Frosted loving cup on baluster-stem. Innholders' Company.
Do.	. .	. . . .	Very small cup like that of 1659 at Marshfield. Sir. T. Thornhill, Bart.
1655	(FW)	. . . .	Plain communion cups and patens. St. Paul, Covent Garden, Lond.
Do.	(WH)	. . . .	Pair of alms-dishes. St. Olave, Old Jewry, Lond.
Do.	(WC)	. . . .	Apostle-spoon (St. Andrew). Octavius Morgan, Esq.
Do.	(IW)	An oval object below	The Blacksmiths' Cup. Sir F. A. Milbank, Bart., M.P.
Do.	(IG)	. . . .	Plain communion cup on baluster-stem. Wythburn, Cumb.
Do.	(DR)	. . . .	Communion cup. Navenby, Linc.
1656	(HG)	. . . .	Tall plain communion flagon. St. Mary, Sudeley Manor, Glouc. Another. Escrick, Yorks.
Do.	WC	As in 1655 . .	Spoon. Rev. T. Staniforth.
Do.	(HN)	Bird with olive branch below.	Communion cup, given 1656. Thornbury Devon.
1657	I·I	As in 1640 . .	Seal-headed spoon. Kensington, Midx.
Do.	Do. .	Do. . . .	Seal-headed spoon. Hackney, Midx.
Do.	HG	As in 1656 . .	Plain rude communion cup, *ex dono* Scotson, 1657. Bermondsey, Surrey.
Do.	(Ꜵ)	. . . .	Plain caudle-cups, ring handles. Clothworkers' Company.

ALPHABET X. 1658—1677.

DATE	MAKER'S MARK		ARTICLE AND OWNER.
1658	(RF)	. . . .	Pint tankard. Messrs. Lambert.
Do.	(GS)	. . . .	Small caudle-cup. Trin. House, Hull.

Y 2

52. Plate of maker's marks, including the *hound sejant*, from Wilfred Joseph Cripps, *Old English Plate, Ecclesiastical, Decorative, and Domestic: Its Makers and Marks*, London, 1878. Early analysis of silver marks was largely detective work using existing silver items to piece together a jigsaw puzzle of date letters and maker's marks.

sold it to the king for £262 10s.[11] In addition to cabinet pieces, the firm also sold the king antique works to augment the buffet of modern silver gilt they had supplied him. To have a section of one's plate room, or perhaps merely a display case in a drawing-room, with an array of Elizabethan silver, or old Nuremberg tankards, was almost *de rigueur:* besides quantities of new silver, the 6th Duke of Bedford purchased from Garrard's in 1817 "a curious antique chased & gilt Salt Cellar" for £31 10s and paid an additional £8 to have it re-gilded. Still in the collection of the Dukes of Bedford at Woburn Abbey, the salt dates from about 1600 and is part of a small group of silver objects by the same unidentified maker who specialized in applied filigree scrollwork.[12]

Reproductions of antique silver began to gain in popularity, while old silver could always be altered or adapted to suit contemporary taste. The carved ivory sleeves which fitted on to German silver-gilt tankards of the seventeenth century were often removed and re-mounted onto modern silver-gilt bodies to make flower vases. But it is not from the British royal collection alone that we can assess how widespread this passion was for both English and foreign antique silver. Auction sales brought a huge number of prestigious items onto the market, which were absorbed by the trade. We only need browse the catalogues of the sales of the Duke of Norfolk in 1816, Queen Charlotte in 1818, William Beckford's Fonthill Abbey in 1823, the Duke of York in 1827, Horace Walpole's Strawberry Hill in 1842, or the Duke of Sussex in 1843. And if that is not convincing enough, there is the sale of the remaining stock of the dissolved firm of Rundell's, also in 1843, and the contents of Stowe House in 1848, both of them full of antiques.

Letters from readers to the *Gentleman's Magazine* during the second half of the eighteenth century show how ignorant people were of silver barely a century old. The reader's attention was drawn to apostle spoons and spool-form trencher salts as curiosities even though they were little more than a hundred years old. A capstan salt was illustrated upside down with its scroll finials mistaken for legs.[13] The first books to describe antique silver objects (often with hilarious inaccuracy) began to appear in the 1840s; one of the first of these was a work devoted to the spoon (fig. 51) in which various antique examples dating from Roman times to the Commonwealth period were illustrated.[14] These books coincided with the increasing popularization of collecting antique silver and a growing curiosity about the meaning of the hallmarks stamped on it.

Marks have been central to silver studies since the earliest days of the market. Hallmarks dated back to 1300 and guaranteed the standard of the silver alloy used in what is a very early form of consumer protection. Until the nineteenth century the secret of the meaning of the various punches was closely guarded by the Worshipful Company of Goldsmiths, which was responsible for running the Assay Office and enforcing the standard; but by the 1850s public curiosity was such that a systematic study of surviving old silver enabled researchers such as Octavius Morgan (1803–1888) and William Chaffers (1811–1892) to compile and publish tables of town marks and date letters.[15] Chaffers, who was himself a dealer in second-hand plate, issued in 1863 *Hallmarks on Gold and Silver Plate*, which went through many editions and was on the shelf of every collector.

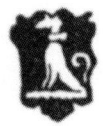

53. The *hound sejant* maker's mark, now attributed to Richard Blackwell (*fl.* 1646–1666). Silver collectors avidly sought the high-quality pieces bearing this maker's mark but only in 2003 was the identity of the man who used it established. *The Silver Society, London*

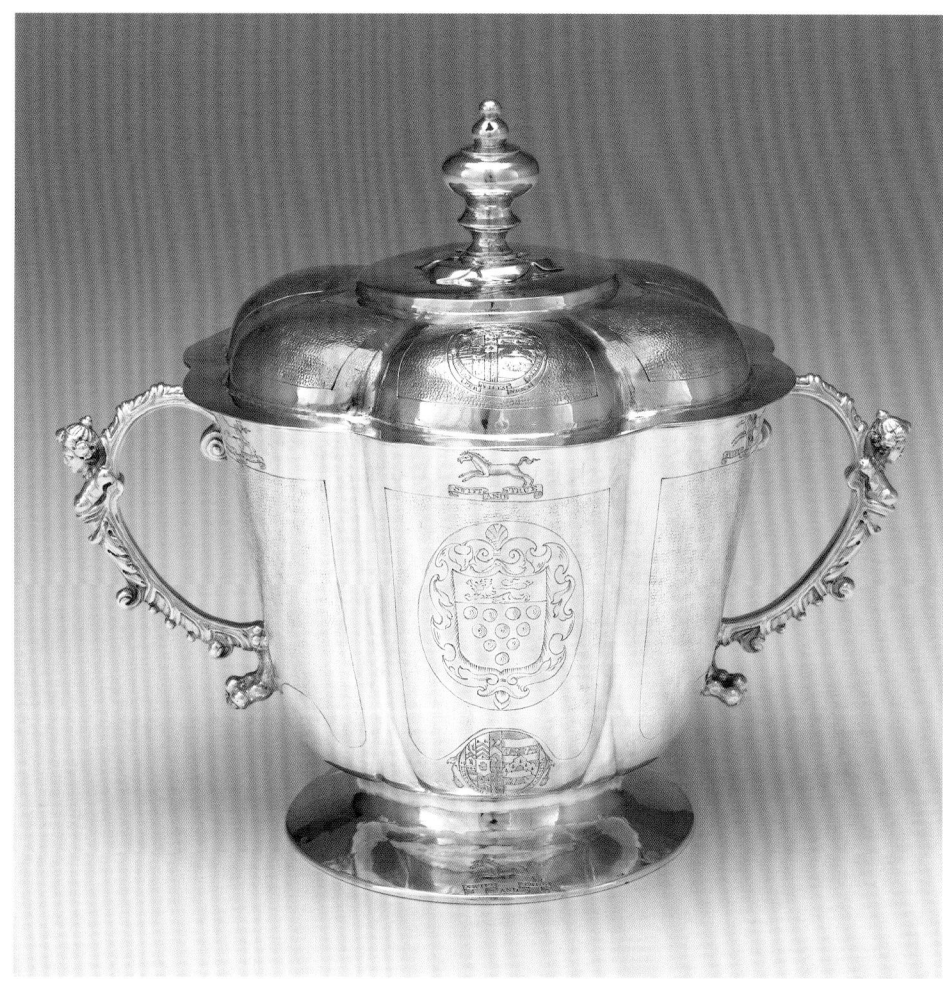

The first book, however, to attempt to chart the development of forms and styles in addition to marks was by William Cripps (1841–1903), who, like Morgan, was a man of independent means. His *Old English Plate* was also a best-seller for the rest of the century (fig. 52). The problem facing these early researchers was the lack of available records revealing the names behind the makers' marks. The Goldsmiths' Company was reluctant to allow their records to be published and right into the twentieth century a painstaking process of comparing the marks on existing pieces in private and public collections with what records were available enabled only some of the marks to be attributed to individuals. Nowadays, even with the Goldsmiths' Company leading the way in research, the picture is still not complete, for their early records of makers' marks were destroyed in a fire at the end of the seventeenth century. Many makers, especially those who used symbols rather than initials in their marks, remain unidentified to this day, although

from time to time researchers uncover some exciting results.

By way of example, the maker who used the mark known as a *hound sejant* (in other words, seated hound) became legendary as the producer of some of the best plate of the 1650s and 1660s (figs. 54–5). The high quality of his output led some authorities to suggest he was a foreign immigrant, probably from Flanders. In 1938 the young Arthur Grimwade noted in his diary that he had seen "a magnificent Commonwealth cup by the greyhound sejant maker — how I would love to trace the man's name," but the truth was not to be revealed until 2003, when the silver scholar Eric J.G. Smith, delving into old records with the zeal of a master sleuth, discovered a record of payments for the town mace of Faversham in Kent to a Richard Blackwell. The mace, still used today by the town corporation, is marked with the *hound sejant*. Smith went on to amass further documentation that enabled him to put together biographical details not only of

54. Two-handled cup and cover, silver, c. 1650, maker's mark a *hound sejant*, for Richard Blackwell. A piece of superb quality, its heraldic engraving documents its early provenance; in the twentieth century it passed through two distinguished English collections, that of Mrs R. Makower and the 3rd Baron Rothschild. Cat. no. 2

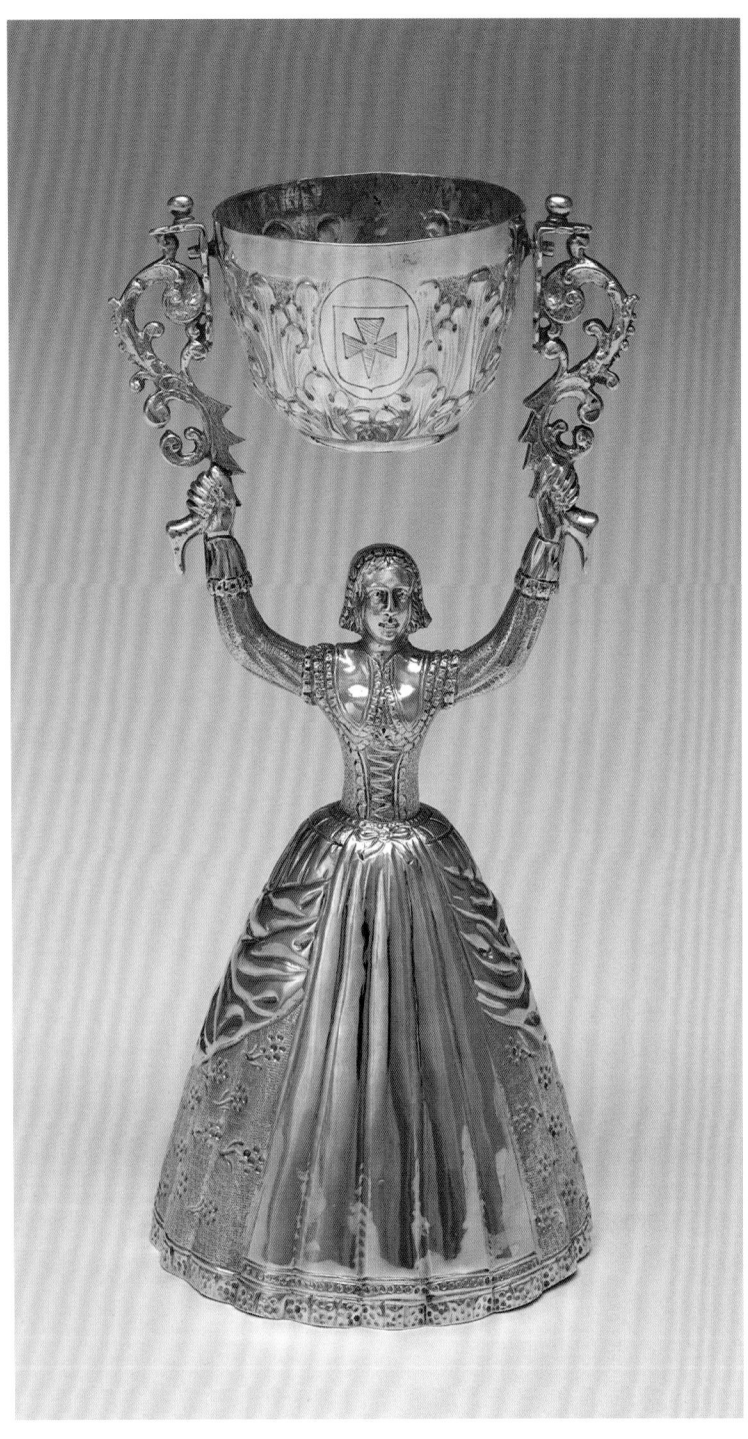

55. Wager cup, silver, c. 1665, maker's mark a *hound sejant*, for Richard Blackwell. An extremely rare survival of an English copy of a German novelty. In drinking contests, it was necessary to drain the contents of the woman's skirt without spilling the liquor in the swivelling cup she holds above her head.
Cat. no. 4

Blackwell but also of his father, also named Richard, and to attribute a further series of marks to the father.[16]

Such information is part of the excitement of the pursuit of antique silver and for silver scholars it opens the way to further research to be done into the structure of the trade in the seventeenth century. But the study of marks has been a two-edged sword. For a collector, undue reliance on the marks struck on a piece of old silver can distract one from studying its form, decoration, and the techniques used in its manufacture. In fact, marks struck on silver can be no more reliable than a signature on a painting. They were often faked in the eighteenth century to avoid sending the item for assay and having to pay the duty. In the nineteenth century, marks were added to new pieces, or to old unmarked ones, to make them more saleable antiques. Perhaps most frustratingly of all, makers' marks are misleading when it comes to identifying the true maker of a piece.

This is because the maker's mark is something of a misnomer, for it signified only the individual who submitted the item for assay. This person might have been the retailer rather than the craftsman in whose workshop the item was made. The mark masks the large network of specialist craftsmen—the designers, modelers, beaters, chasers, engravers, and gilders who, since the Middle Ages, have been involved in the making of silver. Many collectors, however, respond to names, and the antique silver market, like that of Old Masters, puts too great an emphasis on this form of branding even today. Legendary names such as Paul de Lamerie and Paul Storr have, justifiably, been avidly pursued by collectors, but to think of the items bearing their marks as being solely by them and not a collaborative effort is to ignore their genius as businessmen and entrepreneurs in addition to their being artists and craftsmen.

Besides publishing one of the standard works on the history of silver (1911), Sir Charles Jackson, one of the greatest authorities on English silver, also compiled a compendium of marks (1921), which, revised and expanded, remains one of the standard references. The publication of catalogues of important silver collections, beginning with one on Cambridge college plate in 1845, continued with that of the Londesborough Collection in 1860, greatly added to silver scholarship, as did the comprehensive catalogues of exhibitions held from 1862 to the 1930s.

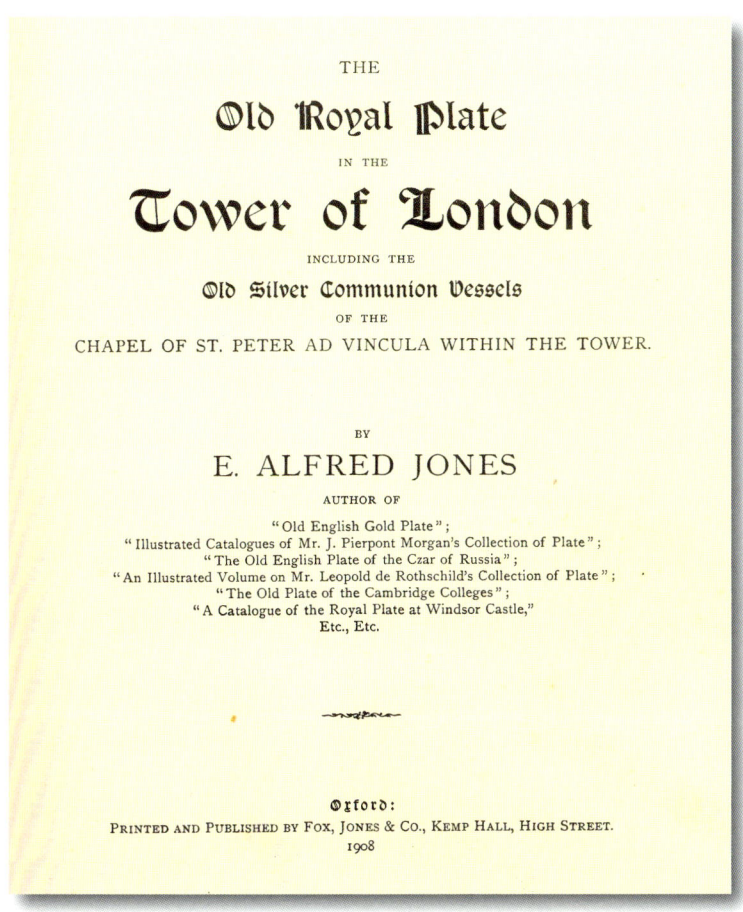

THE

Old Royal Plate

IN THE

Tower of London

INCLUDING THE

Old Silver Communion Vessels

OF THE

CHAPEL OF ST. PETER AD VINCULA WITHIN THE TOWER.

BY

E. ALFRED JONES

AUTHOR OF

"Old English Gold Plate";
"Illustrated Catalogues of Mr. J. Pierpont Morgan's Collection of Plate";
"The Old English Plate of the Czar of Russia";
"An Illustrated Volume on Mr. Leopold de Rothschild's Collection of Plate";
"The Old Plate of the Cambridge Colleges";
"A Catalogue of the Royal Plate at Windsor Castle,"
Etc., Etc.

Oxford:

PRINTED AND PUBLISHED BY FOX, JONES & CO., KEMP HALL, HIGH STREET.
1908

56. Detail of the title page from E. Alfred Jones, *The Old Royal Plate in the Tower of London*, Oxford, 1908. Jones was the author of a number of analytical catalogues of major silver collections in which he documented styles and function as well as marks.

The tradition of systematic cataloguing of silver was begun by E. Alfred Jones (1872–1943) who, from 1907 until his untimely death during the blackout in 1943 (the result of a fall down the grand staircase at Althorp House where he was engaged in cataloguing the Spencer family silver), published more than twenty silver catalogues.[17] Starting with the English plate in the Kremlin, Jones documented the collections of Eton College, the Duke of Portland, William Francis Farrer, J. Pierpont Morgan, Baroness James de Rothschild, Windsor Castle, and the Tower of London, as well as those of a number of Oxford colleges, one volume of the plate of all the Cambridge colleges, and a list of English gold. Jones was instrumental in the exhibition of pre-1739 silver organized to benefit Queen Charlotte's Hospital in 1929. His analytical approach in cataloguing set a standard which was emulated eventually by the auction houses Christie's and Sotheby's. But perhaps Jones's greatest legacy was his best-selling book, *Old Silver of Europe and America*, the first to present a general survey of the silver of different countries.

It first appeared in 1928 and enjoyed huge success on both sides of the Atlantic, no doubt inspiring more than one generation of silver collectors.

By the 1920s the antique silver market had expanded dramatically, in large part through the activities of a number of American collectors, chief among them being legendary newspaper magnate William Randolph Hearst (1863–1951). Much of his silver collection would reappear on the market in the years following the Wall Street crash. The leading auction houses in London held silver auctions at least once a week and the trade supported a large web of runners, brokers, and dealers at all levels. Objects could appear in the country and in a matter of days be in a Bond Street shop, duly recognized, at many times their original price; as one expert noted, "I heard that some years ago, an enormous venison dish of silver, of an unusual place of origin, Newcastle in fact, was sold as plated at a country sale in Sussex. The local auctioneer did not dream that a dish of such a huge size with its cover complete, could possibly be of silver, and, moreover, the Newcastle mint mark deceived him, so that the dealer who purchased the dish took away a great bargain, buying, for ordinary plate, a very heavy silver dish of most unusual date and quality."[18]

At auction, silver was sold by weight, and the bidding (at Christie's this was done in guineas, an obsolete gold coin worth £1 1s—an early form of buyer's premium) was done per ounce. On the fall of the hammer, the sales clerk, at his desk next to the auctioneer, swiftly multiplied the closing bid by the number of ounces and pennyweights in the piece and so calculated the total price. This continued in London until the 1950s.

In the 1930s academic interest in old silver continued to grow, and moreover, there was much concern about the quantities of old silver leaving Britain for America. When the Howard Grace Cup was put up for sale at Christie's by the Duke of Norfolk in 1931, it created a national sensation. The sale was personally attended by the Prime Minister, Ramsay MacDonald, and the director of the Victoria and Albert Museum and, after the cup had been knocked down for £11,000, it was announced that it had been bought by the National Art Collections Fund. MacDonald commented afterwards, "I may definitely state that the cup was to be bought by the nation, no matter what it cost." There was the same buzz of excitement in the air when some six

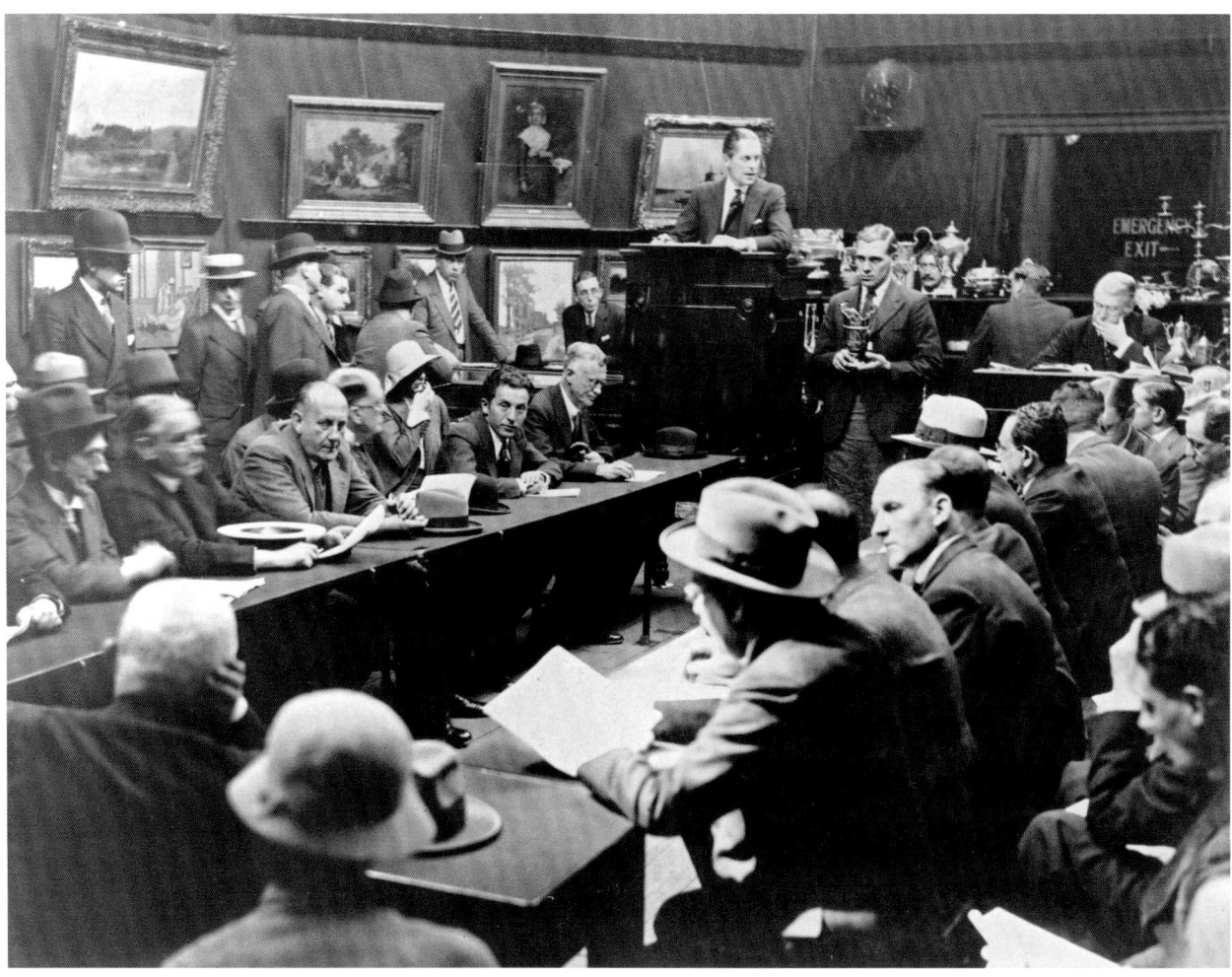

years later an early eighteenth-century monteith, or punch bowl, by the colonial silversmith John Coney of Boston (1656–1722) appeared at auction in New York and the sale was broadcast live on the radio.

In 1932, a lad of nineteen joined Christie's silver department. This was Arthur Grimwade (1913–2004), who was to become recognized as a leading authority in the field, whose reference book, *London Goldsmiths,1697–1837: Their Marks and Lives*, remains a standard work (fig. 50). But Grimwade recalled that when he joined Christie's, a spirit of amateurism reigned and the firm was anxious that their specialists should not be considered as "experts."[19] All that was to change in the ensuing decades as, at both Sotheby's and Christie's, the specialists often became leading figures in their field. In the trade, too, a new type of dealer had emerged who was often considered as much a scholar as a trader. As a form of marketing, it was extremely successful and greatly enhanced knowledge in general. At the time of

the Antique Dealers' Fair at the Grosvenor House Hotel in 1934, it was remarked that "the dealers … have noticed with satisfaction that the collector of today is far more knowledgeable than his predecessor twenty years ago."[20]

In the silver field, one of the first of these scholar/dealers was George How, a former naval commander, who started dealing in Edinburgh in the 1920s but moved to London shortly thereafter (though the trading name remained as How of Edinburgh). He was the author, for Sotheby's, of their 1935 auction catalogue of the Ellis Collection of early spoons which is still a reference work for provincial hallmarks. His wife, Jane, collaborated with him on a monumental three-volume work on spoons and early hallmarks, which was published in the 1950s. Jane How (1915–2004) managed the business after his death until her retirement in the late 1990s (fig. 58). Another influential dealer in this scholarly tradition was Thomas Lumley (1906–1983), who had worked for Sotheby's and afterwards for

57. A silver auction in progress at Christie's, June 28, 1933. Terence McKenna, a director of Christie's and father of Virginia McKenna the actress, conducts the sale, while a youthful Arthur Grimwade, with his back to the camera, organizes the lots behind the desk. Higher taxation in Britain in the years following the Boer War, as well as the Great Depression, brought large quantities of silver onto the market. The ewer being sold is now at the Museum of Fine Arts, Boston.

Commander How before starting his own business in 1936 (fig. 59). In his obituary, he was described by Arthur Grimwade as "a man of exquisite taste in all things."

These key figures were influential in shaping the tastes of collectors and in nurturing connoisseurship. The prevailing taste in the nineteenth century had been "le goût Rothschild." In silver this encompassed highly ornate early German cups and tankards, and English rococo silver. As early as 1876, however, the *Quarterly Review* had declared, "Queen Anne plate is now the rage," and from then until the 1960s the vogue was almost exclusively for plain silver in what was dubbed the "Queen Anne" style (in fact its parameters extended into the 1730s, long after the death of that monarch). Ironically, it was a Rothschild, Victor, 3rd Baron Rothschild (1910–1990), who was one of the leading collectors of this plain silver in the mid-twentieth century (fig. 54).

Especially sought after were octagonal objects (fig. 60), and much rarer objects with nine, or even ten, sides. The emphasis was on line rather than surface decoration, and the patina of the metal. Ironically, these plain pieces had been, at the time of their manufacture, the least expensive to buy, as the fashioning charge was the lowest.

Other influential dealers of the inter-war years included Lionel Crichton (1865–1938) and the firm of Walter H. Willson. Born Lionel Phillips, Crichton had changed his name to avoid confusion with another distinguished firm, S.J. Phillips of Bond Street, and traded in partnership with his brother Philip Phillips as Crichton Brothers. With shops in both London and New York, they counted Queen Mary among their clients.[21] Philip Phillips retired from dealing in 1919 to write a monograph on Paul de Lamerie which appeared in 1935 (fig. 61).

58. Jane Penrice How (1915–2004), seen walking her mastiffs outside St James's Palace, c. 1969. From discreet premises nearby she shaped the taste of several generations of silver collectors, advocating sound scholarship and developing an eye for quality.

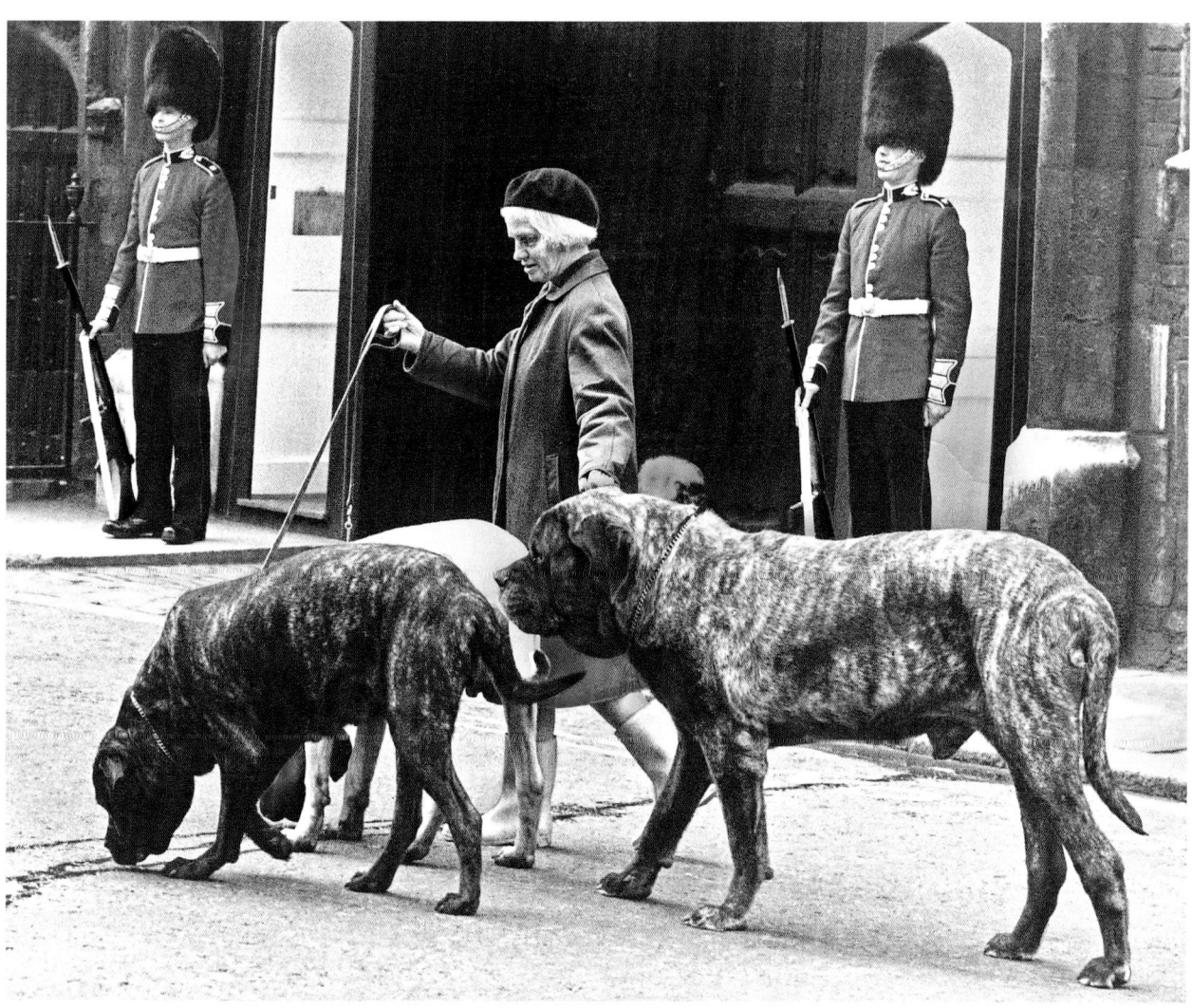

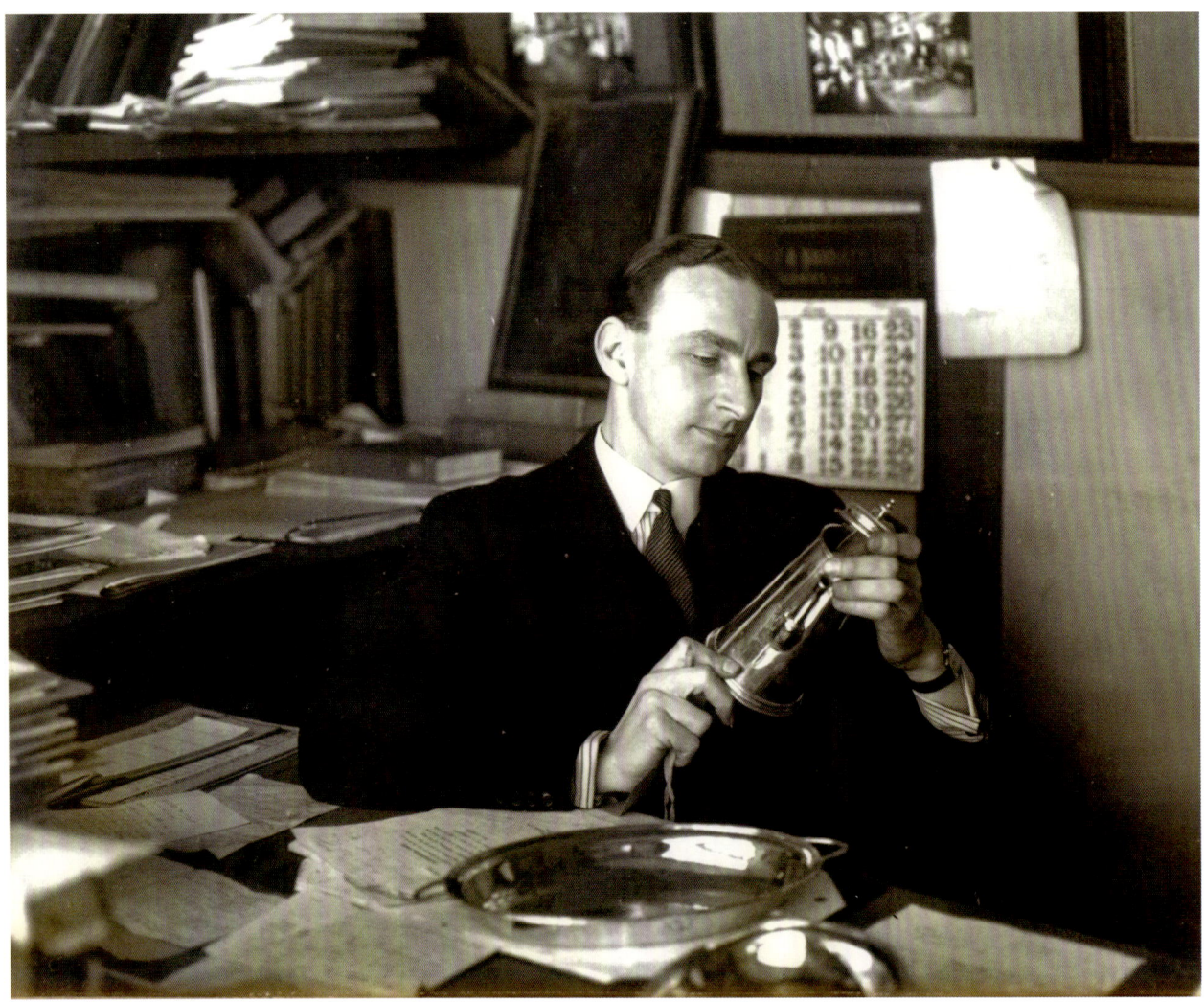

59. Thomas Lumley (1906–1983). Lumley's scholarly approach and connoisseurship shaped the taste of many collectors and museums for over forty years. The Chambers tureens illustrated in fig. 71 and the Heming example in fig. 73 passed through his hands in the 1950s.

Unusually for an eighteenth-century silver-smith, Paul de Lamerie's name was remembered long after he died. The catalogue of the Christie's sale of the Duke of Sussex's collection in 1843 includes "A Superb and very elegant Tea urn 2 feet high, chased with masks, medallions and terminal ornaments in the beautiful taste of Paul L'Emery" (it sold for just above scrap price at 5 shillings an ounce), while a few years later, in 1858, Christie's sold a pair of "Paul Lemere" soup tureens for the Duke of Argyll, also at 5 shillings an ounce. The catalogue of the exhibition held at Ironmongers' Hall in 1861 compared a flask exhibited by Messrs. Lambert to one made "by Paul L'Emere in the reign of King William III, 1688–1703"; apart from the confusion in dates (de Lamerie was not apprenticed until 1703), it shows that de Lamerie's name provided a standard by which silver creations were judged.[22] De Lamerie's mark was one of the only ones identified in the successive editions of Chaffer's *Hallmarks on Gold and Silver Plate*. The 1893 auction catalogue of Admiral Anson's de Lamerie silver (see *A Noble Feast*, pp. 30–3) boasted on its title page that the silver was by "Paul de Lamerie, Each piece bearing his mark, with London hall-mark and date-mark of year." In 1919 the

60. Teapot on lamp stand, silver, wood, London, 1715/16, maker's mark of Joseph Ward. Severely plain silver of the early years of the eighteenth century became the most expensive category of English silver in the inter-war years. Cat. no. 11

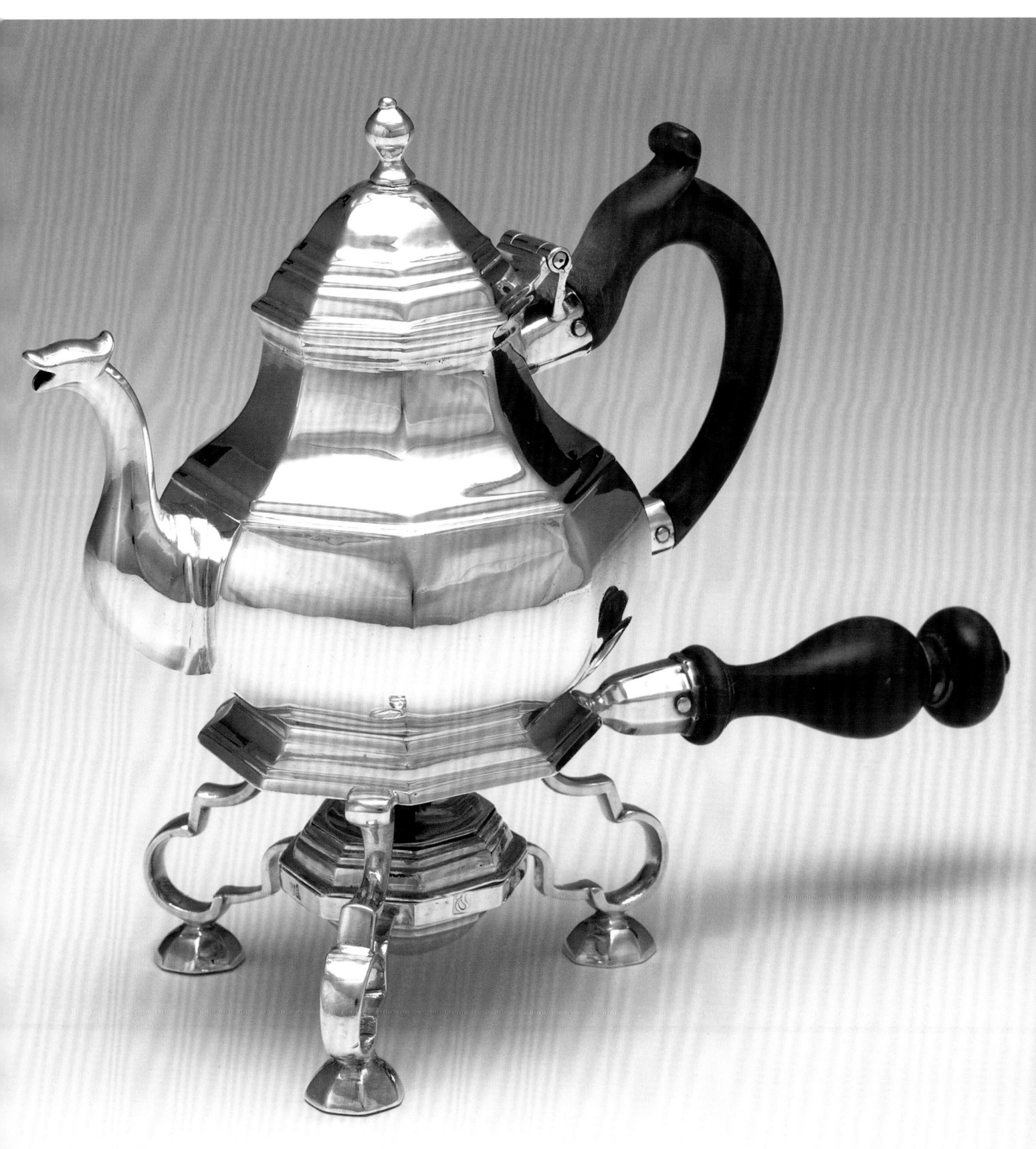

61. Detail of the title page from P.A.S. Phillips, *Paul de Lamerie: Citizen and Goldsmith of London: A Study of His Life and Work A.D. 1688–1751*, London, 1935. As early as the 1840s de Lamerie's name was mentioned in auction catalogues. Phillips's landmark study of his life was the first to be devoted to an English silversmith.

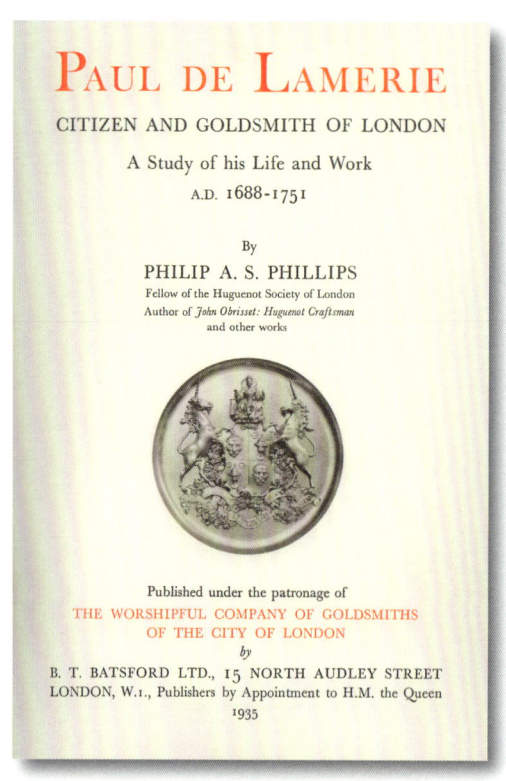

PAUL DE LAMERIE

CITIZEN AND GOLDSMITH OF LONDON

A Study of his Life and Work

A.D. 1688-1751

By

PHILIP A. S. PHILLIPS

Fellow of the Huguenot Society of London
Author of *John Obrisset: Huguenot Craftsman*
and other works

Published under the patronage of
THE WORSHIPFUL COMPANY OF GOLDSMITHS
OF THE CITY OF LONDON
by
B. T. BATSFORD LTD., 15 NORTH AUDLEY STREET
LONDON, W.1., Publishers by Appointment to H.M. the Queen
1935

63. Basket, silver, London, 1742/43, maker's mark of Paul de Lamerie. Scholarship in the early twenty-first century has greatly enhanced our understanding of the design process of the rococo period. Cat. no. 22

62. Basket, silver, London, 1732/33, maker's mark of Paul de Lamerie. Cat. no. 16

Victoria and Albert Museum paid £3,000 at auction for de Lamerie's Newdigate Centerpiece. The rise in interest in plain silver can be seen in the 1924 catalogue of the sale of the Swaythling Collection where de Lamerie's earlier plain works are given the same prominence as his rococo pieces. A pair of de Lamerie candelabra made for Sir Robert Walpole (now in the Gilbert Collection in the Victoria and Albert Museum) sold for £3,000—they had cost £308 in 1893.

In his monograph on Paul de Lamerie, Philip Phillips attempted to elevate his subject to artist

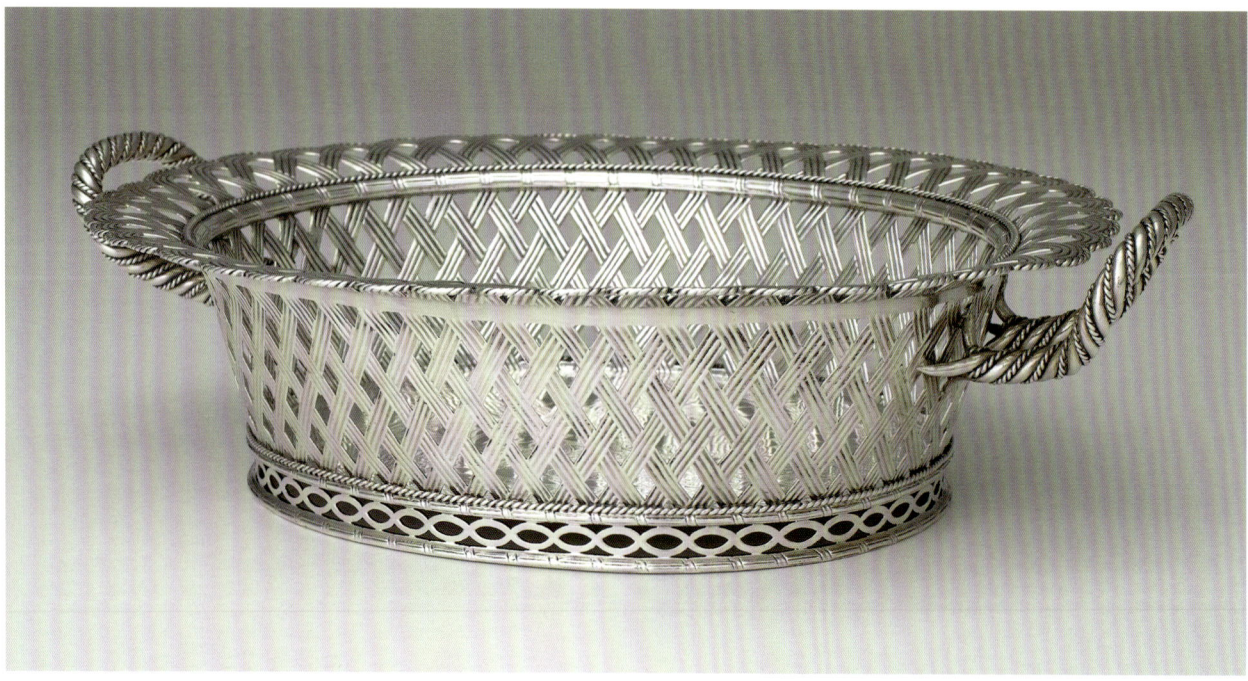

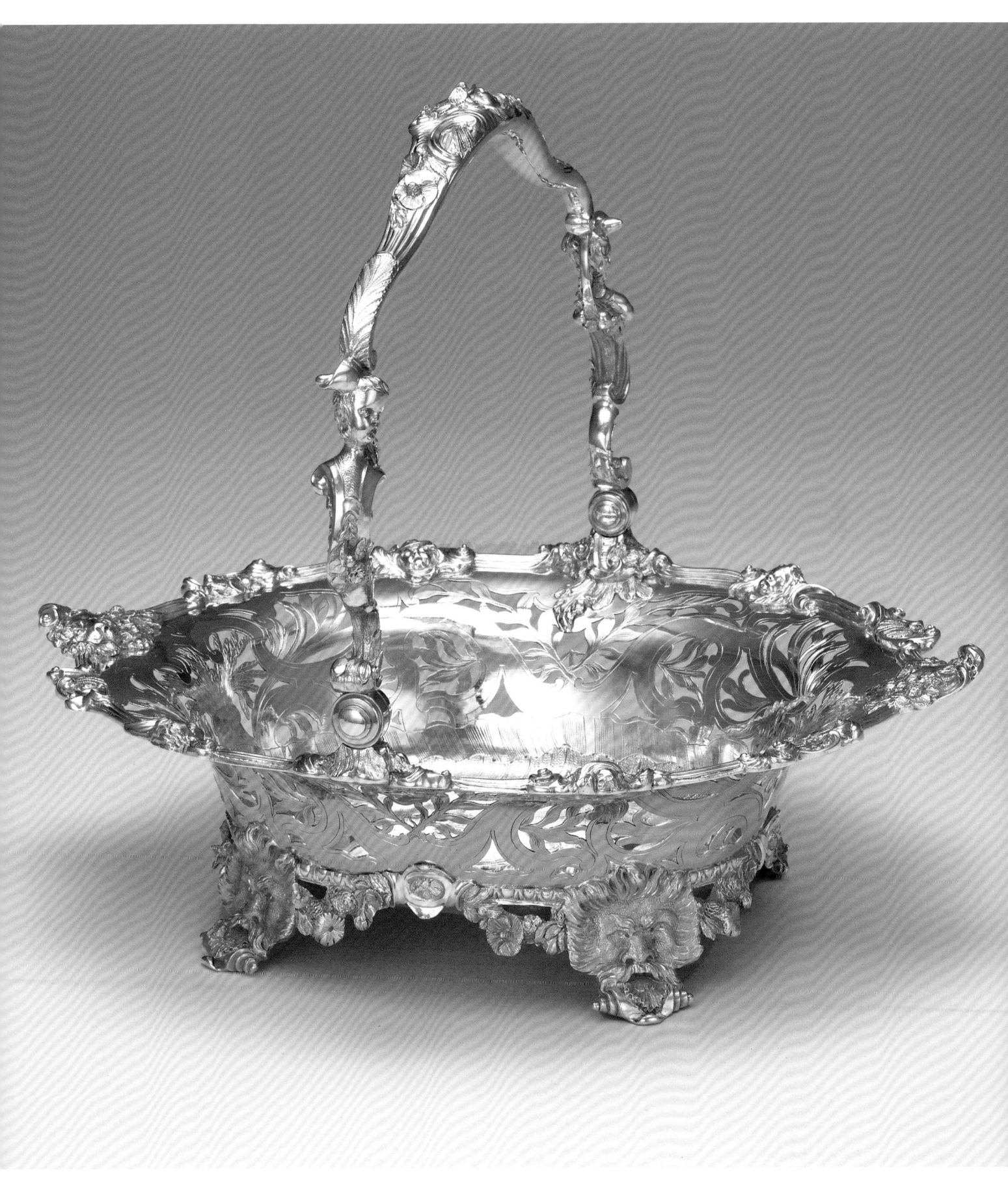

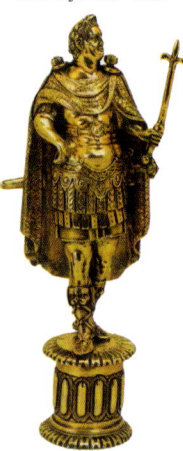

The Morgan Collection

Highly Important English and Continental Silver
and Objects of Vertu

Christie's, New York   Tuesday, October 26, 1982 at 3:30 p.m.

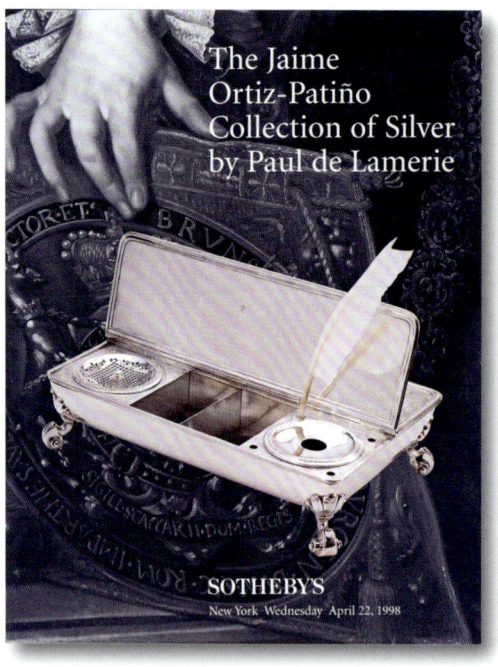

The Jaime
Ortiz-Patiño
Collection of Silver
by Paul de Lamerie

SOTHEBY'S
New York Wednesday April 22, 1998

**64. Cover of the sale
catalogue of the Morgan
Collection, Christie's,
New York, October 26,
1982. Comprising only a
portion of the vast silver
collection of John
Pierpont Morgan, the
sale included important
works by Paul de
Lamerie. Mr. and Mrs.
Gans can be seen
bidding at the sale in
the frontispiece.**

**65. Cover of the sale
catalogue of the Jaime Ortiz-
Patiño Collection, Sotheby's,
New York, April 22, 1998.
The acquisition-to-resale
cycle of collections became
much shorter in the latter half
of the twentieth century; this
major collection, for example,
was formed over a twenty-
year period and sold when the
collector moved on to new
collecting areas. The basket,
fig. 63, comes from this
collection.**

**66. Inkstand, silver,
London, 1741/42,
maker's mark of Paul
de Lamerie.
Cat. no. 21**

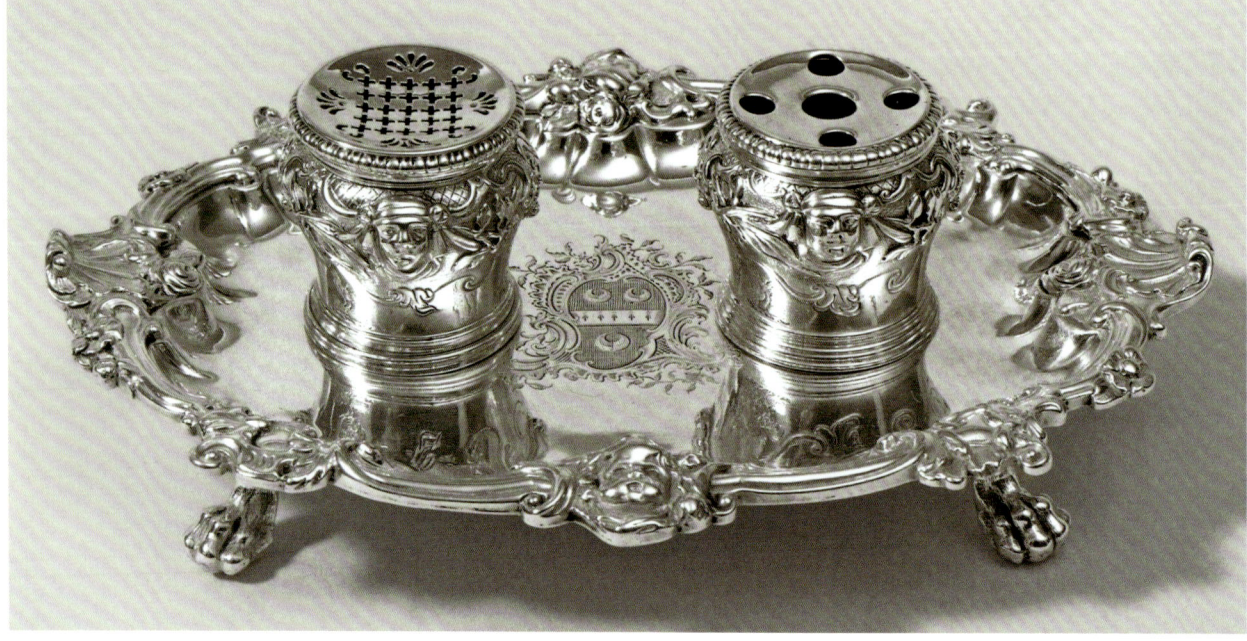

THE MAN AND HIS WORK

IN any attempt to assess the value of a man's work—in whichever of the Arts—in a fair and unbiased manner, as is only his rightful due, it is necessary to put it in its true perspective, to take into account the times in which he worked, to allow for the dictates of passing whims and fashions, to note any extraneous influences, to gauge aright the standard of technique displayed, and finally to consider if the dictum of posterity be right and just.

History can offer many examples of personal initiative and genius being stifled by poverty and lack of opportunity, by prejudice and jealousy, or by misunderstanding and ignorance. This, of course, was not the case with Paul Storr, but one wonders how his technique would have developed had his working life not coincided with one of the great periods of English history, and, above all, had there been no Philip Rundell to inundate him with orders for the Royal Family, for the celebration of a fresh victory, or to fulfil a contract for one of the great houses of a wealthy and aristocratic England.

Considering, then, the degree to which circumstance played a part in Storr's life we can but wonder at the high standard of his work—even when repetition of design got dangerously near that *coup de grâce* of all craftsmen—mass production. It is impossible to point to any piece by Paul Storr as an example of faulty workmanship. We may not approve of the design, we may dislike the proportions, we may criticize unnecessary elaboration of detail, we may consider a piece more suited to marble or bronze than to silver—but bad workmanship: never!

Storr was working from designs drawn by men to whom the nature of gold and silver was practically unknown. Thus Tatham was an architect, Flaxman a sculptor, Stothard a painter and Theed both painter and sculptor. Their *métier* was stone and marble, pottery and porcelain, and classical line-drawings. To transmute from one medium to another demands great skill, and in this Storr was a master. If in judging his work we had to depend solely on his massive and ''grand'' pieces we might dismiss him merely as a fine and clever craftsman, but if we examine his earlier products and some of those simpler domestic objects which appeared from time to time—*parva componere magnis*—we shall see more than the craftsman—we shall see the artist. Paul Storr was the last of the great goldsmiths.

THE CLASSICAL REVIVAL

When in 1792 Storr had completed the period of his apprenticeship almost the first article he produced, in conjunction with William Frisbee, was a two-handled

19

status and ignored the fact that de Lamerie's silver production had been a collaborative effort. Silver scholarship has since recognized the hands of other individuals in pieces bearing de Lamerie's mark, as either engravers or modelers. An exhibition devoted to de Lamerie held at Goldsmiths' Hall in London in 1990 provided an opportunity to compare a wide range of his silver,[23] and by the beginning of the twenty-first century, one individual, the so-called "Maynard Master," had emerged as a separate artistic entity within de Lamerie's work.[24] Such a thing would have been inconceivable fifty years before.

The tyranny of the maker's mark, and the public's love of "branding," had focused attention on major names. Norman Penzer's 1954 book *Paul Storr: The Last of the Goldsmiths* follows the format of Phillips's work on de Lamerie and entirely ignores the fact that the many advanced industrial processes that were involved in producing the silver struck with Storr's mark, as well as its sheer quantity, made it impossible for it to have been created by one man alone. "If in judging his work we had to depend solely on his massive and 'grand' pieces we might dismiss him merely as a fine and clever craftsman, but if we examine his earlier products and some of those

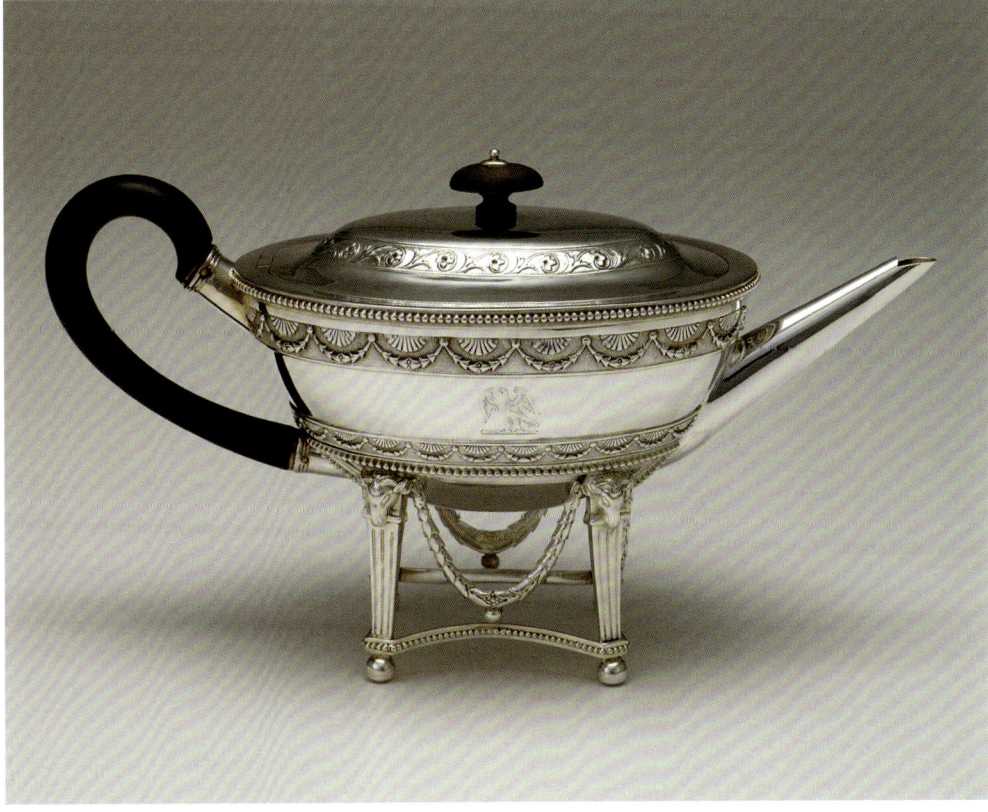

67. The opening to Chapter One from Norman Mosley Penzer's *Paul Storr, the Last of the Goldsmiths*, 1954. An exhaustive study of a major figure in silver production during the first four decades of the nineteenth century, Penzer's book, however, celebrates Storr as an artist rather than a gifted entrepreneur and artistic manager.

68. Teapot on stand, silver, fruitwood, London, 1794/95, maker's mark of Paul Storr. Storr's large output was diverse in style and always of the highest quality, two characteristics vital for collector demand. Cat. no. 31

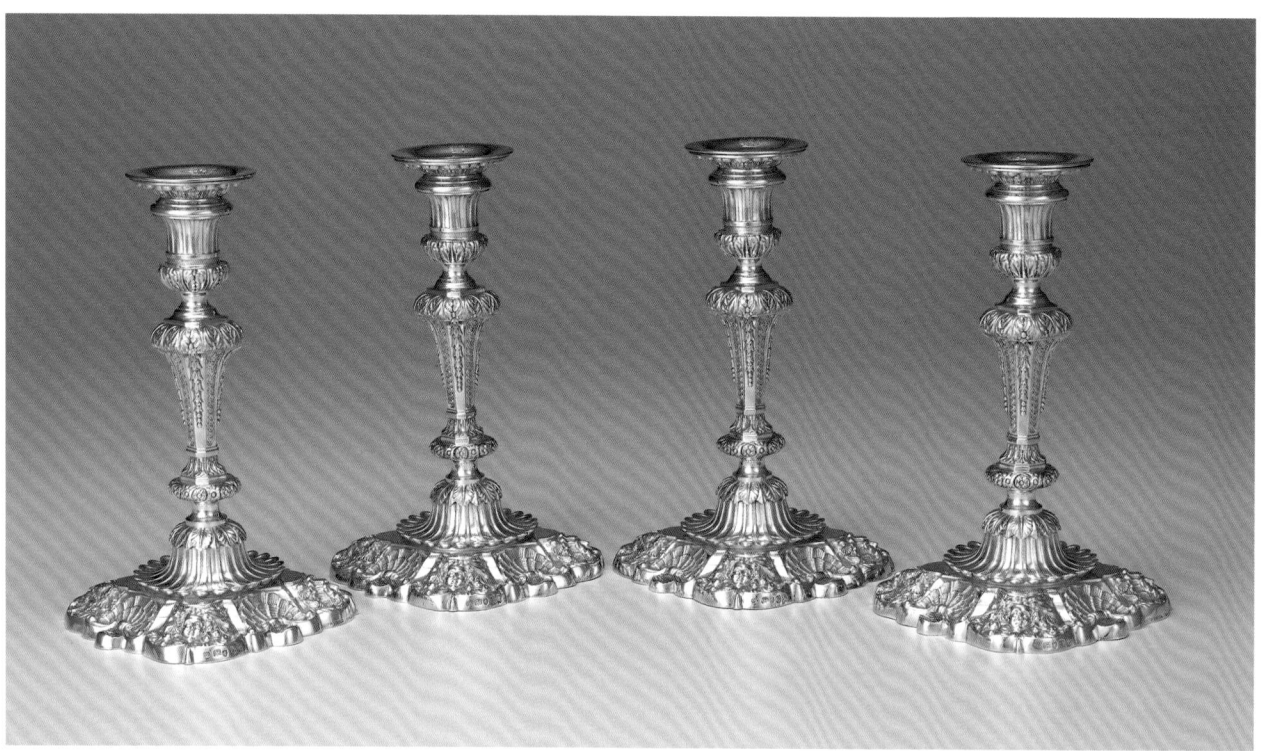

69. Four candlesticks, silver, London, 1815/16, maker's mark of Paul Storr. Inspired by baroque examples of eighty years before, these candlesticks are modeled and cast with great skill. Cat. no. 37

simpler domestic objects which appeared from time to time … we shall see more than the craftsman—we shall see the artist. Paul Storr was the last of the great goldsmiths."[25]

The high point of this nonsense was the publication in 1959 of David S. Shure's book *Hester Bateman: Queen of English Silversmiths*, in which the author asserted that "The Batemans were skilled silversmiths, each capable of selecting a piece of silver and taking it through every process to completion." In fact, the opposite was true. Widowed at an early age, Hester Bateman took over her husband's silver chain-making business, which in time she developed, with the assistance of her three sons, into one of the largest mechanized manufacturers of utilitarian silver in late eighteenth-century London. But to regard Hester Bateman as a craftswoman, creating individual works of art at her bench, as was done for most of the twentieth century, is wrong, and shows a lack of understanding of her prowess as an entrepreneur and businesswoman of tremendous foresight.[26]

Although Paul Storr may not have worked at the bench himself, he was responsible for the creation of works of a virtuosity that is often comparable to work from de Lamerie's workshop. But unlike the de Lamerie market, it was well into the twentieth century before Storr was properly

recognized for his worth and Regency silver in general sold for more than its intrinsic value. In 1932 the young Arthur Grimwade recorded in his diary, "Today I went with Mr B to Princess Beatrice's apartments at Kensington Palace to view a magnificent silver dinner service by Paul Storr which they want to know if we could get more than £1,000 for." Having weighed it, he commented, "The total was just over 5,000 ozs. so we ought easily to get more than £1,000 for the service, even at the low estimate of 4 shillings and 6 pence per oz."[27] A few weeks later, the service sold for just over £1,600, still not much more than scrap, to Vardi, a New York silver dealer. Vardi sold extravagant Regency and Victorian pieces in his shop on 57th Street and it was said that he fostered the idea that he was an illegitimate son of King Edward VII to impress clients.[28] Vardi, along with Maurice Freeman of I. Freeman & Son and Eric Shrubsole of S.J. Shrubsole Corp., did much to promote the taste for Regency silver, and especially the work of Storr, in the United States. Shrubsole remarked years later that the success of his own business had been based on "the three Pauls—Paul de Lamerie, Paul Storr and Paul Revere," the latter the great patriot silversmith.

Another profound influence on collector taste during the post-war period was the appearance at

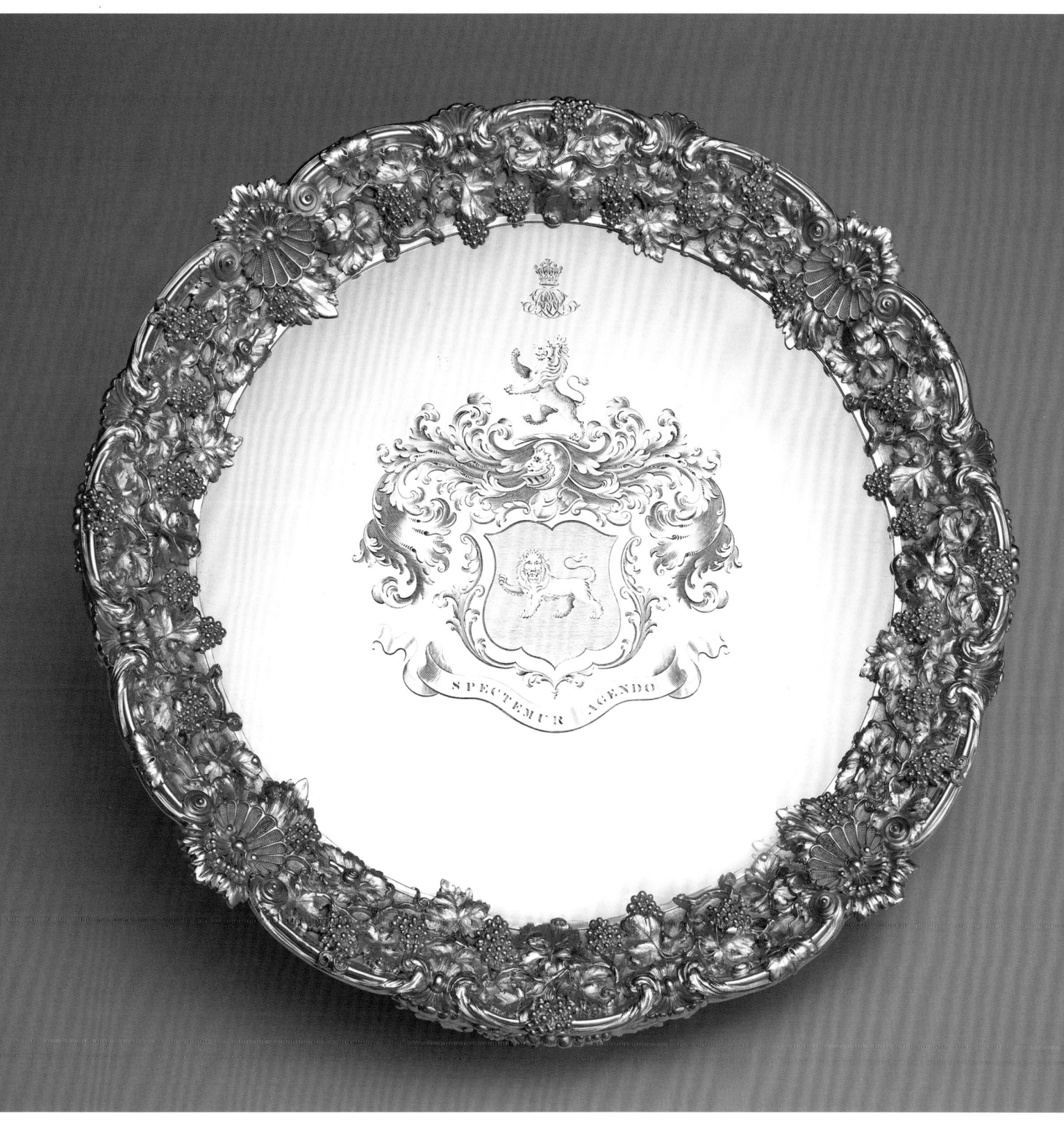

**70. Salver, silver,
London, 1813/14,
maker's mark of Paul
Storr.**
Cat. no. 36

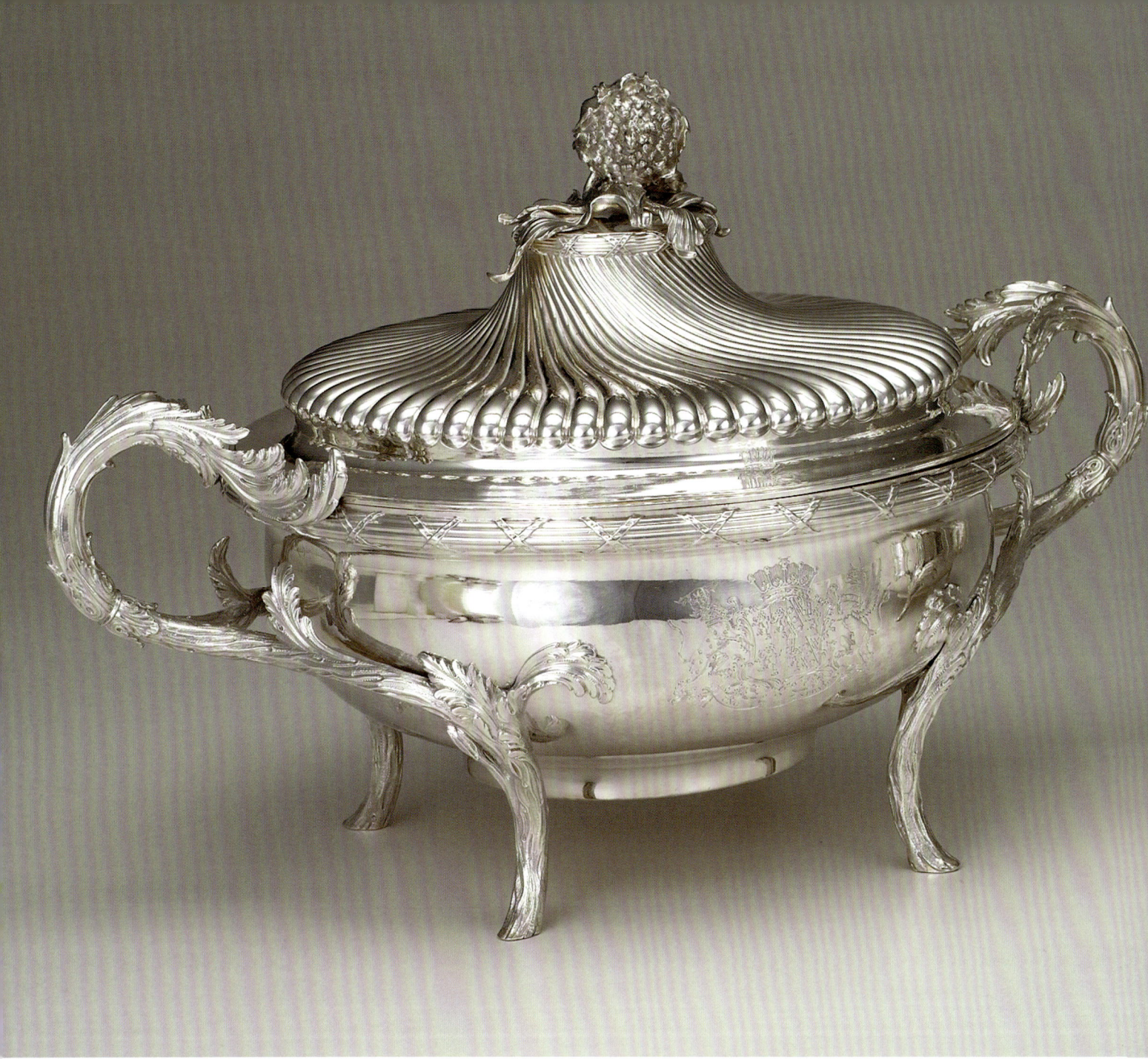

71. Pair of soup tureens and covers, silver, London, 1771/72, maker's mark of Sebastian I & James Crespell, after a design by Sir William Chambers. The complexities not only of silver production in the eighteenth century, but also the design process itself have attracted collectors in recent years. Cat. no. 29

auction of major collections of Regency silver, such as those of Sir William Butlin and the Earl and Countess of Harewood. Billy Butlin, who had made a fortune with his "holiday camps," had formed his collection over a twenty-year period. The Harewood collection of mostly silver-gilt pieces by Storr and others had been commissioned from Rundell, Bridge & Rundell by the 1st Earl of Harewood. Pieces from both sales were acquired by the Memphis collector Morrie Moss, whose collection of Paul Storr silver eventually comprised over two hundred pieces. The collection was well known from a catalogue of it published in 1972.[29] After its sale

en bloc a few years later to the Los Angeles dealer David Orgell, it was distributed amongst a new generation of collectors, among whom were Jerome and Rita Gans, who travelled to California and purchased fourteen items.

During the twentieth century, research by silver scholars delved further into the complexities of silver production and addressed the vexed question of the "maker's mark." The picture has gradually become more focused and in the process the identities of more and more participants in the eighteenth-century silver trade have emerged. Museum installations now go beyond the display of examples of the different types of

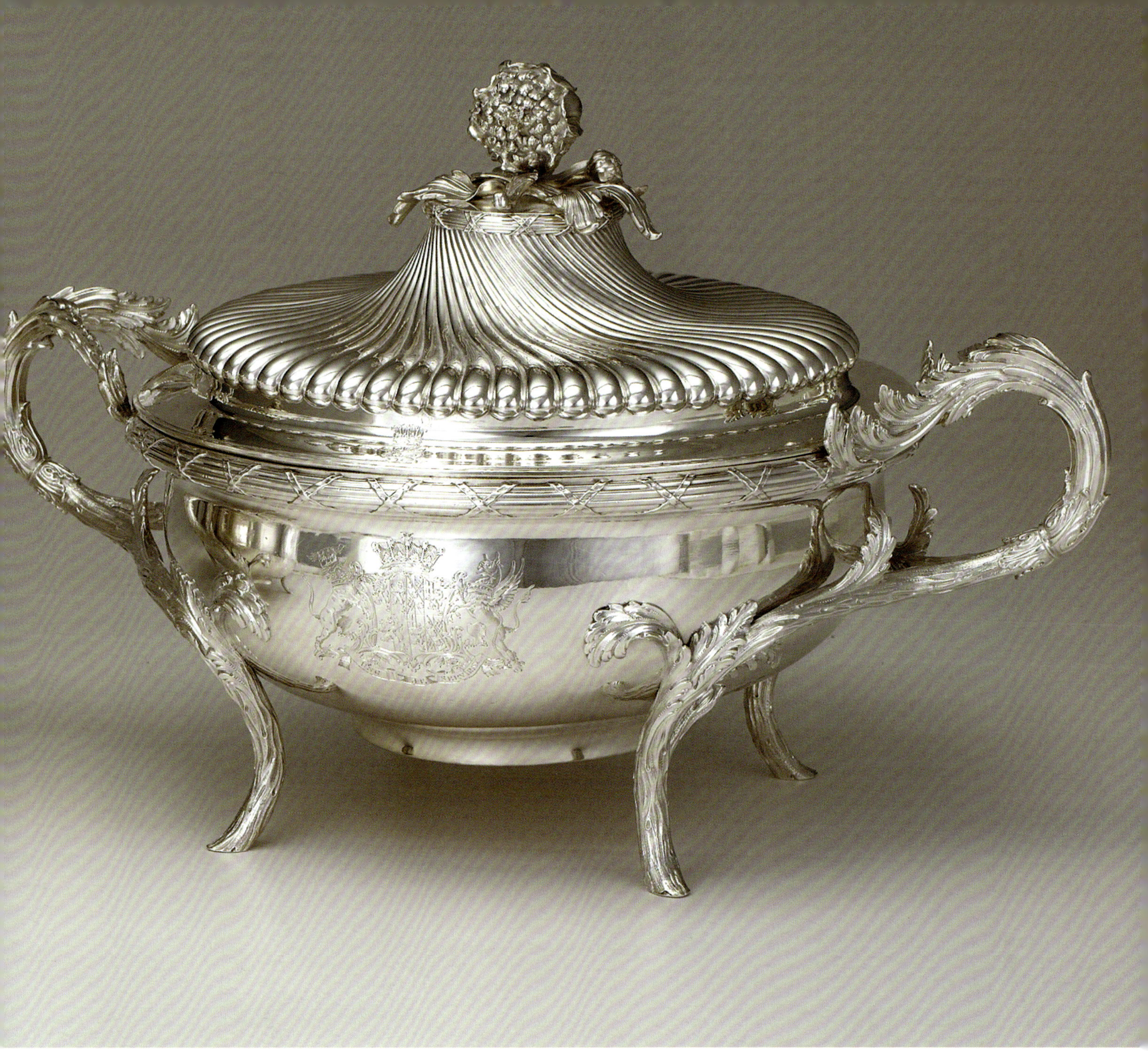

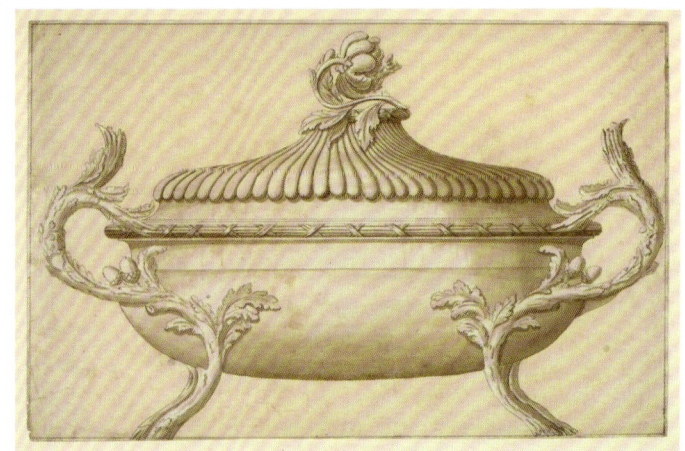

72. John Yenn (1750–1821), after Sir William Chambers (1723–1796), design for a tureen, pen and wash. Silver with documented design, in this case by the Royal Architect Sir William Chambers, has been avidly sought by museums and collectors. *Victoria and Albert Museum, London*

73. Soup tureen, cover, and stand, silver, London, 1780/81, maker's mark of Thomas Heming. Although the "Adam" style had been revived in architecture and interior decoration at the end of the nineteenth century, neoclassical silver was largely ignored by collectors and museums until the end of the twentieth century.
Cat. no. 30

vessel and their successive styles and explore the social context in which silver was used, as well as the process by which designs were transmitted, by way of drawings and models, to the finished product. Research into this has thrown up the identities of many new artists and craftsmen. Of great interest is the role of architects, such as Sir William Chambers (1723–1796) and Robert Adam (1728–1792), as designers of silver. Chambers introduced a French form of naturalism into his dignified models for silverware, well illustrated by the soup tureens he designed for the Earl of Pembroke in the 1770s (fig. 71). Chambers was at the time working on Wilton House, the earl's seat in Wiltshire, and it was only natural that following his work on decorative schemes for some of the rooms there he should have been called upon to design silver. In the case of silver which Chambers designed for another patron, the Duke of Marlborough, we know that Chambers even dealt with the suppliers directly (in this case the retailers Wakelin & Tayler) and

placed the order on the duke's behalf.[30]

Robert Adam's work as a silver designer is known to us from the survival of two hundred or so drawings from his studio in Sir John Soane's Museum in London. Some of these can be matched to surviving objects. But an artist's legacy is often indirect: the designs he draws and gives to a silversmith for execution continue to be used, usually in modified form. The soup tureen from Thomas Heming's workshop (fig. 73), cannot be traced to a drawing by any one artist, but it may be said to be an amalgam of motifs used by Adam and Chambers.

Silver with documented design is now avidly pursued by museums and collectors. The monumental sauce tureens made for the 4th Duke of Newcastle-under-Lyne (in fig. 76), dating from 1807/8, match soup tureens purchased fifty years earlier by Newcastle's grandfather when he was Earl of Lincoln. The soup tureens were in turn second-hand, having been supplied by the retailer George Wickes to Lord Mountford fifteen years

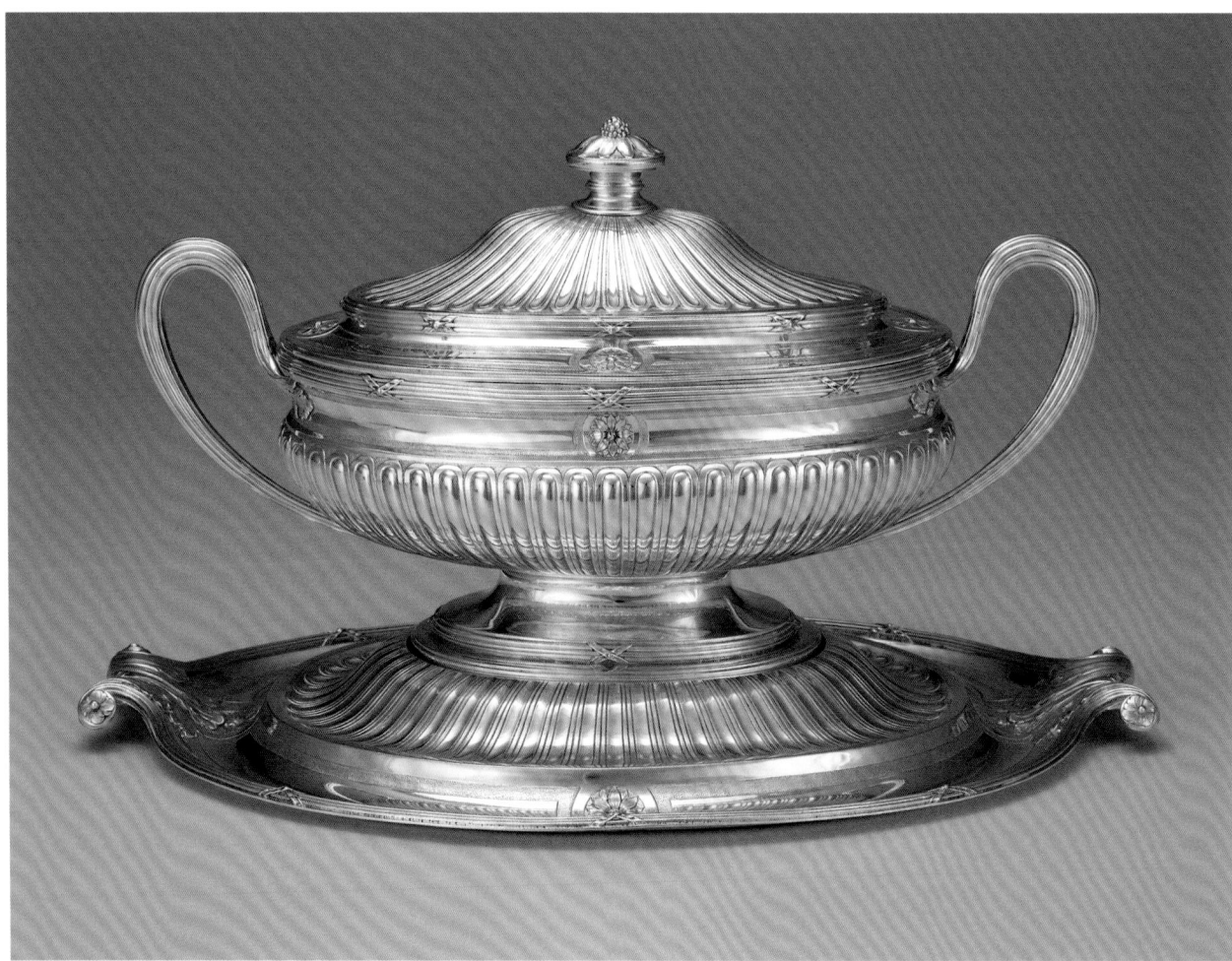

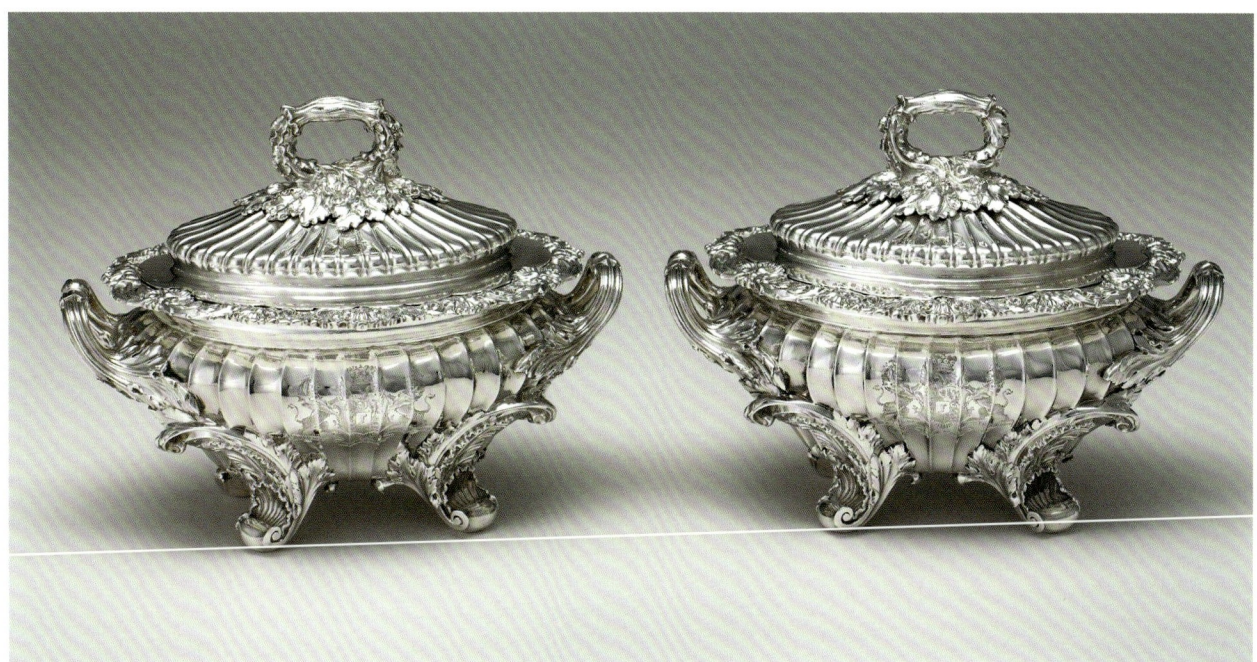

74. Pair of sauce tureens and covers, silver, London, 1823/24, maker's mark of Benjamin Smith II. The "imperial" style promoted by Rundell's and others was completely out of favor in Britain during the period between 1900 and 1960. American collectors were the first to appreciate it. Cat. no. 39

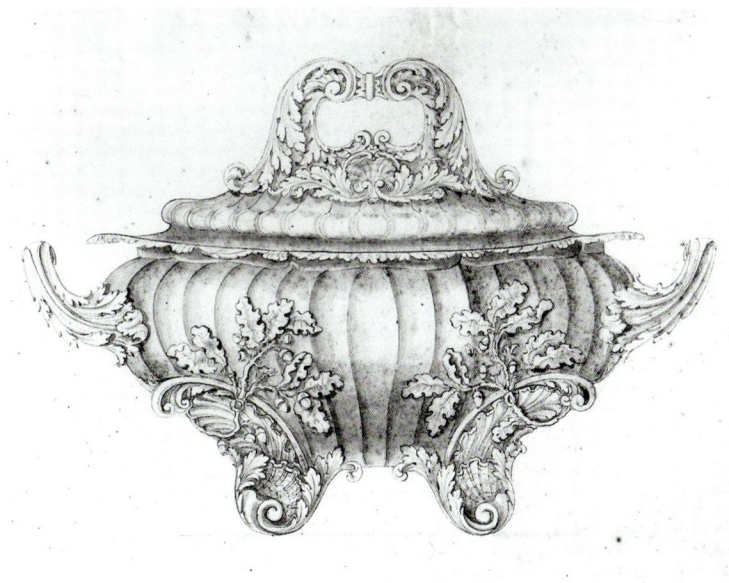

75. Anonymous, early 19th century, design for a tureen and cover, pen and wash. Fuller documentation of silver, in the form of designs, bills and correspondence, has greatly added to our appreciation of early nineteenth-century silver. *Victoria and Albert Museum, London*

before that. Wickes's business ledgers record how Mountford paid a total of £426 for the soup tureens; we also know that Wickes took them back on consignment from Mountford's son, who was in financial difficulties, in 1756 and sold them the following year to Lord Lincoln for £250. The design, by the architect and decorator William Kent (1684–1748), was published by John Vardy in an album of *Some Designs of Mr. Inigo Jones and Mr. Wm. Kent* in 1744 as "A Terrine & Cove for Lord Mountford" (fig. 77). Such detailed

documentation adds a thrilling new dimension to the tureens and for collectors it brings inanimate objects to life.

By the 1970s, when Jerome and Rita Gans began collecting, horizons in the world of silver had broadened considerably. The early twentieth-century fashion for what Vita Sackville-West described as "expensive simplicity," which looked askance at "unnecessary objects,"[31] had been replaced by demand for the best of all periods, even the eclecticism and whimsy of the Victorian

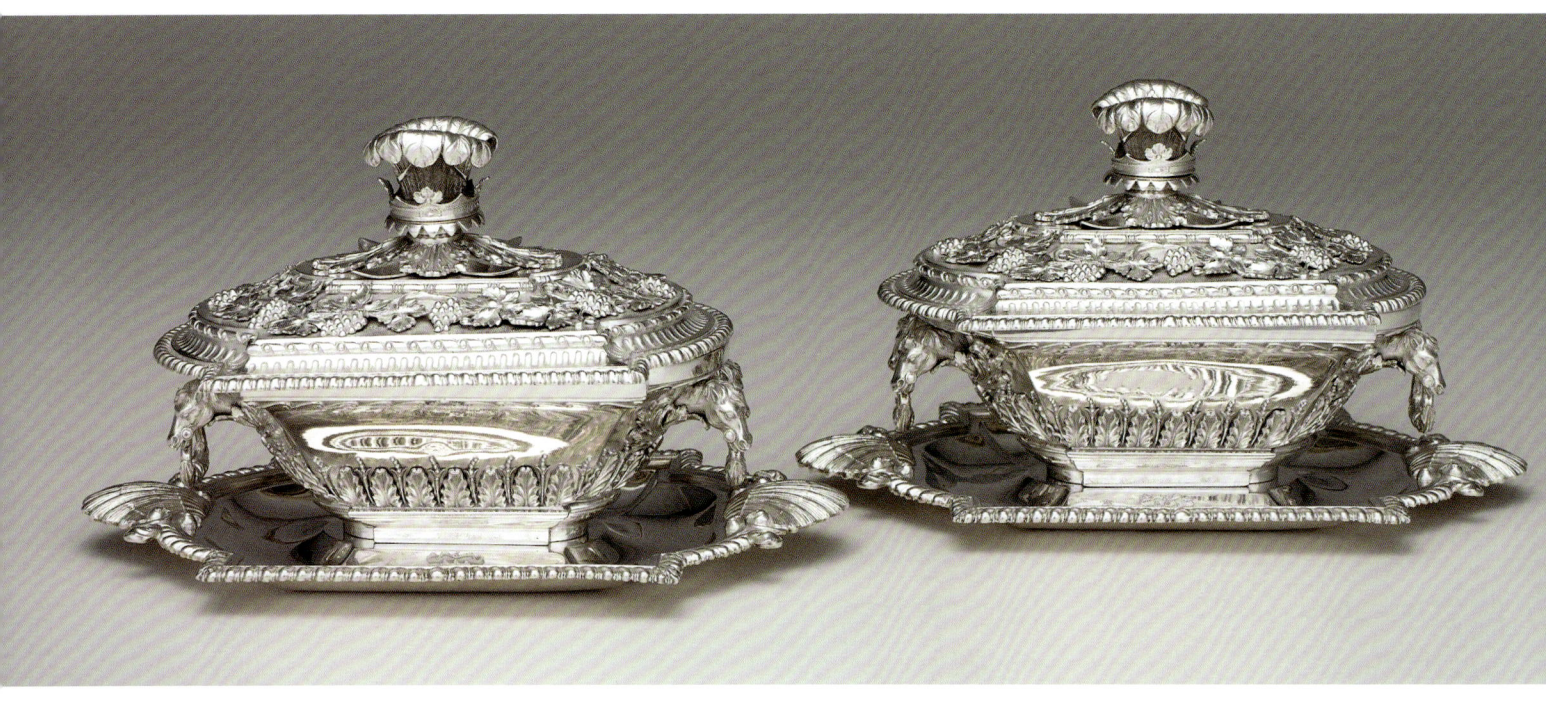

76. Pair of sauce tureens, covers and stands, silver, London, 1807/8, maker's mark of Benjamin Smith II, after a design by William Kent, made for Henry Pelham Pelham-Clinton, 4th Duke of Newcastle-under-Lyne (1785–1851), to match soup tureens acquired by his grandfather from George Wickes in 1757. The many revivals of earlier styles during the early nineteenth century are now seen as an artistic trend in its own right.
Cat. no. 34

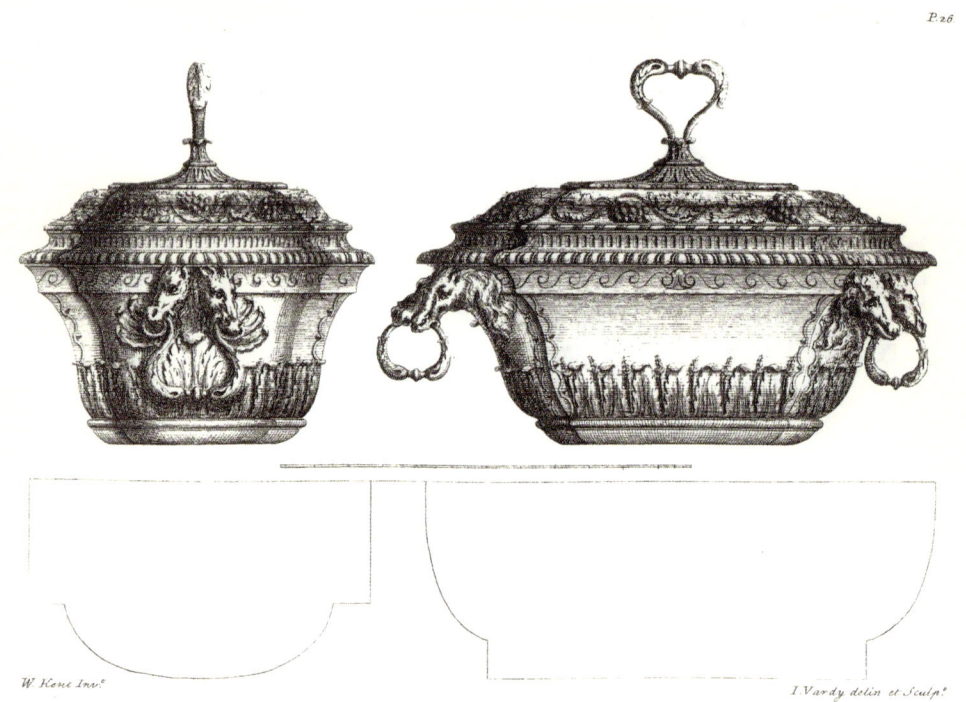

P.26

W. Kent Invt.   I. Vardy delin et Sculpt.

period. In her silver collecting Rita Gans has enthusiastically pursued the finest. But, more than this, she has also bestowed her munificence on silver scholarship in many ways, not least by her financial support of lectures and conferences. Moreover, by giving her collection to the

Virginia Museum of Fine Arts she hopes to inspire a new generation of collectors of antique silver. The excitement of the pursuit is not just about hunting for desirable objects, but also about acquiring knowledge and a better understanding of the silver of the past.

77. Plate from John Vardy's *Some Designs of Mr. Inigo Jones and Mr. Wm. Kent*, London, 1744, "A Terrine & Cover for Lord Mountford."

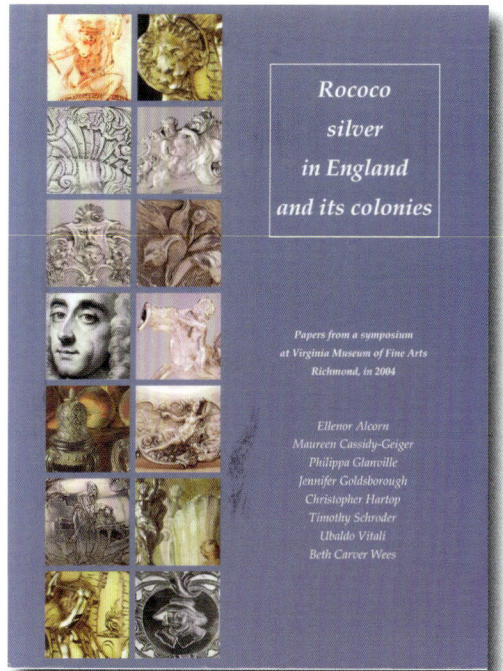

78. Cover of *Rococo Silver in England and Its Colonies: Papers from a Symposium at Virginia Museum of Fine Arts, Richmond, in 2004*, published by the Silver Society in 2006. Silver scholarship at the beginning of the twenty-first century is wide-ranging as well as deep. The publication of books such as this one, funded by Rita Gans, has meant that silver has been studied in the context of other material culture.

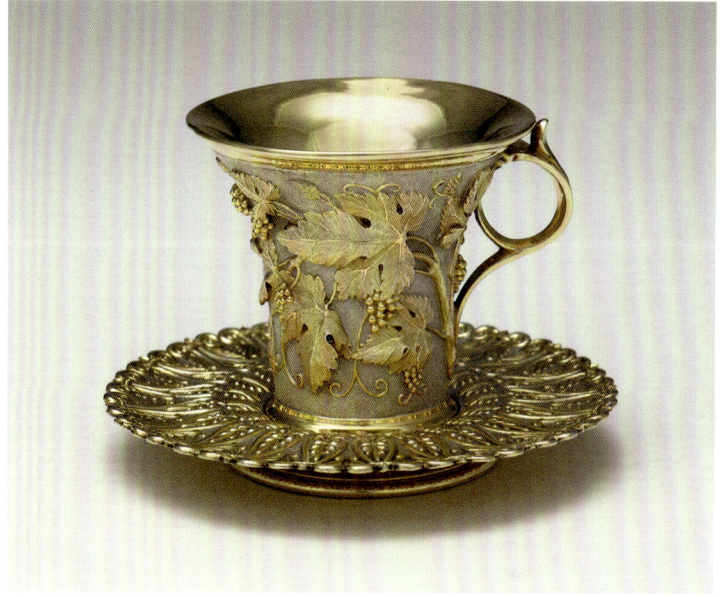

79. Cup and saucer, silver, parcel gilt, London, 1845/46, maker's mark of Elkington & Co. Eclectic Victorian naturalism at its best. Cat. no. 50

Notes

1 Thomas Fuller, *The Holy State, The Profane State*, London, new edn., 1841, Bk. II, chap. VI, p. 66. Fuller's book was first published in 1643.

2 John Earle, *Microcosmography; or, a Piece of the World Discovered*, London, 1811, pp. 20–1, quoted in Wainwright, p. 5. Earle's book was first published in 1628.

3 *Antiquaries*, p. 20.

4 "*The Grumbler, Essay XII*, Complaint of a wife at her husband's rage for antiquities," in Francis Grose, *The Olio*, London, 1796; I am grateful to Ellenor Alcorn and Robert Barker for sharing this book with me.

5 Hartop, 2006, p. 44.

6 *Applebee's Original Weekly Journal*, Saturday, July 16, 1720; I am grateful to Robert Barker for this reference.

7 Oman, p. 19; quoted in Grimwade, pp. 560–1.

8 *Walpole*, p. 127, fig. 145.

9 *Walpole*, cat. nos. 153–4.

10 Oman, p. 19.

11 Hartop, 1995, p. 94.

12 Garrard Ledgers, Archive of Art & Design [V&A], London, AAD/1995/7/39, folio 23.

13 Hartop, 2007b, pp. 32–3; the Harvard Salt, of the 1630s, was as late as the 1850s erroneously illustrated upside down.

14 Habbakuk O. Westman, *The Spoon … Primitive, Egyptian, Roman, Mediæval, and Modern*, London, 1845.

15 For much of the information in this section I am grateful to John Culme and I have drawn extensively on the paper he gave in London in 1985, reprinted as Culme, 1985, and in expanded form in Culme, pp. xvi–xxxvi; see also Steuart Fothringham, p. 114.

16 Grimwade, 1994, p. 118; Smith, pp. 19–35.

17 For these details of Jones's life, I have used the account in Schroder, 2010, vol. 1, p. 25, n. 6, and *The Times*'s somewhat patronizing obituary (August, 27, 1943, p. 7); the story of his accidental death I owe to the silver scholar, Timothy Kent; see also Grimwade, 1994, p. 117.

18 Williamson, p. 153.

19 Grimwade, 1994, p. 131.

20 Harmsworth, p. 12.

21 Glanville, 2005, p. 110.

22 Hartop, 1998, p. 50.

23 Hare, passim.

24 Alcorn, 2006, pp. 29–33.

25 Penzer, p. 19.

26 Shure, p. 12; Hartop, 2007b, pp. 164–5.

27 Grimwade, 1994, p. 17.

28 Told to me in conversation by Eric Shrubsole in the 1990s.

29 See *A Noble Feast*, cat. nos. 44–5, 51, 55–6, 63, 71–3, 78, 82–4, and 89.

30 Harris and Snodin, p. 152.

31 Vita Sackville-West, *The Edwardians*, London, 1930, p. 131.

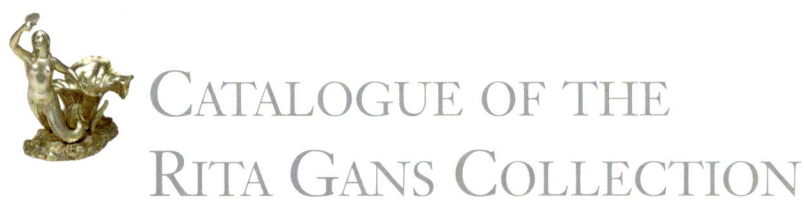

CATALOGUE OF THE RITA GANS COLLECTION

In England, the silver standard was sterling (925 parts pure silver per thousand) until 1697 when the legal (hallmarked) standard was raised to the Britannia standard (958/1000). In 1720 the sterling standard was resumed but the Britannia standard remained optional.

Specific dates of objects are provided by hallmarks, whenever present. The date letter did not change with the calendar. For example, in London, up to 1660, the date letter was usually changed in May of each year; from 1660 to 1975 it was changed on May 29. Dates are therefore given thus: 1665/66.

In this catalogue the term "maker's mark" denotes the mark stamped on an object by the person who submitted it for assay at Goldsmiths' Hall, or at a provincial assay office. This is not necessarily the same person as the one who made the object, and in fact most silver articles made during the period covered by this catalogue were the work of more than one individual. However, it has been decided to retain the term that has traditionally been used.

The size of all objects is given in inches. The equivalent in centimeters (to one decimal place) is given in parentheses. If a measurement shows diameter, it is to the widest point (not foot size). Weights are given in troy ounces and pennyweights, the traditional way of weighing silverware. There are 20 pennyweights (dwt.) in a troy ounce (oz.). Where there is a wooden handle, such as on a coffee pot, a "gross weight" is given. A *scratch weight* is an engraved indication of weight expressed in ounces and pennyweights; this was done, usually in the eighteenth century, for inventory purposes. It is shown here as it appears on the piece.

The following abbreviations are used:
Diam. diameter; H. height; L. length; W. width; Wt. weight.

Provenance includes documented owners; engraved armorials are listed separately. A comma between the names of two owners indicates that the piece passed directly from the first to the second; a semi-colon indicates a gap in documentation.

• 1 •

WOODWOSE SPOON
Silver, parcel gilt
c. 1440
Marks: Leopard's head (How, vol. III, p. 13, line 5, no. 1)
Maker's mark: None
Inscription: Engraved on bowl: *13*

Provenance: S.J. Shrubsole Corp., New York, purchased in 2001

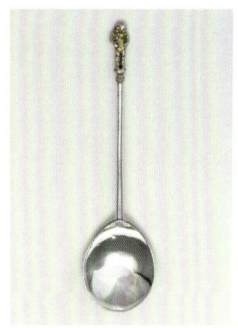

L. 7 ¾ in. (19.6 cm)
Wt. 1 oz. 4 dwt. (43 g)
Accession no.: 2010.13

• 2 •

TWO-HANDLED CUP AND COVER
Silver
c. 1650
Marks: none
Maker's mark: A *hound sejant*, for Richard Blackwell (Jackson, p. 120, line 8)

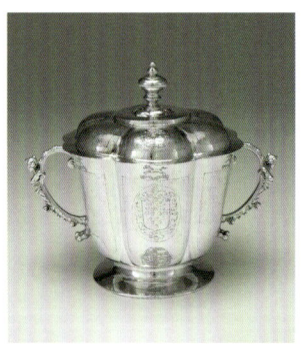

Heraldry: On front: engraved arms of Berkeley; on reverse: engraved arms of Bridgeman; on the cover and repeated on the body: the crest and arms of Fust impaling those of Tooker, as borne by Sir Francis Fust, 5th Bt., of Hill Court, Gloucestershire, who married in 1724 Fanny, daughter of Nicholas Tooker, a Bristol merchant. Fust succeeded his brother in 1728 and died in 1769
Provenance: R.W. Walker, sale, Christie's, London, July 11, 1945, lot 200; The Late Mrs. R. Makower, sale, Sotheby's, London, March 16, 1961, lot 147; Nathaniel, 3rd Baron Rothschild (1910–1990), Teresa, Dowager Lady Rothschild (d. 1996); M.P. Levene Ltd., London, purchased in 1999
Published: Brett, p. 124, no. 411; Smith, p. 28, fig. 11 and p. 42, no. 52

H. 8 ¹³⁄₁₆ in., W. 10 ⁵⁄₁₆ in., D. 7 ⅝ in. (21.9 x 26.2 x 19.4 cm)
Wt. 48 oz. (1493 g)
Scratch wt.: "48=15"
Accession no.: 2010.14a-b

BELL
Silver
c. 1660
Marks: None
Maker's mark: None
Engraved: *CR* below a closed
crown, for King Charles II
(1630–1685)

Provenance: Probably George
Monck, 1st Duke of Albemarle
(1608–1670), then presumably by
descent to Christopher Monck,
2nd Duke of Albemarle (1653–1688), Governor of Jamaica, then
presumably by descent to "Miss Monck", sold by her c. 1850, then by
descent to A Gentleman, sale, Christie's, London, March 11, 1953,
lot 135; Christie's, London, October 12, 1966, lot 47; Partridge Fine
Arts Ltd., London, 1991; The Albert Collection, London,
Christopher Hartop, purchased in 2007
Published: Clayton, p. 36; *Silver at Partridge 1993*, p. 10, no. 5;
Butler, p. 304, no. 374

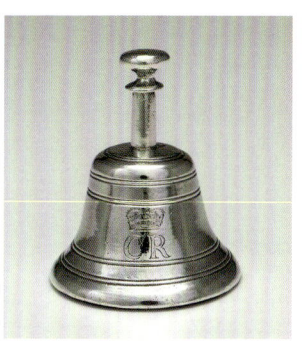

H. 2 ¹¹⁄₁₆ in., diam. 2 ⁷⁄₁₆ in. (6.8 x 6.15 cm)
Wt. 4 oz. 16 dwt. (149 g)
Accession no.: 2010.15

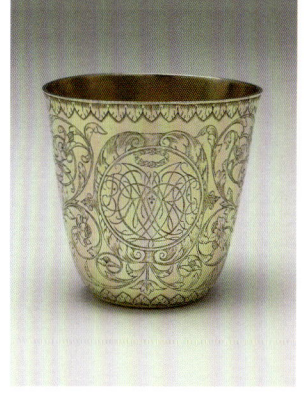

THREE-LEGGED BOWL AND COVER
Silver
Marks: Sterling, London, 1671/72
Maker's mark: *WW* (Jackson, p. 128, line 14)

Heraldry: Engraved crest on body and cover
Provenance: S.J. Shrubsole Corp., New York, purchased in 2001

H. 5 ½ in. (14.0 cm)
Wt. 33 oz. 15 dwt. (1051 g)
Scratch wt. "34 – 5"
Accession no.: 2010.17a-b

WAGER CUP
Silver
c. 1665
Marks: None
Maker's mark: A *hound sejant*, for
Richard Blackwell (Jackson, p.
120, line 8)
Inscription: Engraved: *M / I*F, B
/ G+M*

Heraldry: Engraved arms on
smaller cup probably those of
Maplesden of Kent
Provenance: The Property of a
Lady, sale, Sotheby's, London,
October 24, 1989, lot 520,
Charles F. Poor Collection,
Washington, D.C., Christopher
Hartop, purchased in 2005
Published: Smith, p. 13, no. 57 and p. 25, fig. 6

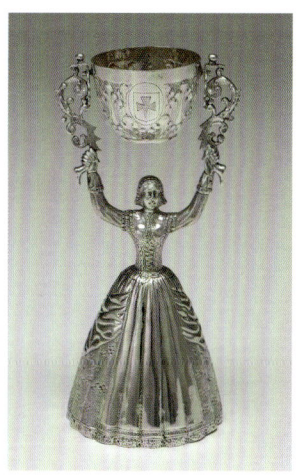

H. 7 ⅛ in., W. (at handles) 3 ⁹⁄₁₆ in., D. 3 ⅛ in. ((18.1 x 9.2 x 8.1 cm)
Wt. 7 oz. 10 dwt. (236 g)
Accession no.: 2010.16

BEAKER
Silver gilt
c. 1690
Marks: None
Maker's mark: *TT*, an annulet between and three annulets above,
probably for Thomas Tysoe

Provenance: Partridge Fine Arts PLC, London, purchased in 2001

H. 3 ¹³⁄₁₆ in. (9.6 cm)
Wt. 5 oz. 5 dwt. (161 g)
Accession no.: 2010.18

7

TANKARD
Silver
Marks: Sterling, London,
1691/92
Maker's mark: David Willaume
(Jackson, p. 132, line 14)

Provenance: S.J. Shrubsole
Corp., 1986; a New York private
collection, Christopher Hartop,
purchased in 2008
Published: Shrubsole, no. 18

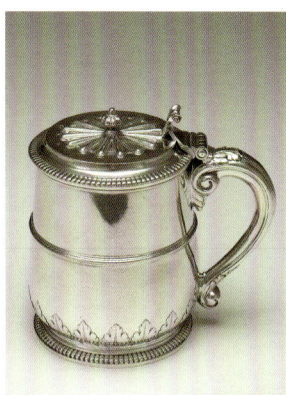

H. 7 ¹³⁄₁₆ in. (19.8 cm)
Wt. 43 oz. 11 dwt. (1355 g)
Accession no.: 2010.19

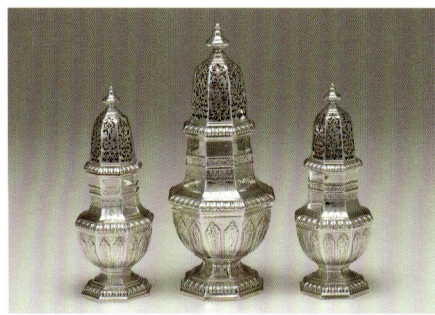

8

SET OF THREE CASTERS FOR SUGAR,
PEPPER, AND MUSTARD
Silver
c. 1705
Marks: None
Maker's mark: The smaller pair, William Fleming (Grimwade,
no. 694)

Heraldry: Engraved crest and motto "MAJOR VIRTUS QVAM
SPLENDOR" of Baillie, as borne by George Baillie of Jerviswood
and Mellerstain (d. 1738), who married Lady Grizel Hume, eldest
daughter of 1st Lord Polwarth in 1692
Provenance: Presumably George Baillie of Jerviswood and
Mellerstain (d. 1738), by descent to his daughter Rachel (d. 1773),
who married c. 1719 Charles, Lord Binning, eldest son of Thomas,
6th Earl of Haddington (1680–1735); by descent to John, 13th Earl
of Haddington, sale, Sotheby's, New York, June 1, 2000, lot 166; a
New York private collector, Christopher Hartop, purchased in 2009

1. H. 9 ⅜ in., diam. 3 ¾ in. (23.5 x 9.6 cm)
2. H. 7 ¼ in., diam. 2 ¹³⁄₁₆ in. (18.5 x 7.2 cm)
3. H. 7 ¼ in., diam. 2 ¾ in. (18.4 x 6.9 cm)
Wt. 24 oz. 8 dwt.; 12 oz. 15 dwt.; 13 oz. 8 dwt. (761; 396; 417 g)
Scratch wt. (2010.20.1) "24"
Accession no.: 2010.20.1a-b–.3a-b

9

PAIR OF
CANDLESTICKS
Silver
Marks: Britannia,
London, 1700/1
Maker's mark: Joseph
Bird (Grimwade, no. 178)

Heraldry: Engraved
arms of a lady, possibly of
Rushton or Kent, and
later linked cipher C with
earl's coronet
Provenance: Private
Collection, Austin, Texas;
Spink & Son Ltd., 1989;
Alastair Dickenson, London, purchased in 2001
Exhibited: Austin, Texas, 1969, no. 30, lent anonymously
Published: Houston, no. 30; *Octagon*, Autumn, 1989, vol. XXVI,
no. 2, p. 43

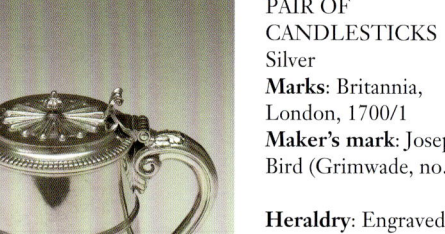

H. 9 ¹⁄₂ in. (23.1 cm)
Wt. 24 oz. 5 dwt.; 24 oz. (754; 749 g)
Accession no.: 2010.21.1–.2

SEVEN CASTERS
Silver
Marks: Britannia,
London, 1705/6
Maker's mark:
Joseph Ward
(Grimwade, no.
2989)

Heraldry:
Engraved arms of
Howe with a
baronet's badge,
probably for Sir
James Howe, 2nd Bt., (1670–1736) of Cold Barwick, Wiltshire
Provenance: Presumably Sir James Howe, 2nd Bt., (1670–1736) of
Cold Barwick, Wiltshire, who married first Elizabeth (d. 1694),
daughter of Edward Nutt, and second Elizabeth, daughter and co-
heiress of Mr. Stratford of Halling, Gloucestershire, then by descent
to Sir James's nephew Henry Lee-Warner of Walsingham Abbey,
Norfolk, by descent to Chandos Brydges Lee-Warner (1863–1944),
the Walsingham Abbey Heirlooms, sale, Christie's, London,
November 30, 1911; George A. Locket, sale, Christie's, London,
April 22–23, 1942; anonymous sale, Sotheby's, London, March 14,
1996, lot 166

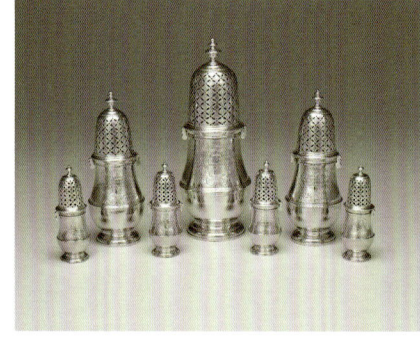

1. H. 9 ¹¹⁄₃₂ in. (23.7 cm)
2–3. H. 7 ⁵⁄₃₂ in. (18.2 cm)
4–7. H. 4 ⁵⁄₁₆ in. (10.9 cm)
Wt. 22 oz.; 11 oz. 18 dwt.; 12 oz.; 3 oz. 12 dwt.; 3 oz. 7 dwt. oz.;
3 oz. 5 dwt.; 3 oz. 10 dwt.; (686; 371; 375; 113; 104; 108; 110 g)
Accession no.: 2010.22.1a-b–.7a-b

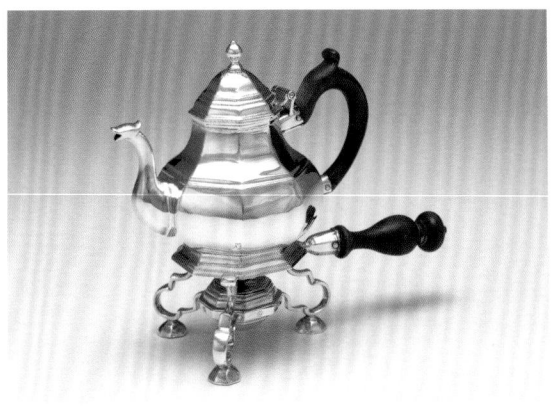

TEAPOT ON LAMP STAND
Silver, wood
Marks: Britannia, London, 1715/16
Maker's mark: Joseph Ward (Grimwade, no. 3856)
Inscription: *G D W*

Provenance: George D. Widener (1861–d. on the *Titanic*, 1912);
S.J. Shrubsole Corp., New York, purchased in 2002

Overall: H. 8 5/32 in., W. 10 ⅜ in., D. 4 ⅝ in. (20.8 x 26.3 x 11.7 cm)
Gross wt. 26 oz. (809 g)
Accession no.: 2010.23a-c

CASTER
Silver
Marks: Britannia, London, 1723/24
Maker's mark: Paul de Lamerie (Hare, no. 3)

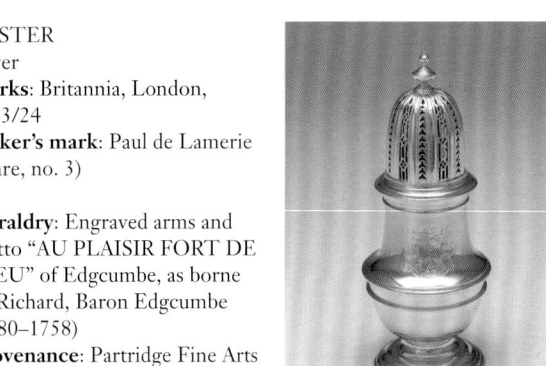

Heraldry: Engraved arms and motto "AU PLAISIR FORT DE DIEU" of Edgcumbe, as borne by Richard, Baron Edgcumbe (1680–1758)
Provenance: Partridge Fine Arts PLC, London, 1991;
S.J. Shrubsole Corp., New York, purchased in 1997
Published: *Silver at Partridge: Recent Acquisitions, 1991*, p. 18, no. 10

H. 9 in., diam. 3 ¹¹⁄₁₆ in. (22.9 x 9.4 cm)
Wt. 24 oz. 6 dwt. (756 g)
Accession no.: 2010.25a-b

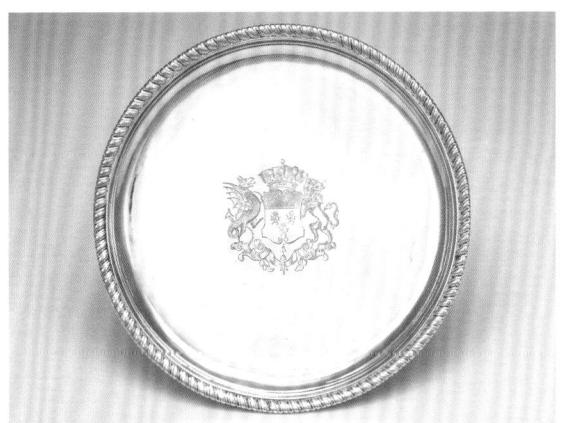

FOOTED SALVER
Silver
Marks. Britannia, London, 1717/18
Maker's mark: Paul de Lamerie (Hare, no. 2)

Heraldry: Engraved arms and supporters of Talbot Yelverton, 1st Earl of Sussex, created earl in 1717
Provenance: M.P. Levene Ltd., London, purchased in 2000

H. 3 ⅜ in., diam. 10 ⅛ in. (8.5 x 25.6 cm)
Wt.: 35 oz. 12 dwt. (1109 g)
Scratch wt.: "36 oz – 13 dwt."
Accession no.: 2010.24

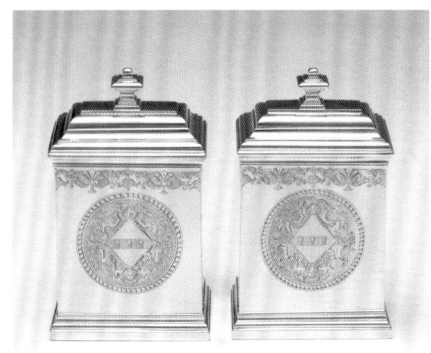

PAIR OF TEA CADDIES
Silver, lead, iron
Marks: Britannia, London, 1724/25
Maker's mark: Paul Crespin (Grimwade, no. 406)

Heraldry: Engraved arms of a lady of the Vernon family
Provenance: S.J. Shrubsole Corp., New York, purchased in 2000

1. H. 5 ³⁄₁₆ in. (13.1 cm)
2. H. 5 ¹⁄₂ in. (12.9 cm)
Gross wt. 13 oz. 16 dwt.; 13 oz. 8 dwt. (429; 419 g)
Scratch wts. "12 – 2"; "11 – 15"
Accession no.: 2010.26.1–.2

• 15 •

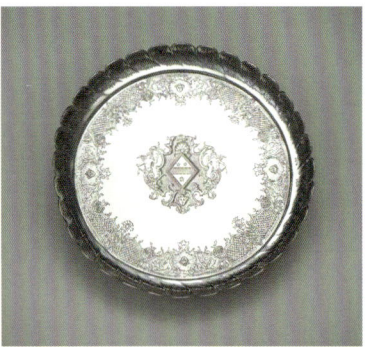

SALVER
Silver
Marks: Britannia, London, 1731/32
Maker's mark: Paul de Lamerie (Hare, no. 3)

Heraldry: Engraved arms of a lady of the Foley family of Worcestershire
Provenance: S.J. Shrubsole Corp., New York, purchased in 1998

Diam. 10 ⅞ in. (27.6 cm)
Wt. 26 oz. 7 dwt. (820 g)
Accession no.: 2010.27

• 17 •

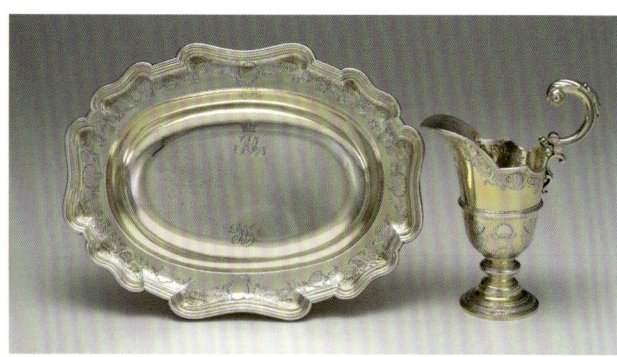

EWER AND BASIN
Silver gilt
Marks: Sterling, London, 1734/35
Maker's mark: John White (Grimwade, no. 1735)

Heraldry: Engraved crown and monogram AR, as borne by Queen Adelaide (1792–1849), consort of William IV; further monogram AC
Provenance: N. & I. Franklin, 2002
Published: N. & I. Franklin catalogue, 2002, p. 21

Basin: H. 2 ½ in., W. 14 ⅞ in., D. 11 ³⁄₁₆ in. (6.4 x 37.8 x 28.5 cm)
Ewer: H. 9 ⅜ in., W. 7 ³⁄₁₆ in., D. 4 ⅛ in. (23.8 x 18.1 x 10.6 cm)
Wt. 45 oz.; 25 oz. 7 dwt. (1401; 789 g)
Scratch wts.: "45 – 0"; "25 – 8"
Accession no.: 2010.29.1–.2

• 16 •

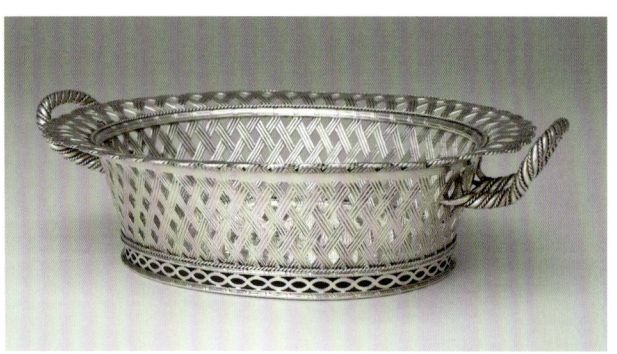

BASKET
Silver
Marks: Sterling, London, 1732/33
Maker's mark: Paul de Lamerie (Hare, no. 4)

Heraldry: Engraved arms of Reynardson, as borne by Samuel Reynardson (b. 1704) of Holywell Hall, Stamford, Lincolnshire, who married in 1732 Sarah, daughter of Sir Randolph Knipe
Provenance: S.J. Shrubsole Corp, New York, 1996; M.P. Levene Ltd., London, purchased in 1997

W. 13 ¹⁵⁄₁₆ in. (35.4 cm)
Wt. 40 oz. 12 dwt. (1263 g)
Accession no.: 2010.28

• 18 •

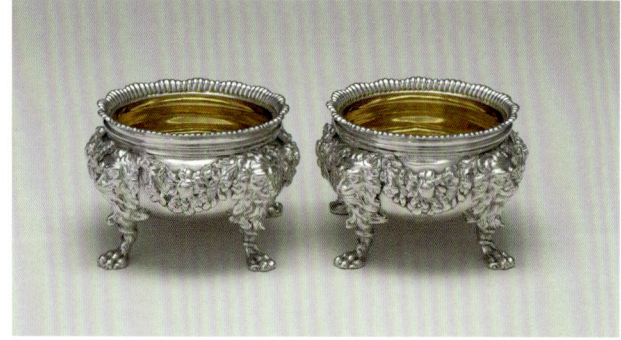

PAIR OF SALTS
Silver, gilt interiors
Marks: Sterling, London, 1734/35
Maker's mark: Paul de Lamerie (Hare, no. 4)

Heraldry: Engraved crest and coronet of the Earls of Shaftesbury
Provenance: Titus Kendall, London, purchased in 1998

H. 2 ¹³⁄₃₂ in., diam. 3 ¾ in. (6.15 x 9.4 cm)
Wt. 11 oz. 2 dwt.; 10 oz. 18 dwt. (348; 339 g)
Accession no.: 2010.30.1–.2

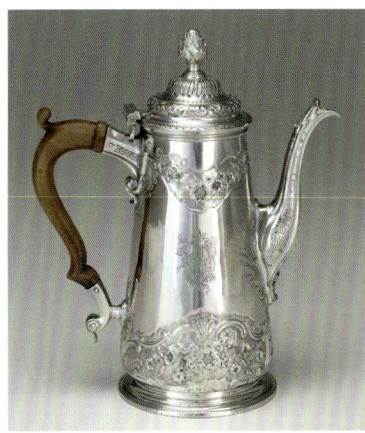

COFFEE POT
Silver, fruitwood
Marks: Sterling, London, 1739/40
Maker's mark: George Wickes (Grimwade, no. 921)

Heraldry: Engraved arms, possibly of Ashton impaling those of Brock
Provenance: Garrard & Co., London, purchased in 1998

H. 9 ⁷⁄₁₆ in., W. 8 ⅛ in., D. 4 ⁵⁄₁₆ in. (24.0 x 20.6 x 11.0 cm)
Gross wt. 27 oz. 15 dwt. (863 g)
Scratch wt. "27 – 3"
Accession no.: 2010.31

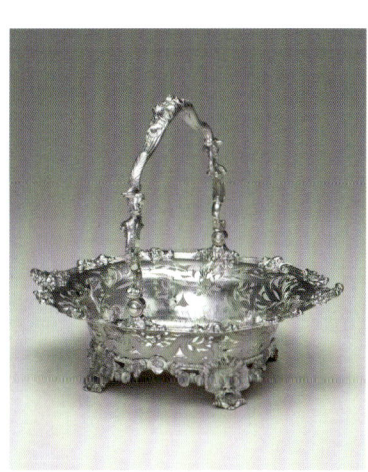

INKSTAND
Silver
Marks: Sterling, London, 1741/42
Maker's mark: Paul de Lamerie (Hare, no. 5)

Heraldry: Engraved arms and crest of Coventry, probably as borne by George William, 8th Earl of Coventry (1722–1809)
Provenance: Presumably George William, 8th Earl of Coventry (1722–1809), probably by descent to George William, 8th Earl of Coventry (1784–1843), who in 1808 married Emma Susanna, daughter of William, 1st Earl Beauchamp, by descent in the Beauchamp family; Partridge Fine Arts PLC, London, 1994; S.J. Shrubsole Corp., New York, purchased in 1997
Published: *Silver at Partridge: Recent Acquisitions, October 1994*, pp. 18–19, no. 13

Stand: H. 1 ⁹⁄₁₆ in., W. 8 ⅝ in., D. 6 ¹¹⁄₁₆ in. (3.9 x 21.9 x 16.8 cm)
Pots: H. 1 ¹³⁄₁₆ in., diam. 2 in. (4.55 x 5.0 cm)
Wt. 23 oz. 15 dwt. (740 g)
Scratch wt. "1 on 25 – 2"
Accession no.: 2010.33.1, .2a-b–.3a-b

CUP AND COVER
Silver gilt
Marks: Sterling, London, 1740/1
Maker's mark: Frederick Kandler (Grimwade, no. 691)

Heraldry: Engraved arms of Windham
Provenance: Presumably John Windham of Waghen, Yorkshire, by descent to his daughter Anne, who married in 1779 Sir William Smith, 7th Bt., by descent to Captain Sir Philip Bowyer-Smyth, Bt., sale, Christie's, London, December 3, 1969, lot 30; Property of a Canadian Collector, sale, Christie's, New York, April 21, 1998, lot 235, M.P. Levene Ltd., London, purchased in 1998
Published: Clayton, *History*, p. 174, no. 3

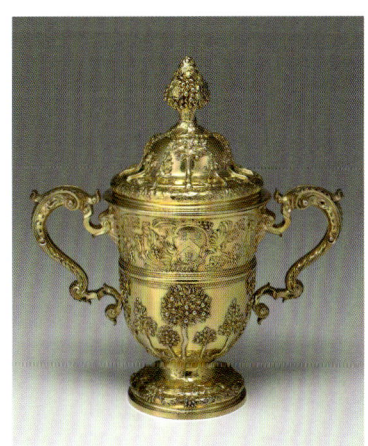

H. 12 ¾ in., W. 11 ⅜ in., D. 6 ⁵⁄₁₆ in. (32.4 x 28.8 x 15.8 cm)
Wt. 76 oz. 16 dwt. (2389 g)
Accession no.: 2010.32a-b

BASKET
Silver
Marks: Sterling, London, 1742/43
Maker's mark: Paul de Lamerie (Hare, no. 5)

Heraldry: Engraved arms of a lady of the Johnson family of Withcot, Leicestershire, almost certainly for Elizabeth Johnson (c. 1688–1754) who inherited the majority of her brother Geoffrey's estate in 1742;
Provenance: John Sheldon, sale, Sotheby's, London, October 24, 1985, lot 100; Jaime Ortiz-Patiño, sale, Sotheby's, New York, April 22, 1998, lot 23, M.P. Levene Ltd., London, purchased in 1998

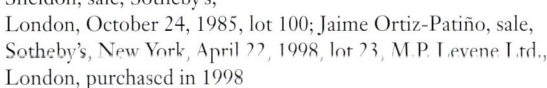

H. 11 ¼ in., W. 13 ¹³⁄₁₆ in., D. 11 ⅝ in. (28.6 x 35.1 x 29.5 cm)
Wt. 62 oz. (1930 g)
Scratch wt. "62 – 5"
Accession no.: 2010.34

• 23 •

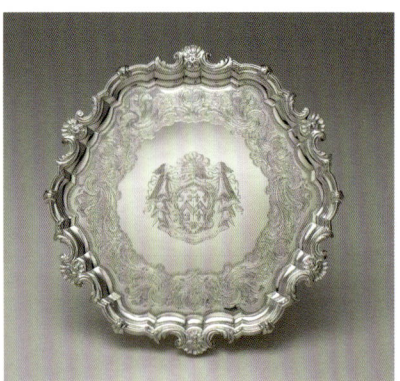

SALVER
Silver
Marks: Sterling, London, 1742/43
Maker's mark: George Wickes (Grimwade, no. 921)

Heraldry: Engraved arms of Lethieullier with a crescent for difference, impaling those of Green, as borne by Manning Lethieullier, second son of William Lethieullier of Beckenham, who married Anne Green
Provenance: Garrard & Co., London, purchased in 1998

Diam. 11 ¹³⁄₁₆ in. (29.9 cm)
Wt. 30 oz. 17 dwt. (960 g)
Scratch wt.: "31 + 0"
Accession no.: 2010.35

• 24 •

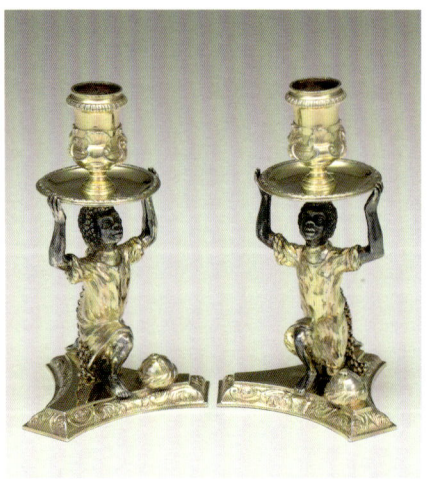

PAIR OF BLACKAMOOR CANDLESTICKS
Silver, parcel gilt, partially oxidized

Marks: Sterling, London, 1745/46
Maker's mark: Isaac Duke (Grimwade, no. 1253)

Provenance: S.J. Shrubsole Corp., New York, purchased in 1998

H. 6 ⁹⁄₁₆ in. (16.7 cm)
Wt. 13 oz. 3 dwt.; 13 oz. (409; 407 g)
Accession no.: 2010.36.1–.2

• 25 •

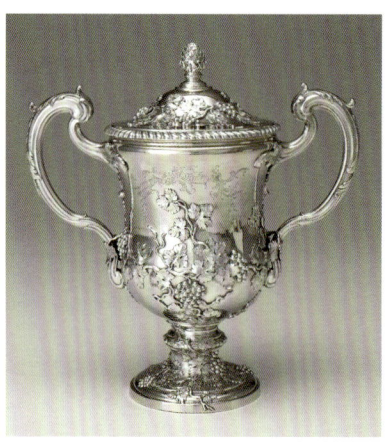

CUP AND COVER
Silver
Marks: Sterling, London, 1746/47
Maker's mark: George Wickes (Grimwade, no. 921)
Inscription: *EX–DONO-CAROLI-HALE-AR & PRIMO-JANUARI / 1746*

Provenance: S.J. Shrubsole Corp., New York, purchased in 1998

H. 11 ¹³⁄₁₆ in., W. 11 ³⁄₁₆ in., D. 6 in. (29.95 x 28.4 x 15.2 cm)
Wt. 73 oz. 13 dwt. (2291 g)
Accession no.: 2010.37a-b

• 26 •

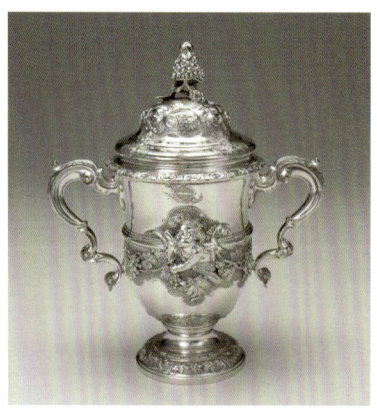

CUP AND COVER
Silver
Marks: Sterling, London, 1750/51
Maker's mark: Paul de Lamerie (Hare, no. 5)

Heraldry: Engraved arms on body, crest on cover, of Slaney, Milton, Staffordshire or Lynam, Ireland
Provenance: S.J. Shrubsole Corp., New York, purchased in 1997

H. 12 ⅞ in., W. 11 in., D. 6 ⅜ in. (32.7 x 28.0 x 16.1 cm)
Gross wt. 75 oz. 5 dwt. (2340 g)
Scratch wt. "75 – 8"
Accession no.: 2010.38a-b

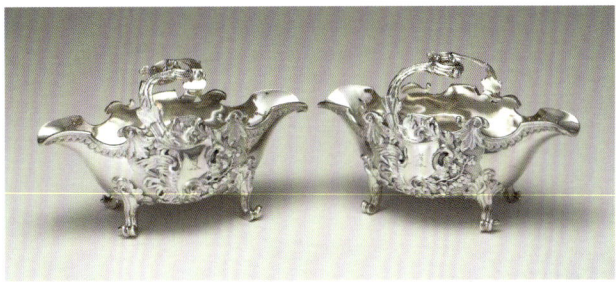

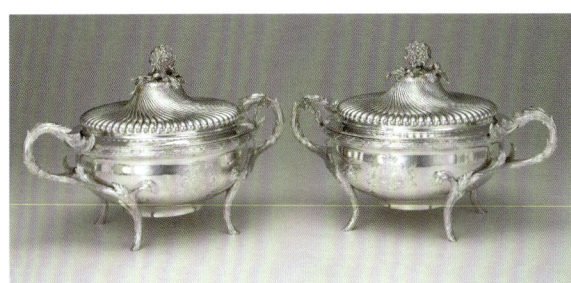

PAIR OF SAUCEBOATS
Silver
Marks: Sterling, London, 1755/56
Maker's mark: Thomas Gilpin (Grimwade, no. 2769)

Heraldry: Later engraved crest of a wyvern's head collared
Provenance: S.J. Shrubsole Corp., New York, purchased in 2000

1. H. 5 ⁵⁄₂ in., W. 9 ¼ in., D. 4 ¹³⁄₁₆ in. (13.4 x 23.5 x 12.2 cm)
2. H. 5 ⅜ in., W. 9 ¼ in., D. 4 ²⁷⁄₃₂ in. (13.7 x 23.45 x 12.2 cm)
Wt. 27 oz. 15 dwt.; 26 oz. (863; 809 g)
Scratch wts.: "No 1 / 27 – 18"; "No 3/ 26 – 2"
Accession no.: 2010.39.1–.2

PAIR OF SOUP TUREENS AND COVERS
Silver
Marks: Sterling, London, 1771/72
Maker's mark: Sebastian I and James Crespell (Grimwade, no. 2497)

Design: After Sir William Chambers (1723–1795)
Heraldry: Engraved arms, crest and motto "UNG JE SERVIRAY" of Herbert, as borne by Henry, 10th Earl of Pembroke (1734–1794)
Provenance: Florence J. Gould, sale, Sotheby's, Monaco, June 26, 1984, lot 1218; A Royal Collection, Alastair Dickenson, London, purchased in 1999
Exhibited: London, Stockholm, 1997, no. 122 (one of the pair)
Published: Young, *Chambers*, pp. 149–50

H. 11 ¹³⁄₁₆ in., W. 18 ¼ in., D. 12 ³⁄₁₆ in. (30.1 x 46.4 x 31.0 cm)
Wt. 156 oz.; 154 oz. 15 dwt. (4864; 4813 g)
Scratch wt. "No 1 156 – 15 No 2 156 – 11"
Accession no.: 2010.41.1a-b–.2a-b

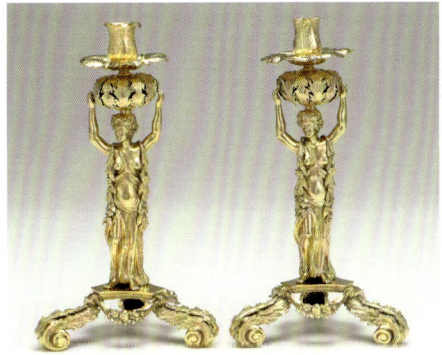

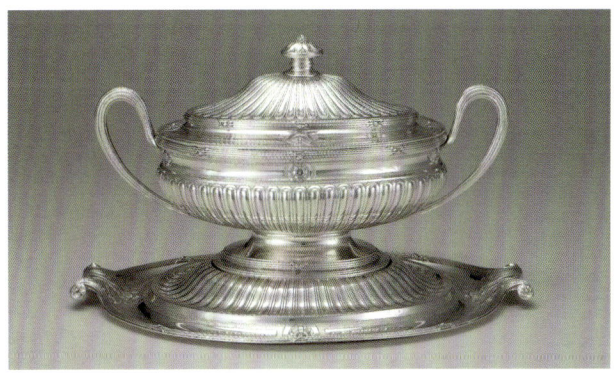

PAIR OF CANDLESTICKS
Silver gilt
Marks: Sterling, London, 1766/67
Maker's mark: Thomas Heming (Grimwade, no. 3828)

Provenance: Presumably John, 3rd Earl of Bute, KG (1713–1792), by descent to John, 7th Marquess of Bute (b. 1958), Works of Art from the Bute Collection, sale, Christie's, London, July 3, 1996, lot 77, N. & I. Franklin, London, purchased in 2008

1. H. 12 ½ in. (30.6 cm)
2. H. 12 ³⁄₁₆ in. (31.0 cm)
Wt. 31 oz. 8 dwt.; 30 oz. 16 dwt. (977; 960 g)
Accession no.: 2010.40.1–.2

SOUP TUREEN, COVER, AND STAND
Silver
Marks: Sterling, London, 1780/81
Maker's mark: Thomas Heming (Grimwade, no. 3828)

Provenance: Thomas Lumley, 1959; S.J. Shrubsole Corp., New York, purchased in 2003
Published: Rowe, p. 71 and pl. 64

Overall: H. 10 ³⁄₁₆ in., W. 18 ¼ in., D. 11 ⅝ in. (25.8 x 46.4 x 29.5 cm)
Tureen: H. 8 ⅞ in., W. 16 ¹⁄₁₆ in., D. 7 ⅝ in. (22.5 x 40.9 x 29.5 cm)
Wt.: total: 131 oz. 18 dwt. (4103 g); tureen and cover: 76 oz. 18 dwt. (2392 g); tray: 55 oz. (1711 g)
Scratch wts.: On tureen: "No 2 79 – 2"; on tray: "No 2 47 – 9"
Accession no.: 2010.42a-c

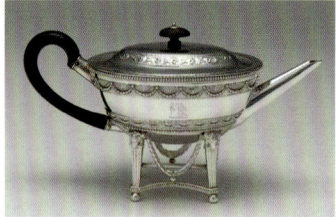

TEAPOT ON STAND
Silver, fruitwood
Marks: Sterling, London, 1794/95
Maker's mark: Paul Storr (Grimwade, no. 2234)

Heraldry: Engraved crest of Aldhouse
Provenance: A Royal Collection, Alastair Dickenson, London, purchased in 1999

Overall: H. 6 ½ in., W. 11 ⁵⁄₁₆ in., D. 4 ¹⁵⁄₁₆ in.
(15.3 x 28.7 x 12.6 cm)
Gross wt. total: 27 oz. 8 dwt. (852 g); teapot: 20 oz. 5 dwt. (629 g);
stand: 7 oz. 4 dwt. (224 g)
Accession no.: 2010.43a-b

32

PAIR OF
CANDLESTICKS
Silver gilt
Marks: Sterling,
London, 1800/1
Maker's mark:
Paul Storr (Grimwade,
no. 2234) for Vulliamy
& Son
Inscription: *Made for
the Abbey at Fonthill /
by Vulliamy & Son /
1800*

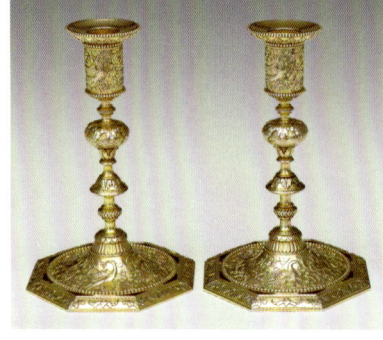

Heraldry: Engraved crests of Beckford and Hamilton
Provenance: William Beckford (1760–1844) [in his abortive sale of
the contents of Fonthill Abbey, Wiltshire, Christie's, October 11,
1822, lot 58], by descent to his daughter Euphemia, who in 1810
married Alexander, 10th Duke of Hamilton (1767–1852), by descent
to Alfred, 13th Duke of Hamilton (1862–1940), sale, Christie's,
London, November 4, 1919, lot 75, Lord Fisher; anonymous sale,
Sotheby's, London, January 23, 1964, lot 19; Christie's, New York,
May 24, 1977, lot 121, Robert H. Smith, Alexandria, Virginia;
Asprey, London, anonymous sale, Christie's, New York, April 15,
1997, lot 273, M.P. Levene Ltd., London, purchased in 1997
Exhibited: New York and London, 2001–2, no. 107
Published: Rutter, 1822, pp. 60–1; Rutter, 1823, p. 66; English and
Maddon, p. 8, plate 7; Redding, vol. II, p. 274; Lansdown, p. 274;
Culme, 1977, p. 64; Snodin and Baker, Part I, p. 743, fig. 22, and
Part II, appendices no. A36; Clayton, *Dictionary*, p. 60, fig. 77; Brett,
p. 247, no. 1111; Schroder, 1988a, p. 326; Truman, 1995, illus. on
dust jacket; Ostergard, pp. 377–8, no. 107

1. H. 6 ¹⁵⁄₁₆ in., W. 4 ⁹⁄₁₆ in., D. 4 ⁹⁄₁₆ in. (17.7 x 11.6 x 11.6 cm)
2. H. 6 ⅞ in., W. 4 ⁹⁄₁₆ in., D. 4 ⁹⁄₁₆ in. (17.5 x 11.6 x 11.6 cm
Wt. 17 oz. 5 dwt.; 17 oz. 8 dwt. (536; 542 g)
Accession no.: 2010.44.1a-b–.2a-b

33

SET OF EIGHT SALTS AND
SPOONS
Silver, gilt interior
Marks: Salts: sterling, London,
1806/7; spoons: sterling, London,
1821/22
Maker's mark: Salts: Digby Scott
and Benjamin Smith (Grimwade,
no. 505) for Rundell, Bridge &
Rundell; Spoons: William Eley I
& William Fearn (Grimwade, no. 3112)

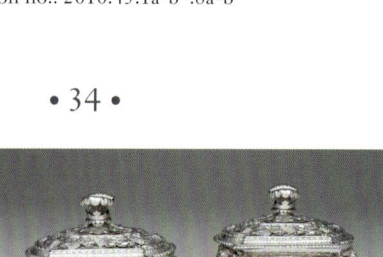

Heraldry: Engraved crest and motto
Provenance: Marks, London, purchased in 1998

Salts:
1a. H. 2 ²⁹⁄₃₂ in., diam. 4 ³⁄₁₆ in. (7.4 x 10.6 cm)
2a. H. 2 ¹⁵⁄₁₆ in., diam. 4 ³⁄₁₆ in. (7.5 x 10.6 cm)
3a–4a. H. 2 ²⁹⁄₃₂ in., diam. 4 ⅛ in. (7.4 x 10.5 cm)
5a. H. 2 ²⁹⁄₃₂ in., diam. 4 ¼ in. (7.4 x 10.6 cm)
6a–8a. H. 2 ²⁹⁄₃₂ in., diam. 4 ⅛ in. (7.4 x 10.5 cm)

Spoons:
1b–8b. L. 4 ⁵⁄₁₆ in. (10.9 cm) (each)

Wt. 1a. 11 oz. 14 dwt.; 2a. 11 oz. 8 dwt.; 3a 11 oz. 17 dwt.; 4a. 12 oz.
4 dwt.; 5a. 12oz. 4 dwt; 6a. 11 oz. 13 dwt.; 7a. 11 oz. 4 dwt.; 8a. 12
oz. 4 dwt. (364; 355; 369; 379; 380; 363; 349; 380 g)
1b. 14 dwt.; 2b. 15 dwt.; 3b. 16 dwt.; 4b. 14 dwt.; 5b. 15 dwt.; 6b. 14
dwt.; 7b. 15 dwt.; 8b. 15 dwt. (22; 23; 26; 22; 23; 24; 22; 23 g)
Accession no.: 2010.45.1a-b–.8a-b

PAIR OF SAUCE
TUREENS,
COVERS, STANDS,
AND LINERS
Silver
Marks: Sterling,
London, 1807/8
Maker's mark:
Benjamin Smith II
(Grimwade, no. 229) for Rundell, Bridge & Rundell

Design: After a design by William Kent (1684–1748)
Heraldry: Engraved armorials of Henry Pelham Pelham-Clinton,
4th Duke of Newcastle-under-Lyne (1785–1851)
Provenance: Henry Pelham Pelham-Clinton, 4th Duke of
Newcastle-under-Lyne (1785–1851); by descent to Henry, 7th Duke
of Newcastle-under-Lyne (1864–1928), sale, Christie's, London, July
7, 1921, lot 20 (a set of eight); Partridge Fine Arts Ltd., London (a
set of eight), 1980; Titus Kendall, London, purchased in 2000
Published: Barr, p. 99, figs. 57a and b (a pair of the set of eight
illustrated)

Overall:
1. H. 5 ¹⁷⁄₃₂ in., W. 10 ¹⁄₁₆ in., D. 6 ⁵⁄₁₆ in. (14.1 x 25.5 x 16.0 cm)
2. H. 5 ¹⁷⁄₃₂ in., W. 10 ⅛ in., 6 ⅜ in. (14.1 x 25.7 x 16.1 cm)
Wt. 62 oz. 10 dwt.; 62 oz. 15 dwt. (1947; 1953 g)
Accession no.: 2010.46.1a-c–.2a-c

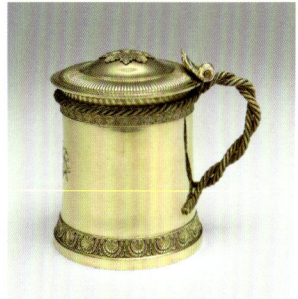

TANKARD
Silver gilt
Marks: Sterling, London, 1811/12
Maker's mark: Benjamin Smith II and James Smith II (Grimwade, no. 238) for Rundell, Bridge & Rundell
Inscription: *This TANKARD was presented / by / DECIMA BARBER / to her excellent friend / HENRY NUNN ESQ^R. / as a small token of / GRATITUDE & ESTEEM*

Heraldry: Engraved arms of Nunn
Provenance: Anonymous sale, Christie's, New York, April 19, 1990, lot 205; a New York private collector, Christopher Hartop, purchased in 2009

H. 7 5/16 in., W. 8 1/8 in., D. 5 7/8 in. (18.55 x 20.6 x 14.9 cm)
Wt. 45 oz. 7 dwt. (1410 g)
Scratch wt. "45 – 10"
Accession no.: 2010.47

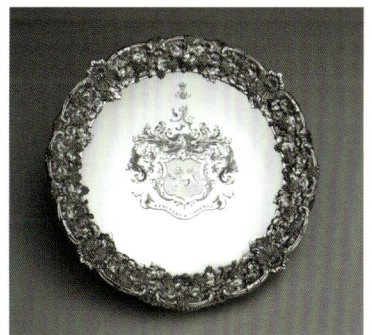

36

SALVER
Silver
Marks: Sterling, London, 1813/14
Maker's mark: Paul Storr (Grimwade, no. 2234) for Rundell, Bridge & Rundell

Heraldry: engraved arms, crest and motto "SPECTEMUR AGENDO," probably for Thompson of Yorkshire, later mirrored cipher and earl's coronet
Provenance: Property of a California Charitable Institution, sale, Christie's, New York, April 11, 1995, lot 232, Garrard & Co., London, purchased in 1998

Diam. 17 1/16 in. (43.3 cm)
Wt. 119 oz. (3702 g)
Accession no.: 2010.48

37

SET OF FOUR CANDLESTICKS
Silver
Marks: Sterling, London, 1815/16
Maker's mark: Paul Storr (Grimwade, no. 2235) for Rundell, Bridge & Rundell
Signature: *RUNDELL BRIDGE ET RUNDELL AURIFICES REGIS ET PRINCIPIS WALLE REGENTIS BRITANNIAS*

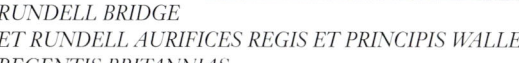

Heraldry: Engraved on the bases and nozzles with a crest
Provenance: S.J. Shrubsole Corp., New York, purchased in 2004

1. H. 9 3/16 in., W. 5 5/8 in., D. 5 1/2 in. (23.3 x 14.3 x 14.0 cm)
2. H. 9 1/16 in., W. 5 5/8 in., D. 5 1/2 in. (23.0 x 14.3 x 14.0 cm
3. H. 9 1/8 in., W. 5 5/8 in., D. 5 1/2 in. (23.3 x 14.3 x 14.0 cm)
4. H. 9 1/8 in., W. 5 5/8 in., D. 5 1/2 in. (23.3 x 14.3 x 14.0 cm)
Wt. 27 oz. 15 dwt.; 27 oz. 9 dwt.; 27 oz. 10 dwt.; 27 oz. 8 dwt.
(862; 854; 856; 852 g)
Accession no.: 2010.49.1a-b–.4a-b

KETTLE
Silver gilt, velvet, sequins, gold thread
Marks: Sterling, London, 1822/23
Maker's mark: Philip Rundell (Grimwade, no. 2228) for Rundell, Bridge & Rundell
Signature: *RUNDELL BRIDGE ET RUNDELL AURIFICES REGIS LONDINI*

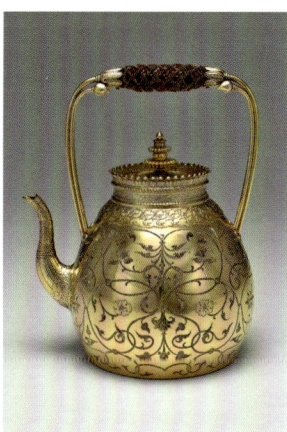

Provenance: William Beckford (1760–1844), by descent to his daughter Euphemia, who in 1810 married Alexander, 10th Duke of Hamilton (1767–1852), by descent to Alfred, 13th Duke of Hamilton (1862–1940); sale, Christie's, London, November 4, 1919, lot 60; Alastair Dickenson, London, purchased in 2001
Published: Hartop, 2005, p. 129, fig. 127

H. 11 5/8 in., W. 9 9/16 in., D. 7 5/8 in. (29.5 x 24.3 x 19.5 cm)
Gross wt. 53 oz. (1649 g)
Accession no.: 2010.50a-b

PAIR OF SAUCE
TUREENS AND
COVERS
Silver
Marks: Sterling,
London, 1823/24
Maker's mark:
Benjamin Smith II
(Grimwade, no. 230)

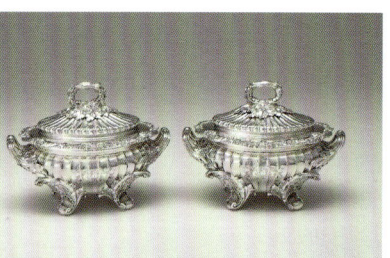

Design: Edward
Hodges Baily (1788–1867)
Heraldry: Engraved arms, crest, supporters and motto "SUAVITER
IN MODO FORTITER IN RE" of Wynn, as borne by Thomas
Wynn, 2nd Baron Newborough (1802–1832)
Provenance: S.J. Shrubsole Corp, New York, purchased in 2004

1. H. 6 ⁵⁄₁₆ in., W. 8 ¼ in., D. 5 ¹¹⁄₁₆ in. (16.0 x 21.0 x 14.4 cm)
2. H. 6 ³⁄₁₆ in., W. 8 ⁹⁄₂ in., D. 5 ⅝ in. (15.7 x 21.0 x 14.3 cm)
Wt. 46 oz. 8 dwt.; 47 oz. 3 dwt. (1444; 1466 g)
Accession no.: 2010.51.1a-b–.2a-b

PAIR OF WINE
COOLERS
Silver
Marks: Sterling, London,
1826/27
Maker's mark:
Robert Garrard II
(Grimwade, no. 2322) for
Garrard & Co.
Signature: *GARRARDS /
Panton Street / LONDON*

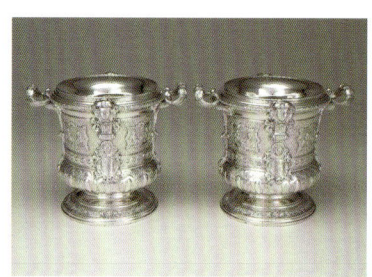

Heraldry: Engraved armorials, crest, and motto of the Order of the
Garter "HONI SOIT QUI MAL Y PENSE," as borne by George
Stanhope, 6th Earl of Chesterfield
Provenance: George Stanhope, 6th Earl of Chesterfield
(1805–1866), by descent to Lady Evelyn Stanhope (1834–1875), who
married in 1861 Henry, 4th Earl of Carnarvon (1831–1890), by
descent to Henry, 7th Earl of Carnarvon (1924–2001), the Highclere
Castle Collection, sale, Sotheby's, London, February 4, 1988, lot
113; an American private collector, S.J. Shrubsole Corp., New York,
purchased in 2007
Exhibited: London, 1991, no. 28, lent by a private collector
Published: Ogilvy, p. 67, no. 28

1. H. 10 ⅝ in., W. 13 ⁷⁄₁₆ in., D. 11 ⅝ in. (27.0 x 34.0 x 29.6 cm)
2. H. 10 ¾ in., W. 13 ⅜ in., D. 11 ⅝ in. (27.3 x 34.0 x 29.5 cm)
Wt. 205 oz. 15 dwt.; 210 oz. 8 dwt. (6402; 6544 g)
Accession no.: 2010.53.1a-c–.2a-c

PAIR OF WINE
COOLERS
Silver, liners fused silver
on copper
Marks: Sterling,
London, 1823/24
Maker's mark: John
Bridge (Grimwade, no.
1172) for Rundell,
Bridge & Rundell
Signature: *RUNDELL
BRIDGE ET RUNDELL
AURIFICES REGIS
LONDINI*

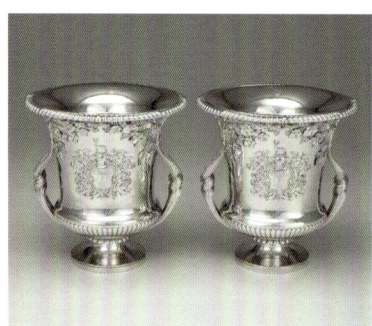

Heraldry: Applied and engraved arms, crest and motto "QUALIS
INCEPTO AB" of Robinson with those of Hobart on an
escutcheon of pretence, as borne by Frederick Robinson
(1782–1859), created Viscount Goderich in 1827 and Earl of Ripon
in 1833
Provenance: S.J. Shrubsole Corp., New York, purchased in 1998

1. H. 10 ⁹⁄₁₆ in., diam. 10 ⁵⁄₁₆ in. (26.9 x 26.2 cm)
2. H. 10 ¹⁷⁄₃₂ in., diam. 10 ⅜ in. (26.8 x 26.3 cm)
Wt. 144 oz.; 144 oz. 10 dwt. (4480; 4499 g)
Accession no.: 2010.52.1a-c–.2a-c

THE NATIONAL CUP
Silver gilt
Marks: Sterling, London,
1826/27
Maker's mark: John Bridge
(Grimwade, no. 1172) for
Rundell, Bridge & Rundell
Signature: *RUNDELL BRIDGE
ET RUNDELL AURIFICES
REGIS LONDINI*
Design: John Flaxman
(1755–1826)

Provenance: S.J. Shrubsole
Corp., New York, purchased
in 1997

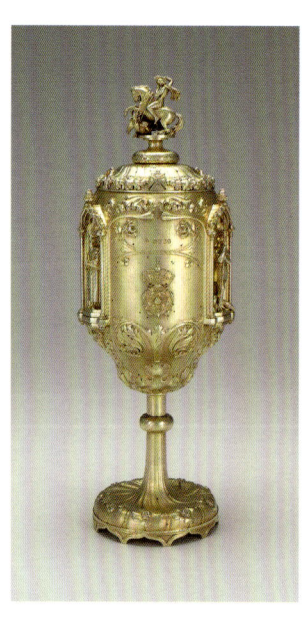

H. 18 ¾ in., diam. 6 ½ in. (47.6 x 16.6 cm)
Wt. 110 oz. 10 dwt. (3440 g)
Accession no.: 2010.54a-b

PAIR OF
SIDEBOARD
DISHES
Silver gilt
Marks: Sterling,
London, 1826/27
Maker's mark:
Paul Storr
(Grimwade, no.
2235) for Storr &
Mortimer
Signature: *STORR & MORTIMER 133*

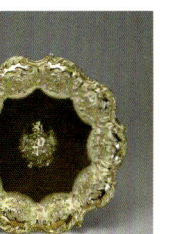

Heraldry: Engraved arms of Beverly or Golding quartering those of Morley
Provenance: A Virginia Private Collector, sale, Sotheby's, New York, April 14, 1999, lot 223, M.P. Levene Ltd., London, purchased in 1999

1. H. 1 ⅜ in., diam. 20 ¹¹⁄₁₆ in. (3.5 x 52.5 cm)
2. H. 1 ⁷⁄₁₆ in., diam. 20 ¹⁹⁄₃₂ in. (3.7 x 52.3 cm)
Wt. 89 oz.; 88 oz. 7 dwt. (2770; 2749 g)
Accession no.: 2010.55.1–.2

GOBLET
Silver gilt
Marks: Sterling, London, 1830/31
Maker's mark: John Bridge
(Grimwade, no. 1172) for Rundell,
Bridge & Rundell
Signature: *RUNDELL BRIDGE ET
RUNDELL AURIFICES REGIS
LONDINI*
Design: Attributed to Augustus
Welby Northmore Pugin (1812–1852)

Provenance: Partridge Fine Arts
PLC, London, purchased in 1998
Published: *Silver at Partridge: Recent
Acquisitions, 1998*, p. 50, no. 30

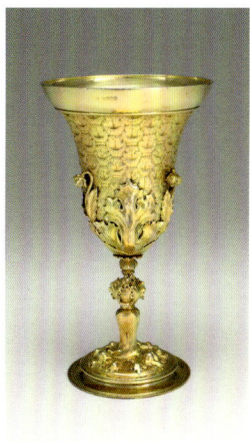

H. 13 ½ in., diam. 7 ¾ in. (34.2 x 19.7 cm)
Wt. 52 oz. 15 dwt. (1642 g)
Accession no.: 2010.57

GOBLET
Silver gilt, rock crystal,
semi-precious stones
The rock crystal, early 17th
century, Milan
Marks: Sterling, London,
1827/28
Maker's mark: John Bridge
(Grimwade, no. 1172) for
Rundell, Bridge & Rundell

Provenance: Partridge Fine Arts
PLC, London, purchased in 2003
Published: *Silver at Partridge:
Recent Acquisitions, 2002*

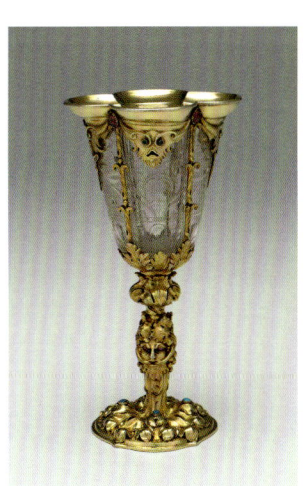

H. 8 ¼ in., W. 4 ½ in., D. 3 ¹³⁄₃₂ in. (22.3 x 11.4 x 9.7 cm)
Gross wt. 18 oz. 10 dwt. (607 g)
Accession no.: 2010.56

JUG
Silver, ivory, gilt interior
Marks: Sterling,
London, 1833/34
Maker's mark: Paul
Storr (Grimwade, no.
2235)

Provenance:
Anonymous sale,
Christie's, New York,
October 20, 1997,
lot 204, M.P. Levene
Ltd., London, purchased
in 1997

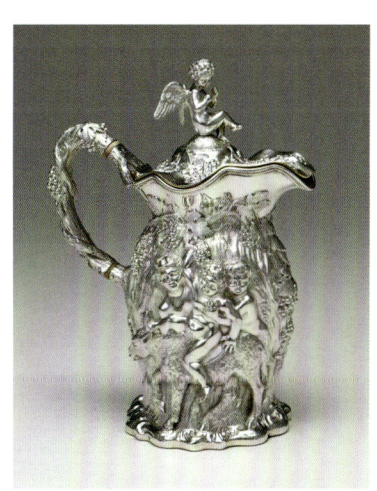

H. 10 in., W. 7 ¹⁵⁄₁₆ in., D. 5 ¹⁄₁₆ in. (25.4 x 20.1 x 12.8 cm)
Gross wt. 66 oz. 9 dwt. (2067 g)
Accession no.: 2010.58

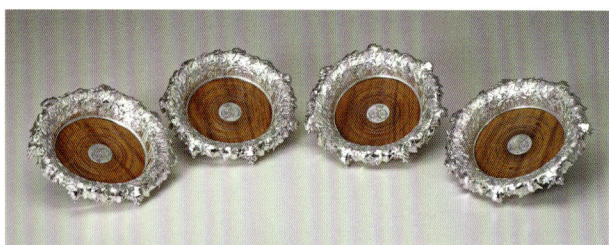

FOUR WINE COASTERS
Silver, wood
Marks: Sterling, London, 1836/37
Maker's mark: John Tapley (Grimwade, no. 1721) for Rundell, Bridge & Co.
Signature: *RUNDELL BRIDGE ET Co. AURIFICES REGIS LONDINI*

Heraldry: Engraved accolé monogram WR within the motto of the Order of the Garter "HONI SOIT QUI MAL Y PENSE" and AR within a wreath, for King William IV (1765–1837) and Queen Adelaide (1792–1849)
Provenance: Garrard & Co., London, purchased in 1998

1. H. 1 ¹⁵⁄₁₆ in., diam. 8 ⅛ in. (4.9 x 20.5 cm)
2. H. 1 ¹⁵⁄₁₆ in., diam. 8 ⅛ in. (4.9 x 20.6 cm)
3. H. 1 ¹⁵⁄₁₆ in., diam. 8 ³⁄₁₆ in.(4.9 x 20.7 cm)
4. H. 1 ¹⁵⁄₁₆ in., diam. 8 ¼ in. (4.9 x 20.9 cm)
Gross wt. 30 oz.; 29 oz. 10 dwt.; 28 oz. 18 dwt.; 28 oz. 8 dwt.
(958; 918; 902; 883 g)
Accession no.: 2010.59.1–.4

PAIR OF SALTS WITH SPOONS
Silver gilt
Marks: Salts: Sterling, London, 1840/41; spoons: Sterling, London, 1871/72
Maker's mark: Salts: John Mortimer and John Hunt (Culme, 8275); spoons: Charles Stuart Harris (Culme, 2446)

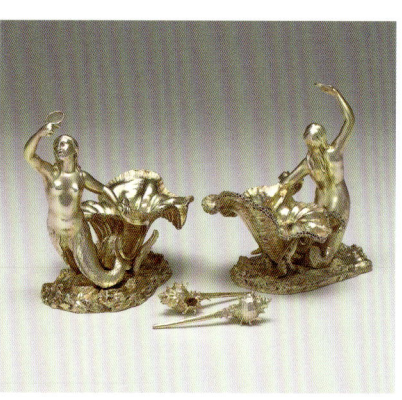

Provenance: Anonymous sale, Sotheby's, New York, April 19, 1991, lot 308; An American Private Collector, sale, Sotheby's, New York, April 14, 1999, lot 219, M.P. Levene Ltd., London, purchased in 1999

Salts:
1. H. 5 ⅞ in., W. 6 ⁹⁄₁₆ in., D. 4 ½ in. (15.0 x 16.6. x 11.4 cm)
2. H. 6 ⁷⁄₃₂ in., W. 6 ⅜ in., D. 4 ¹⁹⁄₃₂ in. (15.7 x 16.1 x 11.8 cm)
Spoons:
1. & 2. L. 3 ⅝ in. (9.0 cm)
Wt. Salts: 26 oz. 5 dwt.; 25 oz. 5 dwt. (817; 786 g)
Spoons: 1 oz.; 1 oz. (32; 32 g)
Accession no.: 2010.61.1a-b–.2a-b

PAIR OF WINE COASTERS
Silver gilt, wood, ivory
Marks: Sterling, London, 1837/38
Maker's mark: Robert Garrard II (Grimwade, no. 2322) for Garrard & Co.
Inscription: *VICT 29th May to 20th June 1837*

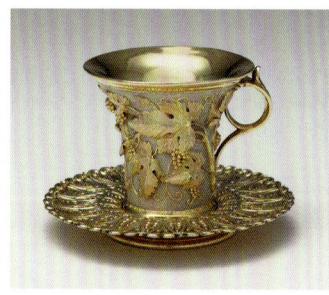

Heraldry: Engraved arms of Fergusson and motto "DULCIUS EX ASPERIS," as borne by Sir James Fergusson, 4th Bt. (1765–1838)
Provenance: Anonymous sale, Sotheby's, London, November 29, 1984, lot 110; anonymous sale, Christie's, New York, April 22, 1993, lot 295; purchased in 1998

1. H. 3 ⅜ in., diam. 6 ½ in. (8.6 x 16.7 cm)
2. H. 3 ⁷⁄₁₆ in., diam. 6 ½ in. (8.7 x 17.7 cm)
Gross wt. 57 oz. 18 dwt.; 57 oz. 15 dwt. (1804; 1797 g)
Accession no.: 2010.60.1–.2

CUP AND SAUCER
Silver, parcel gilt
Marks: Sterling, Birmingham, 1845/46
Maker's mark: Elkington & Co. (Crisp Jones, p. 224, no. 24)

Provenance: Partridge Fine Arts PLC, London, purchased in 2000

Overall: H. 3 ¹⁄₁₆ in., diam. 4 ¾ in. (7.8 x 12.1 cm)
Cup: H. 2 ²³⁄₃₂ in., diam. 3 ⁵⁄₃₂ in. (6.9 x 8.1 cm)
Saucer: H. ²¹⁄₃₂ in., diam. 4 ¾ in. (1.7 x 12.1 cm)
Wt. Cup: 5 oz. 15 dwt. (178 g); saucer: 3 oz. 4 dwt. (100 g)
Accession no.: 2010.62a-b

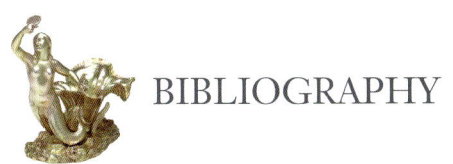

BIBLIOGRAPHY

Further Reading

Alcorn, 2007
Ellenor M. Alcorn, "Boston and the American Taste for British Silver," in Christopher Hartop, *British and Irish Silver in the Fogg Art Museum, Harvard University Art Museums*, Cambridge, Massachusetts, 2007, pp. 17–22

Antiquaries
David Gaimster *et al.*, eds., *Making History: Antiquaries in Britain, 1707–2007*, exh. cat., Royal Academy of Arts, London, 2007

Glanville, 1999
Philippa Glanville, *Silver*, London, 1999

Grimwade, 1994
Arthur G. Grimwade, *Silver for Sale, Christie's in the Thirties*, Norwich, 1994

Hartop, 2005
Christopher Hartop, *Royal Goldsmiths: The Art of Rundell & Bridge, 1797–1843*, exh. cat., Koopman Rare Art, London, 2005

Mowl
Tim Mowl, *William Beckford: Composing for Mozart*, London, 1998

Ostergard
Derek Ostergard, ed., *William Beckford, 1760–1844: An Eye for the Magnificent*, exh. cat., Bard Graduate Center for Studies in the Decorative Arts, Design and Culture, New York, and Dulwich Picture Gallery, London, 2001–2002

Parissien
Steven Parissien, *George IV: The Grand Entertainment*, London, 2001

Roberts
Jane Roberts, ed., *Royal Treasures, a Golden Jubilee Celebration*, exh. cat., the Queen's Gallery, London, 2002

Wainwright
Clive Wainwright, *The Romantic Interior: The British Collector at Home, 1750–1850*, New Haven and London, 1989

Walpole
Michael Snodin, ed., *Horace Walpole's Strawberry Hill*, exh. cat., Yale Center for British Art, New Haven, Connecticut, and Victoria and Albert Museum, London, 2009–2010

Other Works Cited

Alcorn, 1993
Ellenor M. Alcorn, *English Silver in the Museum of Fine Arts, Boston: Silver before 1697*, Museum of Fine Arts, Boston, 1993

Alcorn, 2000
Ellenor M. Alcorn, *English Silver in the Museum of Fine Arts, Boston: Silver from 1697*, Museum of Fine Arts, Boston, 2000

Alcorn, 2006
Ellenor M. Alcorn, *Beyond the Maker's Mark: Paul de Lamerie Silver in the Cahn Collection*, exh. cat., Victoria and Albert Museum, London, and other venues, 2006

Banister, I *and* II
Judith Banister, "Rewards of high office: silver seal cups and salvers–I," *Country Life*, January 29, 1981, and "Pomp from circumstance: silver seal cups and salvers–II," *Country Life*, February 5, 1981

Barr
Elaine Barr, *George Wickes, Royal Goldsmith, 1698–1761*, London, 1980

Bliss
Joseph R. Bliss, *The Jerome and Rita Gans Collection of English Silver on Loan to the Virginia Museum of Fine Arts*, n.d. (but 1992)

Brett
Vanessa Brett, *The Sotheby's Directory of Silver, 1600–1940*, London, 1986

Bury
Shirley Bury, "The Lengthening Shadow of Rundell's: Part 1: Rundell's and their Silversmiths," *Connoisseur*, CLX, February, 1966, pp. 79–85, "The Lengthening Shadow of Rundell's: Part 2: The substance and growth of the Flaxman tradition," CLX, March, 1966, pp. 152–8, and "The Lengthening Shadow of Rundell's: Part 3: The Rundell influence on the Victorian trade," CLX, April, 1966, pp. 218–22

Butler
Robin Butler, *The Albert Collection: Five Hundred Years of British and European Silver*, London, 2004

Christie's Season, 1931
A.C.R. Carter, ed., *Christie's Season, 1931*, London, 1931

Complete Peerage
G.E.C. [George Edward Cockayne], *The Complete Peerage of England, Scotland, Ireland, Great Britain, and the United Kingdom, extant, extinct or dormant*, 13 vols., London, rev. edn., 1910–1959

Crisp Jones
Kenneth Crisp Jones, ed., *The Silversmiths of Birmingham and Their Marks: 1750–1980*, London, 1981

Culme
John Culme, *The Directory of Gold & Silversmiths: Jewellers & Allied Traders 1838–1914 from the London Assay Office Registers*, 2 vols., Woodbridge, 1987

Culme, 1977
John Culme, *Nineteenth-Century Silver*, London, 1977

Culme, 1985
John Culme, "Attitudes to Old Plate, 1750–1900," paper read at the International Silver and Jewellery Fair and Seminar, Dorchester Hotel, London, February, 1985, privately printed, London, 1985, also reprinted in an enlarged version in Culme, pp. xvi–xxxvi

Culme, 1999
English Silver: The Jerome and Rita Gans Collection, Addendum, Richmond, Virginia, 1999

English and Maddox
Edmund Francis English and Willes Maddox, *Views of Lansdown Tower*, Bath, 1844

Gask
Norman Gask, *Old Silver Spoons of England: A Practical Guide for Collectors*, London, 1926

Glanville
Philippa Glanville, "Lionel Crichton and a library acquisition," *Silver Studies: The Journal of the Silver Society*, vol. 19, 2005, pp. 110–11

Grimwade
Arthur G. Grimwade, *London Goldsmiths, 1697–1837: Their Marks and Lives from the Original Registers at Goldsmiths' Hall and Other Sources*, London, 3rd edn., 1990

Grimwade, 1974
Arthur G. Grimwade, *Rococo Silver, 1727–1765*, London, 1974

Hackenbroch
Yvonne Hackenbroch, *English and Other Silver in the Irwin Untermyer Collection*, New York, rev. edn., 1969

Hare
Susan Hare, ed., *Paul de Lamerie: At the Sign of The Golden Ball. An Exhibition of the Work of England's Master Silversmith (1688–1751)*, exh. cat., Goldsmiths' Hall, London, 1990

Harmsworth
Geoffrey Harmsworth, "On Dealers and Collectors," in *The Ninth Antiques Dealers' Fair and Exhibition, 1949, Handbook of Exhibitors*, Grosvenor House, London, 1949, pp. 12–16

Hartop, 1998
Christopher Hartop, "Art and industry in 18th-century London: English silver 1680-1760 from the Alan and Simone Hartman Collection," *Proceedings of the Huguenot Society*, vol. XXVII, no. 1, pp. 50–63

Hartop, 2006
Christopher Hartop, "Patrons and consumers: buying silver in eighteenth-century London," in Vanessa Brett, ed., *Rococo Silver in England and Its Colonies: Papers from a Symposium at Virginia Museum of Fine Arts, Richmond, in 2004*, London, 2006

Hartop, 2007a
Christopher Hartop, *A Noble Feast: English Silver from the Jerome and Rita Gans Collection at the Virginia Museum of Fine Arts*, Richmond, Virginia, 2007

Hartop, 2007b
Christopher Hartop, *British and Irish Silver in the Fogg Art Museum, Harvard University Art Museums*, Cambridge, Massachusetts, 2007

Hartop, 2010
Christopher Hartop, *The Classical Ideal: English Silver, 1760–1840*, exh. cat., Koopman Rare Art, London, 2010

Henderson
James Henderson, *Silver Collecting for Amateurs*, London, rev. edn., 1968

Herrmann
Hermann, Frank, *Sotheby's: Portrait of an Auction House*, London, 1981

Houston
Silver by Paul de Lamerie in America, exh. cat., Museum of Fine Arts, Houston, Texas, 1956

How
G.E.P. and J.P. How, *English and Scottish Silver Spoons, Medieval to Late Stuart, and Pre-Elizabethan Hall-marks on English Plate*, 3 vols., London, 1952

Jackson
Ian Pickford, ed., *Jackson's Silver and Gold Marks of England, Scotland and Ireland*, Woodbridge, 3rd edn., 1989

Jackson, 1911
Charles James Jackson, *An Illustrated History of English Plate*, London, 1911

Keay
Anna Keay, *The Magnificent Monarch: Charles II and the Ceremonies of Power*, London, 2008

Latham and Matthews
Robert Latham and William Matthews, eds., *The Diary of Samuel Pepys*, 11 vols., London, 1970–1983

Lees-Milne
James Lees-Milne, *William Beckford*, London, 1979

Lomax
James Lomax, "Royalty and Silver: The role of the Jewel House in the eighteenth century," *Silver Society Journal*, vol. 11, 1999, pp. 133–9

Lonsdale
Roger Lonsdale, ed., *Vathek*, London, 1970

Lovett
Robert W. Lovett, "Rundell, Bridge and Rundell – An early Company History," *Bulletin of the Business Historical Society*, vol. 23, September, 1949, pp. 150–65

Moss
Morrie A. Moss, *The Lillian and Morrie Moss Collection of Paul Storr Silver*, Miami, 1972

Newman
Harold Newman, *An Illustrated Dictionary of Silverware*, London, 1987

Ogilvy
Julia Ogilvy, ed., *Royal Goldsmiths: The Garrard Heritage*, exh. cat., Garrard, London, 1991

Oman
Charles Oman, "The beginning of silver collecting," in *Proceedings of the Society of Silver Collectors*, no. 8, Summer, 1966, pp. 18–19

Penzer
Norman Mosley Penzer, *Paul Storr: The Last of the Goldsmiths*, London, 1954; reissued as *Paul Storr, 1771–1844: Silversmith and Goldsmith*, London, 1971

Phillips
Philip A.S. Phillips, *Paul de Lamerie: Citizen and Goldsmith of London: A Study of His Life and Work A.D. 1688–1751*, London, 1935

Pinto
Edward H. Pinto, *Treen and other Wood Bygones: An Encyclopedia and Social History*, London, 1969

Redding
Cyrus Redding, *Memoirs of William Beckford*, Bath, 1859

Rococo
Rococo: Art and Design in Hogarth's England, exh. cat., Victoria and Albert Museum, London, 1984

Rococo Silver
Vanessa Brett, ed., *Rococo Silver in England and Its Colonies: Papers from a Symposium at Virginia Museum of Fine Arts, Richmond, in 2004*, London, 2006

Rowe
Robert Rowe, *Adam Silver, 1765–1795*, London, 1965

Rutter, 1822
John Rutter, *A Description of Fonthill and Demesne*, Shaftesbury, 1822

Rutter, 1823
John Rutter, *Fonthill and Its Abbey Delineated*, Shaftesbury, 1823

Schroder, 1988a
Timothy Schroder, *The Gilbert Collection of Gold and Silver*, Los Angeles, 1988

Schroder, 1988b
Timothy Schroder, *The National Trust Book of English Domestic Silver, 1500–1900*, London, 1988

Schroder, 1995
Timothy Schroder, "A royal Tudor rock-crystal and silver-gilt vase," *Burlington Magazine*, June, 1995, pp. 356–66

Schroder, 2009
Timothy Schroder, *British and Continental Gold and Silver in the Ashmolean Museum*, 3 vols., Oxford, 2009

Shrubsole
Bard Langstaff and James McConnaughy, eds., *50 Years on 57th Street*, exh. cat., S.J. Shrubsole Corp., New York, 1986

Shure
David S. Shure, *Hester Bateman: Queen of English Silversmiths*, London, 1959

Sitwell
Harvey Degge Wilmot Sitwell, "The Jewel Office and the Royal Goldsmiths," *Archaeological Journal*, vol. 117, 1960, pp. 131–55

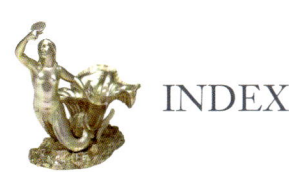

INDEX

Smith
Eric J.G. Smith, "Richard Blackwell & Son,"
Silver Society Journal, vol. 15, 2003,
pp. 19–45

Snodin and Baker
Michael Snodin and Malcolm Baker,
"William Beckford's Silver," *Burlington
Magazine*, part I, November, 1980, and part
II, December, 1980

Steuart Fothringham
Henry Steuart Fothringham, "The over-
optimism of Octavius Morgan," *Silver Society
Journal*, vol. 15, 2003, p. 14

Vardy
John Vardy, ed., *Some Designs of Mr. Inigo
Jones and Mr. Wm. Kent*, London, 1744

Vitali
Ubaldo Vitali, "A quest for the *domus aurea*
in the resurgence of gilding," in Anthony
Phillips and Jeanne Sloane, *Antiquity
Revisited: English and French Silver-gilt from
the Collection of Audrey Love*, exh. cat.,
Christie's, New York, and other venues, 1997

Wees
Beth Carver Wees, *English, Irish, & Scottish
Silver at the Sterling and Francine Clark Art
Institute*, New York, 1997

Williamson
George Charles Williamson, *Stories of an
Expert*, London, 1925

Young
Hilary Young, "Silver, Ormolu and
Ceramics," in John Harris and Michael
Snodin, *Sir William Chambers, Architect to
George III*, exh. cat., Courtauld Gallery,
London/Nationalmuseum, Stockholm, 1997

EXHIBITIONS

Austin, Texas, 1969
*One Hundred Years of English Silver,
1660–1760*, University Art Museum,
University of Texas at Austin and Fort
Worth Art Center–Museum, Fort Worth,
Texas, 1969

London, 1991
Royal Goldsmiths: The Garrard Inheritance,
Garrard & Co., London, 1991

London/Stockholm, 1997
Sir William Chambers, Architect to George III,
Courtauld Gallery, London, and
Nationalmuseum, Stockholm, 1997

PHOTOGRAPHIC CREDITS

COVER PICTURES

Front cover:
**Detail of one of a pair of sauceboats,
silver, London, 1755/56, maker's mark of
Thomas Gilpin. Cat. no. 27**

Front flap:
**Goblet, silver gilt, rock crystal, semi-
precious stones, London, 1827/28,
maker's mark of John Bridge for Rundell,
Bridge & Rundell. Cat. no. 44**

**One of a pair of salts, silver gilt, London,
1840/41, maker's mark of John Mortimer
& John Hunt. Cat. no. 49**

Back cover:
**Kettle, silver gilt, velvet, sequins, gold
thread, London, 1822/23, maker's mark
of Philip Rundell for Rundell, Bridge &
Rundell. Cat. no. 38**

Back flap:
**Two-handled cup and cover, silver,
c. 1650, maker's mark a *hound sejant*,
for Richard Blackwell. Cat. no. 2**